DATE DUE

AP 19'63	OCT 1 '74		
MY 7 '58	MAR 9 1976		
JY 31'63	OCT 8 1976		
AG 16'63			
AP 1 '64	MAR 1 6 1977		
	MAR 1 3 1978		
JY 31 '64	MAY 0 1 1978		
NO 19'65	NOV 1 9 1979		
	FEB 2 7 1980		
NO 15'66	MAR 0 4 1981		
DE 2 '66			
JA 2 AM	NOV 1 9 1990		
OC 6 '67	DEC 1 0 1990		
OC 20'67	MAY 1 6 2004		
OC 30'70	FEB 1 1 2008		
DE 1 '70	MAR 0 1 2008		
OC 24 72			
MAR 1 5 1973			
OC 16 73			
MY 21 74			
GAYLORD			PRINTED IN U.S.A.

EUGENE V. DEBS
Socialist for President

MEN AND MOVEMENTS SERIES

Men and Movements

CONSCIENCE IN POLITICS
Adlai E. Stevenson in the 1950's
    STUART GERRY BROWN, 1961

NORMAN THOMAS
Respectable Rebel
    MURRAY B. SEIDLER, 1961

GIFFORD PINCHOT
Bull Moose Progressive
    MARTIN L. FAUSOLD, 1961

HENRY A. WALLACE
Quixotic Crusade 1948
    KARL M. SCHMIDT, 1960

OSWALD GARRISON VILLARD
Liberal of the 1920's
    D. JOY HUMES, 1960

EUGENE V. DEBS

Socialist for President

H. WAYNE MORGAN

Syracuse University Press · 1962

Manufactured in the United States of America
Printed by Vail-Ballou Press, Inc., Binghamton, N.Y.

TO
MY MOTHER
AND FATHER

Preface

Few Americans today remember a time when the Socialist Party of America was a power of any proportions in politics. They have forgotten or never knew that a scant two generations ago the socialists were the third party of American politics; that they were a considerable force in local and state politics; and that many of the "radical" policies which they advocated have become standard fixtures in the American system.

In mid-twentieth century, the American socialists have fallen on evil days. The First World War divided the party into quarreling sects which sapped its remaining life and ruined its cohesiveness as an organization. The disillusionment that followed the war, the collapse of progressive sentiment, the frivolity of the 1920's, the Great Depression and its cure, the New Deal, the Second World War, a permanent cold war—these have served in their separate and collective ways to deaden any popular appeal the once important Socialist Party of America might have had. At the height of its influence in 1912, the party's presidential candidate polled nearly 6 per cent of the vote in the face of two other powerful liberal vote-getters; forty years later the vote was hardly a courtesy one. In 1912, more than a thousand socialists held elective office; forty years later the number was close to zero.

If the Socialist Party seems to have no future, it at least has a past. No student of American history of the period between 1890 and 1920 can help being struck by the immense quantities of socialist literature printed and distributed. Popular as well as learned magazines before the World War were filled with speculation about the future of socialism. Politicians as well as scholars worried that socialism would invade American society and triumph unless checked. Hundreds if not thousands of leading community men were interested in the theory and often in the practice of socialism, and they sometimes translated that interest into a vote for Eugene Debs between 1900 and 1920.

The history books that extol the campaign exploits of William Jennings Bryan, Theodore Roosevelt, and Woodrow Wilson often fail to record that the most famous American socialist, Eugene Victor Debs, waged five presidential campaigns between 1900 and 1920. Historians have failed to exploit the rich body of material left behind in the wake of those campaigns, or to show the extent to which socialist electioneering succeeded or influenced American life.

Whatever success the Socialist Party had in national politics between those years was due in large part to the man who carried the party's banner. Buoyed up by the waves of protest and reform of those years, Debs shrewdly capitalized on new forces to present his message to hundreds of thousands of Americans during the course of his campaigns. No man gave more to American socialism than he. Despite his romantic sentimentality and lack of profound insight into the forces at work in his time, Debs was a thoroughly practical man, a politician in close touch with the masses.

My purpose in writing this book is to chart the course

of the socialists in national politics between 1900 and 1925. I have attempted to write neither a biography of Debs nor a history of American socialism. The socialists employed political methods, and gained successes that are in themselves well worth studying. Aside from the intrinsic interest of socialist politics, the party's successes proved two things: the mission of minor parties in American history has been to force major parties to accept the least radical portions of their programs; and the socialists succeeded in a free society, a thing which is no small tribute to both the socialists themselves and their opponents. Though suffering much persecution, which ultimately contributed to the party's demise, the socialists nevertheless worked in a remarkably free atmosphere during their heyday between 1900 and 1912. Their history in American politics is not essentially one of suppression, but of hard work and at least limited success.

I have been assisted in preparing this book by many people and institutions. I wish to thank Mrs. Sylvia Angrist, executrix of the estate of the late Miss Nina Hillquit, for permission to quote from the papers of Morris Hillquit. I wish to thank especially the staffs of the Bancroft Library at the University of California at Berkeley; the Tamiment Institute in New York, formerly the Rand School of Social Science; the manuscripts division of the Library of Congress; the newspaper division of the Library of Congress; Miss Mattie Russell and her staff at Duke University; the staff of the Denver Public Library; and Miss Josephine Harper and her staff at the State Historical Society of Wisconsin. The staffs of the Honnold Library in Claremont, California; the Arizona Pioneer Historical Society in Tucson; and the State Historical Society of Colorado in Denver also gave me their time and cooperation. Portions of this work have appeared in *The American Quarterly, Mid-America,* and *The Indiana Magazine of History,* and I am indebted to the editors of those journals for permission to reprint that material here. I wish also to thank Miss Michele Vandersyde of the Syracuse University Press, whose untiring editorial labors have greatly improved the text. For whatever errors may remain, I alone am responsible.

H. WAYNE MORGAN

Austin, Texas

Contents

Do you know that all the progress
in the whole world's history has been
made by minorities? I have somehow
been fortunately all of my life in
the minority. I have thought again
and again that if I ever find myself
in the majority I will know that I
have outlived myself. There is something
magnificent about having the courage
to stand with a few and for a principle
and to fight for it without fear or
favor, developing all your latent
powers, expanding to the proportionate
end, rising to your true stature,
no matter whose respect you may
forfeit as long as you keep your own.

Eugene V. Debs, 1924

I

Eugene V. Debs and the Rise of American Socialism

Liberty, be it known, is for those only who dare strike the blow to secure and retain the priceless boon.
Eugene V. Debs, 1895

The very character and principles of Eugene Victor Debs made a Debs legend inevitable. No man of such warm temperament, colorful personality and unorthodox beliefs could escape becoming a legend in America. Born in the great, frontier Indiana of 1855, he seemed to possess from birth the traces of radicalism that spring so often from that great watershed of discontent. Named after two radical writers favored by his Alsatian father, Eugene Sue and Victor Hugo, the boy seemed destined from the first to follow unorthodox lines.

Terre Haute, Indiana, his birthplace, was then a frontier settlement, a railhead and center for commerce and transport. The veil of memory cast a spell over it for him in later years, when he recalled it as a place of tall sycamores and carefree days. In truth it was muddy and dusty, rutted and ramshackle, populated by as many varieties of men as there were nationalities, a rough western town made rougher by railroad influences.[1]

1

The railroad's steel rails symbolized much for the boy, and fascinated him whose future was to be tied so intimately to their expansion and the commerce they carried. Like the railroads, the young Debs grew rapidly in all directions, but chiefly up, until he stood at a lean and gangling six feet, endowed with a winning personality, an amiable charm, and a desire to combat the injustice he saw around him. He made friends easily, was generous to a fault, and even as a young man seemed marked for success in some avenue of public life.

Public life and the glamor of the outside world were far from his youthful thoughts; his first problem was making a living. The boy was drawn to the railroaders like steel filings to a magnet, but his father frowned on such ambitions. The Debs family had followed a long, hard road to respectable middle-class prosperity, and the elder Debs wanted his sons to make their mark in a profession. He himself had worked at many jobs, and suffered all the tortures and frustrations that beset the immigrant, settling at last to ownership of a small grocery store in Terre Haute. He was a kindly, gentle man, who exercised a great influence on his eldest son. A wide reader and avid social critic, he impressed upon the young Eugene the necessity of understanding the world around him.

Eugene worked for a time in his father's store, but tired of the routine. The restlessness of adventure was in his blood; the railroad was too close, its whistle too intriguing to allow him to count cookies and measure cloth for housewives. He devoted much of his excess energy to reading, and read widely if not deeply, drinking at the same fountains as his father, filled early with the rhetoric and reasoning of social protest and the romantic view of life. He favored Hugo among the novelists, Robert Ingersoll among the popular philosophers, and action in everything.

Without family approval, he started work on the railroad in 1870, beginning at the bottom of the ladder, working his way up as floor boy, oiler, and finally into the locomotive cab with the firemen and engineers.[2] It was not an easy life even for the lean, hardened young man. Bad weather, poor equipment, erratic schedules and the unforeseen combined with low wages and long hours to make the railroaders a tough group. Drinking, gambling, and the roughest horseplay were their pastimes. The young Debs entered into all of this gladly. He found in the men around him a hard core of principle, a feeling of camaraderie inspired by common hardships, and he greatly admired their courage, sense of honor, and general outlook. He made many lasting friendships, each of which strengthened his belief that men were basically good and that evil was the product of the social system, rather than human nature.

Despite his long hours and grueling schedule, Debs continued to read widely, attended many lectures in Terre Haute and other cities along the railroad, and absorbed much of the radical thought of his day. His mother's protests, however, finally triumphed over his love for the railroad and he left his job because she feared that he would be killed or maimed, the common lot of many railroaders.

Yet his neighbors marked him for progress. In 1879 he was elected city clerk of Terre Haute with the support of the local political boss, and won a second term in 1881, though the rest of the ticket went down to defeat. If he thought of politics in those days, he thought of himself as a Democrat. The routine of office did not exhaust his energies and he continued his studies and his interests in radical politics and labor affairs. In 1880 he reluctantly became secretary-treasurer of the Brotherhood of Locomotive Firemen and editor of the *Firemen's Magazine*. It was no sinecure, for the union was weak, bankrupt, and disorganized. But Debs applied his energies to the task and within a year the debts were paid, membership was growing, and the future seemed bright.

Debs allowed the Democrats to run him for the state legislature in 1884. Thinking that he could help his union followers, and utterly unaware of the political process, he plunged into public life again. In 1885, he maneuvered a bill through the lower house providing that railroads compensate their employees when injured through no fault of their own. The bill died a lingering death in the upper house and the experience was such a shock to Debs that he refused to run for re-election, feeling that he had failed his followers. He turned from party politics and never afterwards had any faith in parliamentary process under the old parties.[3]

His heart was not in politics, however; the union brotherhood claimed it. Throughout the 1880's he worked steadily to build up the union, devoting time, health, money to the cause. He worked eighteen hours a day, full of idealism as well as the practical belief that he could help his men. At that time he knew little if anything of socialism and was committed to the craft unionism which he vehemently condemned in a few years.[4]

He devoted much of his time to the *Locomotive Fire-*

men's Magazine, and he learned there a facility of pen and ease of expression which helped him much later. The Debs of 1890 was not the Debs of 1900. His general tenor was that of a Christian moralist, exhorting his readers to improve themselves through sobriety, thrift, self-help, and hard work.[5] He even listed appropriate examples of self-made men for his readers to emulate.[6] When Jay Gould died Debs thought it appropriate to say a few kind words, and pointed out that although Gould had done many bad things, he had treated his men with consideration.[7]

If Debs thought of socialism it was with a negative edge on his mind, dismissing it as a utopian scheme, generally irrelevant to the workers' present needs.[8] He who would later preach the class struggle as the source of social conflict saw little of it in these years. On the eve of the great depression of 1893, which drastically altered his outlook, he wrote:

> We indulge in none of the current vagaries about a conflict between capital and labor. There are capitalists who fight labor; we do not anticipate any diminution of their numbers, but, we do expect to see them checkmated in their schemes of piracy.[9]

Partly because of exhaustion and overwork, Debs repeatedly begged to be released from his work with the union. More significant, however, was his growing conviction that craft unionism was outmoded and that a new and broader system of organization was necessary if labor was to move forward. The cruel Panic of 1893 brought hardship and suffering to thousands and impressed upon Debs the inherent weaknesses and cruelties

of the economic system. Before that, however, he had thought of a railroad union based on industrial, not craft, lines; a union to which all railroaders, regardless of their jobs, would be united for a common cause. He saw that unity was the key to success, for if all the railroad workers struck, not just the firemen or switchmen, management would be brought to terms much faster.

From these first thoughts the American Railway Union was born. Joined by many craft unionists and sympathizers who felt the same way, Debs began organizing his one big union. He was astonished by his success, for applications for membership and local charters came in faster than he and his limited staff could handle them. He worked prodigally and successfully through the autumn and winter of 1893, facing opposition from craft unionists and capitalists alike. As the depression deepened, the membership lists grew. In the spring of 1894, the ARU won a sensational strike against James J. Hill's Great Northern Railroad without violence and with unity despite blandishments from all sides. The ARU, it seemed, had come to stay, and so had its leader, Eugene V. Debs.

But that was not to be, for 1894 was a cruel year in American history and none felt that cruelty more than the employees of the Pullman Palace Car Company in the model town of Pullman, Illinois. Every aspect of the paternalism sponsored by George Pullman was evident in the town, yet its workers were not happy. Cuts in orders compelled cuts in wages, Mr. Pullman said, and cuts were made. Chicago tensed; labor trouble was in the air. The workers who made the Palace Cars were technically not railroaders, but occupational bonds overrode technical differences and strong ties of sympathy held the two groups together. Finding their conditions intolerable, the Pullman workers finally struck in desperation and called for the support of fellow workers.[10] Debs was invited to investigate the situation, and though he was not inclined to lead his fledgling union into a massive strike, he visited Pullman, Illinois, talked with the workers, and came away convinced that their cause was just. "The paternalism of Pullman is the same as the interest of a slave holder in his human chattels. You are striking to avert slavery and degradation," he told the workers.[11]

Strong as his sympathies were, Debs hesitated to join the strike. He knew that a full scale labor war was in the making, that his union was not as strong as it seemed, and that times were hard, which meant that the company could count on strike breakers and government influence. But if he hesitated, his men did not. They took the issue from his hands by voting to join the strike. Reluctantly, Debs agreed, and issued a call for a general strike to the railroad brotherhoods, who declined to join the ARU.[12] In late June, 1894, Chicago prepared for the worst.

From Debs' point of view, the strike was an immediate success. Trains carrying Pullman cars were sidetracked; little rail traffic moved except mail trains, and the ARU lines held firmly. In a matter of days the greatest strike of the century was firmly entrenched, with remarkably little violence, but with neither side inclined to surrender. The union asked for arbitration, but Pullman gave a classic answer: "There is nothing to arbitrate." Debs directed the strike from his Chicago headquarters, enjoining his men to avoid violence, which could only boomerang against them. He was busy, and his tall, balding figure, his rapid stride, and ready handshake were familiar sights to his men as he made his rounds of the strike headquarters.

The company was not idle. Strikebreakers were easy to find because of hard times; special company approved deputy marshals were sworn in to protect railroad property; private detectives watched Debs and other union officials. Governor John P. Altgeld of Illinois, already stigmatized by his pardon of the Haymarket anarchists, was notified that state militia might be needed; the governor, for all his sympathies toward labor, was ready to prevent violence and enforce the law.

As the strike wore on into July, tempers flared and tension mounted. A city already filled with the kindling of discontented workers now bore the added danger of a national strike. Pressures were applied from elsewhere as delays in rail shipments affected all parts of the country. Railroad property was destroyed, cars fired, tracks blocked and trains overturned or derailed in and around Chicago. The companies charged that the strikers were at fault; the strikers charged that hired company thugs burned old and heavily insured railroad cars, blaming the violence on the union. The General Managers' Association, an organization of railroad owners, used ample funds, the press, and contingents of agents to sustain their position.

Attorney General Richard Olney, himself a former corporation counsel, prominent in railroad work before he entered Cleveland's cabinet, thought first and foremost of protecting property. He had no sympathy with the strike and welcomed the chance to crush it. On July 2, a sweeping court injunction, which Debs called "a Gatling gun on paper," forbade further interference with trains on the grounds that interstate commerce and the mails were disrupted. The union leaders were in effect enjoined from further activity. It was the death knell of the strike.

Olney persuaded President Cleveland to order federal troops into Chicago on the grounds that rioting and looting were rampant and that Illinois officials were powerless. Despite Governor Altgeld's vehement protests, Cleveland did so and the end of the strike was in sight.[13] Debs had not counted on federal intervention. The strikers' funds were low and their strength nearly exhausted; press and public opinion opposed them; the government moved to suppress them; and their leaders stood in the shadow of a court injunction that threatened to break up the ARU.

In quelling the strike, Cleveland acted in good faith within the limits of his knowledge, but in truth he misunderstood the situation. He leaned almost exclusively on Olney's advice, and the Attorney General cleverly stacked the cards against the strikers from the first. It was a time of troubles for the President, but he illustrated in his inflexibility during the Pullman strike and in his disregard for the local situation a narrow view of his responsibilities. In this, as in other actions, he conceived his role as a negative one. He was not a callous man, nor did he dislike labor; in his way he wished as much for the workers as did Debs. But Cleveland's massive figure was not so easily swayed by emotion, and his chief virtue was his chief weakness—an intractable will that defined duty but which at the same time often misguided and restricted his powers for good. The personal courage for which he was famous was often merely a form of stubbornness, a dangerous stubbornness when based upon meager information and misunderstanding.

The outcome of the strike, which quickly collapsed

as troops assisted in clearing the rail yards and helped companies suppress strikers, was catastrophic for Debs and the ARU. It meant the union's death, for its members were now systematically blacklisted from railroad work and the bankrupt union could not ease its members' plight. Debs himself, with other leaders, faced a jail sentence.

Debs' confidence in his cause never wavered, even as the strikers were driven to earth, but the experience was a revelation to him. He was proud of the union's conduct; it had avoided violence and the men had stood together remarkably well. This proved to him his theory of the superior strength of industrial unionism. The strikers had held their ground until the power of the government crushed them; here was the secret of success for any movement. The strike had also proved, however, that the government would subvert the judicial process to enforce its will and that individual rights were jeopardized by a government sympathetic to corporate interests. For Debs the greatest blow of the whole affair was the violation of his personal rights. Clearly, he must sharpen his interest in politics.[14]

But the struggle disclosed an even deeper truth to Debs, for all the doubts and suspicions he had felt about the economic and social system crystallized. Even now, though not quite a socialist, he could at least appreciate the direction of socialist propaganda. The tramp of soldiers' feet showed the gulf between the haves and the have-nots, and "in the gleam of every bayonet and the flash of every rifle *the class struggle was revealed.*"[15] If he was not yet convinced, the road to socialism beckoned.

Debs was duly arrested and tried for contempt of court; defense by the already prominent Clarence Darrow did not save him.[16] He was sentenced to six months in jail for contempt and conspiracy to obstruct the mails. Confined to jail in Woodstock, Illinois, he put his time to good use. He received an immense quantity of mail and a steady stream of visitors. Among the latter were Victor Berger and other socialists who gave him literature and arguments on the merits of socialism, trying to win him to their cause. He was a famous man, identified with labor and political radicalism, and his capture would be a dramatic coup for socialism. Debs listened politely and was impressed, but he clung persistently to his old beliefs. He would think it over, and his mind was open.

His release from jail was the signal for further work and he turned his energies to helping his former followers. Yet he could not escape politics entirely. The dramatic campaign of 1896, when it seemed to him clear that the gage of battle was flung down between capital and labor, found him in the thick of it.

It was rumored that he would accept the Populist nomination, and that his friends were hard at work for it. A number of newspapers and groups favored his selection within the Peoples Party. Debs himself, while optimistically but fruitlessly working to revive the ARU, also lent a willing ear to such talk, and worked a good deal for the Populists.[17] Debs pleaded, however, that he was not a politician, that he was too poor to run, and that his first loyalty was to labor. "To make it still stronger, I would not accept the nomination if I knew that I could get the office, because a successful politician is nothing more than a bundle of compromises."[18]

"Clearly"

Yet when the Populists met in July, 1896 it was reported that his followers secured over 400 pledges of support from the 1,300 delegates.[19] Like it or not, his name was a drawing card in many Populist circles. Then, as later, Debs would doubtless have accepted a "draft"; it was not in him to reject what he thought was the voice of the people. Yet he was hesitant. Did he wish to ally himself with a reform party that would save capitalism? His mind was already working with a different theory. Assuming that he might be considered, he instructed his followers to endorse William Jennings Bryan, the Democratic nominee, and to work for unity in the campaign.[20] To his chagrin, Debs had supported Cleveland in 1888 and 1892, and was now wary of Democratic politicians, but he supported Bryan hoping that free silver would be only one reform issue and that a Democratic victory would help labor. He himself wrote Bryan:

> With millions of others of your countrymen I congratulate you most heartily upon being the People's standard bearer in the great uprising of the masses against the classes. You are at this hour the hope of the Republic, the central figure of the civilized world. In the arduous campaign before you the millions will rally to your standard and you will lead them to glorious victory. The people love and trust you—they believe in you as you believe in them, and under your administration the rule of the money power will be broken and the gold barons of Europe will no longer run the American government.[21]

Thus he accepted all the clichés of the silverites and threw himself into the campaign against gold and what he considered plutocracy. In his heart he knew that it was a choice of evils, but like many he trusted for the moment in Bryan and the people's wish.

He knew less of silver even than the average Democrat, and devoted his speeches to labor and its cause. The further he proceeded the more he realized that the Populists and Democrats were only reformers, prisoners of a single idea, devoid of a coherent and comprehensive program of reform. He concluded that reform of existing capitalism was not enough. He was ready for socialism.[22] Despite opposition from many labor leaders who felt that he hurt labor's cause, Debs spoke extensively in the Midwest, capitalizing on his own fame and on the sentiment of the hour to advance Bryan's cause.[23] He spoke with eloquence to many gatherings, attended by men in overalls and their Sunday best alike, preaching change and even revolt. Heads nodded and his rhetoric rose in wrath against the "masters." Although he disliked Democrats, remembering Cleveland, to him as to many others, Bryan was a different story, a white hope for a new order.[24]

McKinley's victory in November was only one of several events that proved to Debs that the old system needed drastic revision if the people were to rise to plenty and progress. That change could come about only through socialism. On January 1, 1897, he announced in a lead editorial in the *Railway Times* that he had accepted socialism. Berger and other socialists, his own reading and reflection, and events of the last few years had convinced him that capitalism was justly doomed and that the new order would be based on a socialism flowing from common ownership and common rule.[25]

It is doubtful that what he read influenced him as much

as what he saw. From first to last he had no taste for theory. A natural bent for the romantic and idealistic, a genuine dislike of the economic and social poverty he saw around him, and an aching desire to help his fellow men moved him to cast his lot with socialism. The Pullman strike was the central event of his early career for it convinced him that there was a class struggle in America and that mankind could move forward only when capitalism was replaced by socialism. On these assumptions, he was ready to do battle for a new cause.

The socialist movement which he joined was far from powerful, but it had potential. Its origins lay deep in American history, in the idealistic experiments, the limited utopias, the Brook Farms and Oneidas and other visionary communities. These early experiments were important—every movement has its ancestors—for they showed that some of socialism was indigenous to the American experiment. But the real impulse toward organized socialism rose with industrialization and economic expansion after the Civil War, which created factory work and factory workers, social discontent, and opportunity for agitation.

Organized socialism in the United States did not prosper mightily, but one important party arose, the Socialist Labor Party. Its base was the immigrants who flooded into the eastern industrial centers, particularly New York City, in the 1870's and 1880's. It was a small party, suffering from its lack of attachment to the trade union movement, and prey to factionalism which sapped its strength. The SLP was formed in 1877, and took advantage of the large numbers of German socialists and sympathizers in the East.[26] The SLP leaders believed in "boring from within" the established trade unions and worked assiduously in that direction. The party entered politics in a limited way in the late 1870's and early 1880's and scored enough success in some eastern municipalities to warrant its hope of a bright future as a political force. In 1880, much to their later chagrin, the SLP membership supported the Greenback candidate for President, but failed to capture the loose and ineffective organization of that party.[27]

Hard times in the mid-1870's gave the socialists fields in which to work, and they cooperated with the Knights of Labor and other union groups. The great coal and rail strikes of that decade found them often in the thick of labor and political struggles.[28] But they suffered from their doctrinal quarrels and from their failure to understand the American economic and social system and they never captured control of the unions which might have given them an entering wedge to successful political organization and social power. In 1886 they cast their unwelcomed lot with Henry George in his famous race for the mayoralty of New York.[29] His defeat embittered the SLP and turned most of the party membership away from cooperation with reform groups.

In 1892, the SLP nominated Simon Wing of Boston for President, and Charles Matchett of New York for Vice-President. Running on tickets in six states, they received 21,512 votes, hardly enough to usher in the long awaited millennium, but sufficient to spark hope.[30] The party was especially active in New York, and in its early days Tammany thought so little of socialist candidates that it hired urchins to pelt SLP men with eggs and stones as a show of contempt.[31] Socialist Labor Party tickets entered numerous local political contests but drew little publicity from the press, which chose to ignore them.[32]

The SLP produced one great figure—to whom it owed much of its success and most of its failure—the stocky, bearded, scholarly and purposeful Daniel DeLeon. Born in the Dutch West Indies in 1852, he came to America for his education and taught law and diplomacy at Columbia University. Widely read in history, political science, philosophy, and sociology, he flirted with radicalism in the 1870's. Reading Marx, he was converted and sacrificed a promising career to dedicate himself to the task of establishing a sect of pure Marxists in the United States, committed to industrial unionism and political action. His hand shaped the SLP and he brooked no opposition. Those he attacked hated him, and his savage pen impaled many a friendship on fine points of doctrine. "The New York Pope," as he was called, never hesitated to purge those whom he considered poor Marxists. He had all the rigidity, passion and belief of the true fanatic. Unhappily for him, in a country which disliked theoretical dogma, he knew little else. In Europe he might have become a leading light, but in America he became instead a dogmatic crank.[33] Debs disliked DeLeon's dogmatism and the two seldom agreed. William D. "Big Bill" Haywood summed it up years later when he said that DeLeon was "the theorizing professor," while Debs was the spokesman of the working class; it was DeLeon's purpose to indoctrinate, Debs' to convert.[34]

By the late 1890's, the SLP reached the height of its influence. In politics its success was limited, in labor organization it was a failure due to DeLeon's establishment of a rival union to the American Federation of

Labor after failing to win that organization. Factional-ism was rife within the party's ranks and the rigid doc-trinal demands and hairsplitting practiced by the De-Leonites drove more and more people away yearly. Clearly the SLP was ready for changes.

It was not to DeLeon and the SLP that Debs turned when he wanted advice on socialism but to the small group of socialists around Victor Berger in Milwaukee. The stolid, Germanic Berger, whose dignified, stocky appear-ance belied his Austrian origins, was among those who first interested Debs in socialism and though the years were to separate them, Debs greatly admired Berger as he began his career as a socialist. Berger, like DeLeon, was an immigrant and had worked as a common laborer and school teacher before organizing a remarkably effec-tive political machine in Milwaukee. His work with the German element in that city paid great dividends and "The Bear," as friends called him, was cautious and astute enough to know how fast to move.[35]

In the months after his release from jail and after the campaign of 1896, Debs drifted until his pronouncements in favor of socialism in 1897. He had enough to do; he was busy lecturing, paying off the ARU debt, helping blacklisted friends and union followers, and finishing up the ARU's business. He was obviously uncertain in choos-ing his kind of socialism. On the one hand he could not face the rigidity of DeLeon; on the other hand he was not sure that Berger's rather academic socialism appealed to him either.

Inevitably he turned to utopian colonization schemes. He joined a movement to a plant a colony of socialists in some sparsely-populated western state in the hope that in time growing socialist influence would dominate the state and influence the rest of the nation. Such a plan naturally appealed to the romantic and sentimental Debs who was inclined to believe what he wanted to believe. Furthermore, it was an excellent way of providing for his old ARU followers, many of whom were in dire straits. In June, 1897, he agreed with the ARU convention which formed the Social Democracy of America, with colonization as its aim, and lent his energies to raising funds for the group. Conversion to colonization did not turn him from political action, however, and he insisted that the new group was politically oriented. "Were the colonization plans to prove a failure it would not stop the Social Democracy movement," he assured skeptical socialist friends.[36] He believed sincerely that the campaign of 1900 would bring the socialists to the forefront, and that the commonwealth would be inaugurated in 1904. He even labored under the naive misapprehension that the SLP, the Social Democracy and other socialist groups would easily cooperate in the scheme.[37]

It was plain to all who cared to see that the colonization plans were a failure; funds were scarce, opinion divided, the West a long way off. Yet Debs' dream died hard. He was anxious to help his ARU followers and seemed desperate to prove that his idealism could be made practical. Throughout 1897 and 1898 he vacillated between the political actionists and the colonizers. Friends knew that he was more and more drawn to political action but he hesitated to abandon the colonists lest he destroy their last hope. By June, 1898, the two groups in the Social Democracy came to a parting of the ways. As one observer put it, "People cannot be kept enthusiastic in 44 states over the prospect of establishing a model common-wealth in the 45th on easy monthly payments." [38] In the convention of that month, the colonists overrode objections and voted to continue their efforts. The vote was a signal for the political actionists to bolt and form a new party. At an early hour in the morning, under Berger's leadership, they did so. Debs was conveniently ill in his hotel room, but sent word of his support to the political actionists and the Social Democratic Party was launched.[39]

In the months that followed, the outlines of the new Social Democratic Party emerged. It was a genuinely socialistic party, based on the idea of a cooperative common-wealth, political agitation, propaganda, work with labor unions, belief in the class struggle and other communal ideas inherited from the pattern of European socialism as altered to fit the American situation. A set of "immediate demands" satisfied the Berger element, which wanted to proceed slowly in their transformation of capitalism. To all of this Debs gave his support, glad that the vexing colonization question was settled and anxious to begin his work with the new party. Significantly, he himself participated little in the organization of the new party; theory and formal organization were never his forte. He left that to others and planned instead to preach a popular socialism that would appeal to the masses. He threw himself into his work with a will and undertook an extensive tour which carried him as far as Texas and through the Midwest. By September, 1898, thanks largely to his efforts and reputation, twelve states boasted SDP organizations.[40]

Though Debs took little note of doctrinal matters, others did, and the new SDP was but a fledgling when divisions of opinion arose, a pattern that was to plague the

American socialist movement all of its life. The rough factional outlines into which the party settled in the next decade were evident even in 1898. Though the socialists always resisted easy classification, two basic geographic wings contended within the party, the more conservative easterners centered in New York, and the more radical westerners operating in Chicago and further west in the Rocky Mountains. The conservative Bergerites were generally somewhere in between, allying themselves more with New York than with Denver.

More than geography divided the socialists, however. The conservatives like Berger were willing to cooperate on a limited scale with local reform elements in order to attain political office and to institute their mild "immediate demands." They believed largely in "step at a time socialism." They disliked craft unionism symbolized by the seemingly successful AFL, but were seldom willing to antagonize these same unions if it meant political defeat.

The left wing, or so-called revolutionary socialists, who claimed Debs' support, were far less tractable, demanded a truly socialistic political platform, and were spiteful toward craft unions and the hated AFL. They "bored from within," much to the annoyance of the craft unionists, and did not hesitate to destroy an organization for their own purposes. Genuine radical socialism was their aim and fine points of conduct did not deter them.

It was, in the end, a question of means and time. The "Slowcialists," as the conservatives were called, would go slow, work hard and depend on organization and compromise for success at the polls to implement socialism in stages. The revolutionists wanted a constant drive, lettered in red, for the full socialist program at once. The end was the same, the cooperative commonwealth, only the means differed. Yet the means were crucial, since they defined the type of socialism envisioned, and were thus worth fighting for; hence the constant struggle for power among leaders within the party. Factionalism was the curse that finally brought socialism to ruin, and was inherent in the very circumstances of its establishment.

Debs greatly disliked party gatherings and did his best to rise above factions. He had no stomach for doctrinal haggling and no will to fight socialists. He much preferred the color, glamor and excitement of the lecture circuit to the convention hall or planning board. He felt uncomfortable in the midst of theorists, yet he himself in his way fashioned a social philosophy which was a curious blend of American and European doctrine, of individualism and collectivism, of idealism and realism.[41]

In truth he knew little of the academic theories of socialism or the formal discipline of Marx or other socialist thinkers, but the goal for which he strove was the same as theirs and, once converted to socialism, he accepted the basic tenets of the creed without reservation. Early in his career as a socialist he founded his social theory on a few principles to which he adhered throughout his life. The political, social, and economic system which he envisaged and for which he worked was nothing less than a utopia, a heavenly city. He had no elaborate design for it, except to base it on common wealth and cooperation.

He believed that industrial capitalism and the profit motive it inspired were the roots of all evil, for they created a system which oppressed the individual and enabled some men to profit unjustly from the labor of others.

If capitalism could be replaced by a more humane co-operative socialism, the whole social system, the very nature of man and his world, could be changed for the better. A basic paradox in all of Debs' thinking was his quest for greater individual freedom and development through the adoption of an equalitarian cooperative society.

This belief that capitalism was evil and in a transitional phase motivated Debs' attack on the economic system of his day. "The day of individual effort, of small tools, free competition, hand labor, long hours and meagre results is gone never to return," he said bluntly in 1904. "The civilization reared upon this old foundation is crumbling." [42] Men were bad because the system was bad; he was an environmentalist of the simplest type. For that reason he did not hate the capitalist, for he, like the worker, was merely a product of the system. "We shouldn't forget that many capitalists are born capitalists just as many workers are born workers, and the former are creatures of their environment and circumstance in precisely the same sense as the latter." [43] Change the system and you change the men; that was his answer.

His personal sentimentality and his wish to believe in his fellow men blended with a genuine belief in the goodness of men to raise his theory to an exalted vision. "Love and labor in alliance, working together, have transforming, redeeming and emancipating power," he said. "Under their benign sway the world can be made better and brighter." [44] He would have agreed heartily with the socialist editor who wrote: " 'You can't change human nature,' says the shallow thinker. The deuce we can't? Well, just give me a chance and if I don't change it, I'll change its manifestations, which is the same thing for all practical purposes of socialism." [45]

Debs devoted his whole career to agitating for a revolution which never came but in which he never lost faith. A second paradox of his thinking was his distrust of violence though he preached revolution. In truth, there was little substance to the menacing shadows cast by his revolutionary talk, for he believed that socialism could and would be adopted through the ballot in America; he never envisaged an upheaval comparable to the Russian revolution. His steadfast belief in socialist political action rested upon the assumption that once the workers were aroused and educated, they would vote socialism into being. "[The Ballot] can give our civilization its crowning glory—the cooperative commonwealth." [46] He was radical in the end he wished to attain more than in the means by which he wished to attain it. If anything, he was representative of a generation of American reformers who sought revolutionary ends by orderly and peaceful means. His reliance on common sense, education, the ballot instead of the bullet, placed him in the mainstream of American radicalism.

The coming commonwealth was real to him, as it was to other dedicated socialists of the day, and he believed in what he taught. Man could be made new again, the world could be made beautiful:

> When the bread and butter problem is solved and all men and women and children the world around are rendered secure from dread of war and fear of want, then the mind and soul will be free to develop as they

never were before. We shall have a literature and an
art such as the troubled heart and brain of man never
before conceived. We shall have beautiful houses
and happy homes such as want could never foster or
drudgery secure. We shall have beautiful thoughts
and sentiments, and a divinity in religion, such as
man weighted down by the machine could never have
imagined.[47]

Such was his vision, and to him it was as real as the sordid
world around him.

If Debs was aware of the contradictions, the naivete,
the lack of realism in his social theories he did not admit
it; in fact, he probably reflected little upon them. He
spoke his beliefs for all to hear, not asking that they agree,
asking only that they understand. It was easy for him to
cling to his ideals for he participated little in the party
organization, had almost nothing to do with party doctrine, and spent most of his time among people who agreed
with him and who were easily swayed by his words. His
mission was to evangelize socialism, to verbalize as one
the protest of many, to be the Great Agitator of his day.
"Ink pots have never been inviting to me," he told a friend
late in life, "but I cannot say the same of the platform.
That is my forte." [48]

It is easy to dismiss as unrealistic much of what the
early twentieth century American socialists felt, yet as
they stood at the door of a new century it seemed they
had every reason to be hopeful. Socialism the world around
prospered mightily, borne upward on the wave of industrialization that created capitalist and worker. In America the socialists profited from other protest movements,

first from Populism and then from Progressivism. They adapted to the American idiom and devised an organization which accommodated every shade of the red spectrum. In an age of confidence in the worth of man, in a time of belief in progress and the ultimate conquest of evil and poverty, the socialists preached a doctrine that attracted many who would later be repelled.[49] They were gripped by a vision no less real than that which moved the early Christians. For them the kingdom was indeed at hand; capitalism was crumbling before a new and higher order of life. The thunder of Populist discontent, they thought, foretold the death of the capitalist system. In the gathering groundswell of Progressive revolt, they perceived the tidal wave that would cleanse America of capitalistic evil. Only this consuming belief can explain the ferocity with which they debated fine points of procedure, for it mattered what kind of socialism was adopted. Many of the socialists, like Debs himself, had forged their personal beliefs in harsh fires of experience. Academic dreamers and practical workers alike believed in the coming commonwealth. As Marx had said, history was on their side; they need only watch and work.

Debs came to American socialism at a time when it needed his qualities most. He gave to it his color, enthusiasm, boundless energy, and American ideals. He became a figure around whom socialists of every stripe could rally in times of crisis. He brought a national reputation and important connections with the labor movement and the common people. The socialists could indeed be proud of having captured his allegiance. He was one with his new comrades in the belief that the future belonged to socialism. The year 1900 saw the birth of a new century and a new force in American politics and it marked the rise of Eugene Debs as a political leader. In more ways than one this was a new century. Underneath the seeming content of America, ferment was at work. Eugene Debs was to have a leading role against the backdrop of the new century and the restless men it produced.

II

The Promise of American
Socialism: The Campaign of 1900

*Promising indeed is the outlook for Social-
ism in the United States. The very con-
templation of the prospect is a well-spring
of inspiration.*

Eugene V. Debs, 1900

In the golden age of American socialism, prior to the
World War, there was nothing quite like a socialist convention. Such gatherings focused the discontents and differences of opinion of the membership and few conventions passed without invective and violence, often over the
most trivial of points. The SLP had more than its share
of the masters of invective, and its conventions and organizational meetings on every level were often scenes of
tumult and shouting.

By 1898–1899 the stresses and strains in the fabric
of DeLeon's SLP were all too plain. Though the party enjoyed rising membership and encouraging electoral success on local levels, appearances of growth and unity were
deceptive. Inside the party a strong rebellion against De-
Leon's tyrannical leadership was brewing. As the party
convention in New York approached in 1899, a group led
by Morris Hillquit prepared to make themselves known
or break away from their comrades. Angered by DeLeon's

increasingly pedantic "scientific socialism" and his tyrannical manner, disgusted by the failure of his dual union
policy, believing that their conciliation toward the AFL
was ready to bear fruit, and anxious to emphasize political
action, a potent group rallied around Hillquit to contest
the master's control of the party.

Hillquit was an able leader, destined to be a ranking
member of the American socialist movement. Born in
Riga, Latvia, he emigrated to America where he studied
and practiced law while dabbling in radical politics. His
dislike of capitalism and belief in socialism did not prevent
his amassing a lucrative law practice. A deft compromiser,
a skilful manipulator with an exhaustive understanding
of parliamentary procedure, and a hard driving, if somewhat chilly, personality, he was marked for party leadership. Though appearing to be liberal, he was in fact a conservative socialist, and time drew him and Berger together
as the leading "Slowcialists" of their day. In 1900 his role
in the SLP was that of the new leader, and he fulfilled it
well.

The New York convention of July, 1899, was a classic
event in socialist annals.[1] The Hillquit faction, dubbed
"Kangaroos" by their opponents, were determined to oust
the DeLeonites from party control; the latter were equally
determined to remain in control. The result was a brawl
on the convention floor that cost smashed furniture, broken
heads, and bloody noses for both groups. The Hillquit
faction rallied after being forcibly ousted by the De-
Leonites and formed a new SLP, claiming all the privileges of the old; each side promptly purged the other and
claimed exclusive control of the party press, membership
lists, and organization.[2] To the astonishment of SLP

members in other states, the New York party degenerated into a permanent brawl. Invective boiled over; where two or three socialists gathered together there was a fight. Two identical issues of *The People* appeared, one published by each group, each blasting the other; there were two SLP organizations, each claiming the full membership of the original party; purges were wholesale.

The Kangaroo faction organized its members along what it considered socialist lines, insisted that political action was the key to success, and adopted a more tractable attitude toward the AFL, whose capture for socialism it deemed likely in the future. In November, 1899, both factions of the SLP prepared to nominate candidates for the New York elections. DeLeon quickly carried his case to the capitalist courts, who upheld his control of the party and his right to use the name and the organization.

Weary of bickering and aware that they could hardly win over the courts, the Kangaroos turned instead to the formation of a new union party with the rising SDP of Berger and Debs. Hints had been in the air since July and many SDP members were frankly desirous of unity; it was rumored that Debs himself favored such a movement.

Accordingly, the Kangaroos convened in Rochester, New York, late in January, 1900, where with as much amity as there had been enmity in July, they fashioned a new platform and nominated a presidential slate. Job Harriman of California and Max Hayes of Ohio were chosen for the Presidency and Vice-Presidency respectively. In point of fact, the Kangaroos did not intend to run their ticket, but used it as a blade to turn a compromise with the Social Democrats, whose convention was scheduled for early spring. To achieve this end, a committee was chosen to deal with the SDP for unity of the two groups and nomination of a joint slate for the presidential election of 1900. They confidently awaited the outcome of their negotiations with the SDP.

They did not wait long, for the SDP national convention met in March, 1900, in Indianapolis to nominate a presidential slate and attend to party business. The years between 1898 and 1900 were times of transition and hard work for the Social Democrats, but the delegates to the national convention were proud of the organization they had built against heavy odds. On the surface it was a minor party, claiming only 5,000 members, but it had come a long and relatively prosperous way through the toils of party strife and public apathy.

In the months after its organization in 1898, the SDP literally ran on a shoe string, or to be more accurate, a watch chain, for when funds were exhausted, Debs' younger brother Theodore pawned his watch to pay postage and office rent until dues were collected. Party officials in Chicago and New York dined at free lunch counters and spent odd hours pasting socialist stickers on the elevated railway.[4]

Hard times did not dampen spirits nor deter SDP efforts. Debs early suggested that in areas where there was no SDP local, socialists might vote for SLP candidates rather than waste their votes on capitalist reform candidates, but this was a move born of desperation and a policy that ended as quickly as the SDP organization could be built.[5] Between 1898 and 1900, Debs was on the road constantly in an effort to strengthen the party organization and recruit members, speaking at country crossroads and county fairs, city auditoriums and on the lecture circuit, preceded everywhere by his reputation. His efforts repaid handsome dividends. He persuaded many independent socialist groups to form SDP locals, establishing nuclei in several states. He even entered an opening wedge for socialism in the solid South by winning the independent socialists of Tennessee, Arkansas and Texas to the SDP banner.[6]

The SDP was especially active and successful politically in Massachusetts and Wisconsin. In the former state, the party made a considerable show of strength in Haverhill, where disaffected workers in shoe and textile factories sympathized with socialism. In December, 1897, James F. Carey of Haverhill, allied with the local SLP, was elected to the city council. In January, 1898, he was elected president of the Common Council. The touchy DeLeonites sniffed treason in the air, accused Carey of deserting socialism for political office, demanded that he enact the commonwealth at once, and finally expelled him for "opportunism." [7] It was a familiar story in socialist politics, but Debs took advantage of SLP troubles and visited Carey in company with Sylvester Keliher, another SDP organizer. The two men persuaded Carey to join the SDP and help organize a local. In November, 1898, Carey and a friend, Louis Scates, were elected to the state legislature by the disgruntled workers on the SDP ticket and public interest rose.[8] A month later John Chase was elected mayor of Haverhill on the SDP ticket.[9] "The mere casting of these 2,500 votes has done more to direct attention to Socialism than could have been done with any other means," wrote Julius Wayland in the *Appeal to Reason*.[10] These successes were at best minor, yet to the socialists, grasping at straws and eager to use every means to advance their cause, they portended the coming revolution. If they were not important politically, such victories were important as morale builders.

The party officially refused to sanction voting for reform candidates and urged socialists everywhere to vote the socialist ticket and to put forward socialist candidates and platforms whenever possible.[11] Every triumph, however small, was a tonic to socialism everywhere and a seed from which later success might sprout.

In Milwaukee, Victor Berger's growing socialist machine began to bear fruit that later made it famous. Astutely working with the city's large immigrant population, especially the Germans, Berger devised a socialist program based on gradualism that appealed to many dissatisfied elements. He enlisted the aid and help of prominent reformers, ran his own newspaper and propaganda service, and labored night and day to perfect a political organization that could challenge the Republicans and Democrats. In the spring of 1898, the Milwaukee SDP put forward a full slate of candidates for the city election. Standing on a tempered socialist platform boasting its reform tendencies and lack of radicalism, they won nearly six per cent of the total vote.[12]

Elsewhere in 1898 the socialists made hopeful beginnings. Socialist candidates ran in the fall elections in Massachusetts, New Hampshire, Maryland, New York, Wisconsin, Indiana and Missouri, polling 12,000 votes. Massachusetts won most of the party's laurels, but SDP candidates were successful elsewhere also; in January, 1900, the party headquarters announced that twenty members had been elected to public office, and confidently asserted that this was but the beginning of the coming avalanche.[13] It was an obvious exaggeration, but not without its significance. If nothing else, the victories proved that the party could win with work and organization, and also that the party was committed to political action as well as mass propaganda and work with labor unions.

As the SDP national convention of March, 1900, approached, the demand for unity with the SLP Kangaroos was growing among the rank and file members of both groups. Though the National Executive Board of the SDP distrusted Hillquit's faction, they issued a formal but chilly call for unity early in 1900. Debs himself, in an anomalous and vacillating position, favored unity but vigorously attacked the SLP men for what he considered defamation of his name.[14] On the one hand he desired unity, but his alliance with Berger, who did not, and his long dislike of DeLeon and anyone connected with the SLP warned him to go slow.

The Social Democrats did not send representatives to the Kangaroo convention in 1900, despite an invitation, and sent instead only their formal call for unity. Hillquit replied in effect that his men were willing but would not accept dictation. Aware that the rank and file of the SDP favored unity, realizing that they promised much in the way of coordinated campaign work, and hopeful that Debs would use his influence for unity, they too bided their time.[15] Meanwhile, the SDP headquarters was flooded with letters and petitions demanding unity between the two groups. Clearly it was the topic of the hour in socialist circles. If it was important to the rank and file, who presumably discussed it around their firesides and at their local meetings, something would have to be done.

The SDP National Executive Board, who hoped that

in time the dissident Kangaroos would drop singly into their laps without risking public fusion, were disappointed in their plan, for the general demand for immediate unity was too strong.[16] Outmaneuvered, the NEB agreed to permit Kangaroo delegates to attend the national convention and the reluctant SDP leaders expressed the vague hope that their efforts "may in due season be crowned with success." [17] The Kangaroos, who had already adopted a resolution favoring unity and appointed a unity committee, accepted with alacrity.

The sixty-seven delegates who came to Indianapolis for the national convention of the Social Democratic Party in March, 1900, represented thirty-two states and a membership of almost 5,000.[18] The boisterous welcome which they accorded the Kangaroo delegates indicated their desire for unity and frowns from the party leaders did not dampen their enthusiasm for the project. Hillquit and other Kangaroos were invited to share the platform and could speak but not vote during the proceedings. Business was barely in order when Debs moved that a committee retire to consider unity.[19]

The committee duly reported not one but two reports, as might have been expected. The majority report favored unity only with retention of the name "Social Democratic Party," and in general reflected the recalcitrance of the men around Berger, who were still suspicious of the Kangaroos. In their opinion, like the pope in the French proverb, who ate of DeLeon died of him. The minority report was milder, only suggesting that the name "Social Democratic Party" be adopted. It was a question of tone, not of content. Berger strongly supported the majority report, insisting that the Kangaroos must be taken on SDP terms, and rallied strong support. Hillquit would not swallow dictation, pointing out that the former SLP men were not beggars. Conciliation, at which Hillquit was a master, triumphed with Debs' support and the minority report was adopted. A committee on unity was appointed to meet with a similar Kangaroo committee and the prospects of unity seemed bright.

This accomplished, the convention turned to nominate a presidential slate. The Social Democrats confidently expected Debs to accept their nomination by acclamation; he was the logical candidate, a national figure, an experienced speaker, a man with a ready audience in labor and liberal circles. Moreover, his tendency toward unity with the Kangaroos would help ease the difficult work of the unity committee. But Debs dismayed everyone concerned by positively refusing the nomination. He cited his repeated promises never to seek office, his debts, and his dislike of campaigning.[20]

The convention was in chaos when someone nominated Harriman and Hayes, the Kangaroo candidates, on the grounds that they were the next best thing to Debs, and it might promote unity.[21] Berger saw Hillquit's fine hand in the action. Panic-stricken lest the nomination go by default to the suspected Kangaroos, who were not even Social Democrats, the conservative Social Democrats maneuvered a hasty adjournment to gain time and devise a plan.

It was suggested that a committee of leaders consult on the nomination and Hillquit quickly agreed, aware of his bargaining position. Berger was more cautious but finally succumbed to pressure, and seven Social Democrats joined Hillquit, Harriman, and G. B. Benham of California in the old Occidental Hotel for a conference on the nomination.[22] Hillquit at once offered to support the name "Social Democratic Party" if the SDP would nominate Harriman and Hayes. Berger backed and filled, protesting that Debs' friends were pressuring him and that he might yet accept the nomination. He asked if the Kangaroos would accept the name "Social Democratic Party" if Debs agreed to run, and Hillquit and Harriman agreed. The meeting then adjourned to permit Berger to talk with Debs.

Meanwhile, Debs' friends had converged on him in his hotel room, filling it with smoke and protests. He was still adamant. His lank frame sprawled across the bed, he listened to their pleas, walked around a while to cool off, thought it over, and then succumbed; he would run.[23] Jubilant, the Debs men rushed to Berger with the good news just as he left Hillquit. Both were taken aback for they had assumed that it would take some time to persuade Debs. Suspicion flared in Hillquit's mind that Berger had bargained knowing that Debs would run. The suspicion lingered, but faded now in the glow of success; a sigh of relief went up over a vexing problem presumably settled.

"Debs Forced To Take It," ran the headline of the *Indianapolis Press* of March 9, 1900, as he and Harriman were nominated for President and Vice-President respectively.[24] Debs addressed the delegates with his customary emotional rhetoric and insisted that he had been sincere in his first refusal. "But now, with your united voices ringing in my ears, with your impassioned appeals burning and glowing in my breast and your eyes searching the depths of my soul, I am brought to realize that in your voice is a supreme command of duty." [25] It promised to be a colorful and dramatic campaign for the fledgling socialists.

The platform on which Debs stood was a compromise of revolutionary and evolutionary socialism, designed to appeal to all socialists. While proclaiming the party's adherence to socialism and calling for a cooperative commonwealth, it also contained demands for women's suffrage, public works for the unemployed, national labor laws, direct legislation, and a host of other reform measures.[26]

With their business transacted, the delegates adjourned and returned home to work for the unity which they confidently expected and to prepare for the coming campaign. Debs himself returned to Terre Haute, hoping to rest before plunging into the maelstrom. Even by 1900 he had been on enough speaking tours to know that they were exhausting and held few rewards save the knowledge that the cause was advanced. He lost no time in displaying his talents. Terre Haute knew him as a lovable man, even if he was a socialist, and he was open to every charge of glad-handing and baby-kissing because of his personality and natural effervescence. A large crowd gathered at the railroad station to welcome him home, some curious, some eager to congratulate him. He doffed his hat, bowed and smilingly made his way through the crowd, shaking hands, when he spied a colored porter he knew. Vaulting blithely over a railing, he extended his arms and cried out: "Why, bless my heart, Bob, it's good to see you." [27] In an age that savored dignity in its presidential candidates, thus did Eugene Debs begin his first national campaign.

The weeks after the national convention were doldrums, for it was too early to begin campaigning. But if it was quiet in public, socialists on the inner councils knew better, for the vexing unity question now rose to the fore. Hopes that the national convention had settled the issue were shattered by the floods of denunciation, charges and countercharges that shortly enveloped the unity committee.

The committee met in New York on March 25, 1900. Berger was significantly and eloquently absent, though able lieutenants spoke for him. His chief spokesman at the conference, Frederic Heath, denounced the Kangaroos for allegedly breaking their promises and withdrew. The remaining delegates compromised and drew up a "treaty of union" which called for a party referendum on the unity question and established working unity for the presidential campaign. There was to be no official party press, but certain papers were to be subsidized by party headquarters. Springfield, Massachusetts was chosen party headquarters as a compromise between New York and Chicago, while the latter city was to be the center of campaign direction. The "treaty" amalgamated the two platforms and endorsed Debs and Harriman.[28]

Assurances that it was all over but the shouting were in vain as the NEB of the SDP charged that the Kangaroos were still dealing in bad faith; Berger and others steadily attacked the ex-DeLeonites for their dogmatism and impeded the unity referendum.[29] Party members from coast to coast were confused. On May 12, the NEB of the SDP announced that its party members had refused to endorse unity with the Kangaroos.[30] Not to be deterred, the unity committee sent out ballots of its own to both the Kangaroos and the regular SDP membership.

The Kangaroos had the advantage from the first, for

many prominent SDP members and leaders favored unity despite Berger's protests. "I have already heard from enough places to assure us that the hardest workers in our party are for union and our NEB will get a shock that will surprise them," one Social Democrat wrote Hillquit.[31] John Chase and others cautioned against further public quarreling since that played into the NEB's hands, and counseled everyone to work for the future and to forego debate.[32] Both the advice and tactics were sounder than those pursued by the Bergerites.

Debs took little part in the discussion, but those desiring unity used his name freely. In truth he vacillated, for while he favored unity and speedy compromise, he still did not trust the DeLeonites. He opposed any cooperation with the regular SLP and was still stung by the attacks on him in DeLeon's press.[33] Late in May, Debs attended a unity conference with leaders of both groups. Hillquit attacked the recalcitrant SDP spokesmen. Debs, as usual, wished a hasty compromise and suggested that practical unity be adopted for the campaign and that the details be worked out later. Hillquit hotly rejected this as an effort to use the Kangaroos in crucial areas without giving them credit or voice in the party.[34] The meeting adjourned where it had begun, awaiting results from the party referendum.

The socialists did not wait long. During June and July the vote trickled into party headquarters. The sentiment for unity grew stronger as the campaign season approached, and most members of both groups were tired of bickering and anxious to join their strength.[35] Early in July the totals were announced; both the SDP rank and file and the Kangaroos had voted overwhelmingly for unity. The NEB's protests were waved aside and the Kangaroos accepted the results as final. On July 13 and 14, the Kangaroo leaders held their last meeting, turned over their records to the new Springfield headquarters, chose William Butscher as party secretary, and notified Debs and Harriman of their nomination on a joint ticket.[36]

The question was: Would Debs accept? His acceptance would cut the ground from under the NEB and destroy their position, making unity a fact. Debs did not disappoint his followers and accepted the nomination over strong protest from Berger and others. In point of fact, he was sick of the whole endless quarrel and had hard words for all parties concerned. "There are fools and fanatics on our side as well as the other who would sacrifice the ticket and sink the movement to gratify their miserable 2x4 spite and resentment," he wrote Frederic Heath in defense of his acceptance. "It has been said that war is hell and the same is true of the man who is the candidate of such dwarfish creatures. You know under what circumstances I accepted the nomination. Besides a thousand other objections I had to it, it knocked me out of at least $2000 financially and from that day to this hell has been popping around my ears in token of grateful appreciation of my sacrifice." At long last he decided to exercise the leadership that was rightfully his, and was determined to rise above factions. "I have made up my mind to do as I please, that is to say, as I think right and if the wild men who nominated me do not like it all they have to do is to nominate somebody else to dance on with hobnail shoes." [37] The show of unity had duly impressed Debs; he could hardly afford, as Hillquit and others had foreseen, to spurn a nomination from a united group, even if it meant stepping on toes in the Berger camp.[38]

On July 31, he formally accepted the joint nomination and sounded a clear call for unity. "Let us dismiss all minor considerations and unite in every state and territory, from end to end of the land in one mighty effort to hasten the end of capitalism and the inauguration of the cooperative commonwealth." [39] Privately he was just as emphatic. "I have accepted the ratification of my nomination by the Springfield party," he wrote Heath. "I did it in the interest of the Socialist movement compared with which all parties so far developed in this country amount to less than nothing. Had I done otherwise, I would have been as small and contemptible and as unworthy of the position I occupy as those in the other party our people are making so much fuss about." [40]

Both groups were fully alive to the importance of Debs' acceptance. His national figure now became the pole around which opinion in both factions crystallized; the unity movement was in full sway. "Debs' letter may be cunning [?] but it acknowledges a unity committee, referendum vote, and a national secretary with headquarters at Springfield, Mass.," Butscher wrote. "This is the best thing that could have happened for us and will materially strengthen us by making those who were on the fence flop over." [41]

The situation now was at best confused, and many socialists rubbed their eyes. There was only one SLP, that of DeLeon, but there were two SDP organizations, the Bergerites in Chicago and Milwaukee, and the new "united Party" in Springfield. Fortunately for the cause, everyone was weary of the bickering; the main issue was the party name and that had been decided in favor of the SDP. The subterranean fear that the Kangaroos would dominate the party evaporated from all but the die-hards, and party members everywhere prepared to join hands for the campaign.

The business at hand, after all, was the presidential race and the party rank and file fell to the task with a will, casting aside for the moment at least quarrels and quibbles over doctrine and organization. The rank and file now looked to Debs for a spirited and effective campaign and he did not disappoint them. They could not hope to win, but the same belief in their cause that inspired them to found their party now urged them to make every vote count for socialism. In a cause such as this, with his gifts for propaganda and personal contact, Debs was highly effective. He gladly abandoned the council table for the more exciting and, to him, more rewarding lecture circuit and campaign stump.

Even as the smoke of committee battles rose, socialists in city and state were not idle. May Day brought unusual demonstrations of workers in New York and Chicago, and many Debs and Harriman banners fluttered in the marching ranks of workers.[42] The socialists were under no illusions as to their strength, but they missed no opportunity to make their influence felt. Strikes brought socialist agitators, richly supplied with literature and lung power, to take advantage of disaffection. In the East, party workers tried to win union support, while in the West and Midwest agitators appealed to more radical elements to join the procession to utopia behind Debs and Harriman. Occasional arrests of socialists were grist for the party's mills and socialists welcomed the publicity. "I think [Max] Hayes' arrest will result in great good to the cause although rather inconvenient for Max," Butscher wrote a field worker. "You ought to make good use of it as propaganda among the workmen." [43]

Money was a problem to the socialists. Their scant resources were badly strained throughout the campaign and despite prosperity among workers they gathered little funds. "No contributions coming in for the Nat'l Campaign Fund," the tireless Butscher wrote. "This should be boomed up and the comrades' attention be brought to it." [44] Campaign donors' names were printed in the party press with calls for more money.[45] In fighting capitalism it was, unhappily, necessary to fight fire with fire.

Before the campaign was launched an organization was outlined and filled in as well as possible. Chicago boasted a campaign committee, and Springfield acted as a clearing house for information and literature and operated a speakers' bureau. Sixteen speakers worked from the Springfield office, touring the East and Midwest.[46] "Encouraging news is coming from all quarters and speakers are always in demand," Butscher noted.[47]

The written as well as the spoken word concerned the party. The socialist press was never formally controlled by the party, but remained in the hands of various groups and individuals. Unlike DeLeon, the party organization did not demand an official organ, though various leaders such as Berger operated newspapers. The lack of central control afforded a flexibility and effectiveness in the socialist press that the SLP never attained. Debs was fully alive to the importance of newspaper coverage and warned that the regular press would ignore his campaign and circulate slander and defamation against him when possible.[48] Despite its weakness in numbers and relatively small circulation, the socialist press did its best throughout the campaign and was effective locally.

As fall weather approached and the campaign intensified, lithographs, campaign buttons, photographs of Debs, and even cartoons available cheaply at bundle prices, flowed from both Springfield and Chicago, though the latter headquarters distributed most of the campaign literature.[49] The party did not rely on literature so much in its first national campaign as it did later. The candidate himself was its most potent advertisement.

Debs' tours early in the summer carried him to farflung points in the East and Midwest and he made no effort to maintain contact with either party headquarters. It was all he could do to meet his speaking engagements, answer the correspondence that followed him, shake all the hands extended to him, and sandwich rest in between train rides and speeches.[50] He had no assistants and all the tiresome details fell on his own shoulders.

But these drawbacks did not hinder him. Fired with enthusiasm for his cause, eager to join battle with the Democrats and Republicans, anxious to take his message to America, he threw himself into the campaign with all his famous energy. Even before the scheduled fall opening of the campaign, he toured eastern industrial centers and poured his famous brand of radicalism into willing ears. As he began the campaign he disclaimed any intention of seeking personal advancement. Mindful that charges of coyness and vacillation might be thrown at him for his original attitude toward the nomination, he took pains to make his stand clear. "I seek no personal preferment and I claim consideration only as a representative of the principles of international class conscious socialism," he told a crowd. "In that capacity and that alone I appeal to the working class and my countrymen for support." [51] At every chance, he affirmed his and his party's radical sympathies, and was anxious not to be identified with reform groups.

On the eve of the formal campaign he warned readers that though socialism had been tarred with the brush of anarchism, mob rule, violence and calumny, it would ultimately triumph. He warned his followers that the regular parties would stop at nothing to hold down the socialist vote in 1900.[52] Such assertions were evidence of Debs' incurable optimism, for while local authorities sometimes harassed or jailed socialist speakers and organizers, the party was not prominent enough in the campaign to attract much attention from either Democrats or Republicans.

Those who hoped that the socialist campaign would never get off the ground, however, were disappointed. As September and campaign weather drew near rumors floated that Debs would withdraw in favor of Bryan. The socialist candidate emphatically stated that he would not. "Comrade Harriman and I have been nominated as candidates for Vice-President and President respectively of the Social Democratic Party and we shall stand as such candidates to be voted upon on election day, all reports and rumors to the contrary notwithstanding." [53] Later stories that socialists would desert to Bryan and that the Republicans were secretly financing the socialists drew withering fire from Debs. "The Republican papers declare that Socialists will vote for Bryan while the Democratic press charges that Socialists are in the pay of Mark Hanna.

THESE OLD CAMPAIGN LIARS KNOW BETTER, BUT THEY UNDERSTAND EACH OTHER." [54]

On September 29, Debs and the Christian Socialist, George D. Herron, veteran of many a good crusade, formally opened the socialist campaign with a mass meeting in Chicago's Music Hall. Pictures, placards and lantern transparencies lighted the procession of 3,500 marchers who converged on the hall singing socialist songs and chanting for Debs and Harriman. Long before Debs was ready to speak the hall was packed, alive with red banners and streamers. When Debs appeared on the platform a delegation of former ARU members presented him with a huge bouquet of red roses and while the expectant crowd cheered wildly, Debs smiled and nodded, waiting for the tumult to subside. The speech and festivities which followed lasted until nearly midnight and set the tone for the larger rallies on Debs' tours. [55]

Employing all the florid rhetoric and personal color which became famous, Debs introduced his audience to socialism as he understood it. No Marxist epigrams greeted the attendants, there was no display of learning, no desire to hew a doctrinal line; rather, they heard an exposition of socialism based on a radicalism tempered by American beliefs and experiences in the labor movement. If the logic was weak the presentation compensated for it and despite a lengthy speech, Debs held his audience. Into every word and phrase he poured the passion born of belief that capitalism was evil and that socialism was good. The conviction that men could be made new again by socialism radiated from every sentence, and to hear him "was to listen to a hammer riveting a chamber in Hell for the oppressors of the poor," a sympathetic observer noted. [56]

Presidential campaigns are by definition exciting, but that of 1900 was not nearly as stirring as that of 1896. A unified Republican Party unanimously renominated President McKinley while his old foe, William Jennings Bryan, a little older but little wiser, bore the Democratic standard. Bryan insisted that free silver was still an issue, despite the verdict of 1896, and his stand provoked Thomas B. Reed to remark that "Bryan had rather be wrong than president." But silver, the Commoner notwithstanding, fell by the wayside as the public and orators alike fastened attention on trust regulation and imperialism as the chief issues of the campaign.

Debs had scant patience for his opponents and sharp words for their pretensions. To the socialists the two older parties were branches on the same tree. "The republican politicians are satisfied to bleed a few deeply. The democratic politicians, being of a smaller stamp, want to dribble many. Both are anxious that capitalism, the source of ill gotten wealth, shall remain forever," intoned an official socialist publication.[57] McKinley's identification with capitalism was plain for all to see, the party said, and Bryan's pretensions to the contrary were false. "He clings to capitalism as a drowning man to a straw. His watchword is prosperity for the middle classes at the expense of the large capitalists, 'and the devil take the hindmost— the laborer.' "[58] Debs put his own attitude in a nutshell when he appealed for labor's vote. "The differences between the Republican and the Democratic parties involve no issue, no principle in which the working class has any interest, and whether the spoils be distributed by Hanna and Platt, or by Croker and Tammany Hall is all the same to it [*sic*]."[59]

While President McKinley stayed comfortably at home attending to official duties and refusing to campaign, his vice-presidential running mate, Theodore Roosevelt, trailed Bryan across the country with hundreds of whistle stop speeches and appearances. Debs had a particular dislike for the flamboyant Rough Rider and, suspecting his liberal pretensions, missed few chances to snipe at him. He recalled to one audience that years before he had seen Roosevelt board a train dressed as a cowboy. "I did not like him then and I see no reason for revising my opinion," he said tersely.[60] The feeling, it may be imagined, was mutual.

Debs' suspicion of his reform-minded comrades hardened into dislike in years ahead, but even in 1900 he refused to cooperate with reform elements and wanted a genuinely socialistic party. Thus he had harsh words for the municipal reformers who presaged the coming progressive movement. Talk that the socialists might support Samuel "Golden Rule" Jones of Toledo nettled Debs. Jones may have helped his city and reformed his municipal government, but to Debs he was no better than Bryan. "You may still be esteemed as the modern apostle of the 'Golden Rule,' at least until the election is over," he said in Jones' own city, "but I cannot imagine how you can enjoy mental serenity when you contemplate your connection with and your activity for a party explicitly committed by its own platform to revive, renew and continue forever the competitive strife you have so fervently denounced." [61] To Debs socialist purity was better than temporary gains and he consistently denounced alliances with reform groups during the campaign.

The socialists took a decided stand on the trust issue.

From the first they did not view trust formation as evil; their quarrel was with the owners of the trusts. Industrial concentration was inevitable under capitalism; the fault lay not in the trusts but in the men who misused them.[62] While it was divided as to the ultimate disposition of the trusts, the "Slowcialists" feeling that they could be acquired slowly on state and local levels, the radical socialists demanding their immediate expropriation, the party was at least united in opposing "trust busting" as a reactionary program designed to insure the survival of outmoded competition. Once the trusts were placed under cooperative control, their efficient and increased production would benefit the many, not the few. As for the middle class, "It is but natural that a squeezed pig should squeal. The shopkeeper and the manufacturer coming out of the bankruptcy court would endeavor to enlist public sympathy, but the march of progress cannot be stopped because the unfit are eliminated." [63]

To the socialists imperialism was not an issue either, for it was merely another aspect of capitalism. Surplus goods must be marketed abroad; the need for raw materials also drove capitalists to expansion. "Our sympathy with struggling Cuba and Puerto Rico, and our fraternal interest in the poor Filipino is excited by our concern for the capitalists' surplus wealth." [64] Chauncey Depew, prominent New York Republican, remarked in passing that the United States had five per cent of the oriental trade and needed fifty per cent. "The getting of the other 45 per cent constitutes the white man's burden at the present time," Debs sneered.[65]

Because they believed that capitalism had destroyed the American dream of equality and individual opportunity, the socialists decried its further advance. Paradoxically they called for a collective society to insure individual security. Like most American protest groups, their call at first was for a return to former purity.[66] Debs agreed with all this. Marxism may have come to America from Europe and the Social Democrats may have been modeled on European patterns, but for better or worse all their actions and theories filtered through American experience. Because DeLeon fitted American issues with European principles he failed in his quest for pure Marxism. Debs would not make the same mistake; he gladly adopted the techniques and attitudes that spelled success in American politics, while refusing to compromise on fundamental issues. He fought for freedom and equality, a higher form of genuine democracy than America had ever known. He would have agreed heartily with the pen that wrote: "Democracy and Plutocracy cannot continue to exist together in the State. Democracy must be given new life or cease to be." [67] That new life was socialism.

Based as it was on the working class, the Socialist Party directed its chief appeal to that group. Long disputes with the older craft unions had inured socialists to disappointment in their labor work, but they combined the campaign with organizational work which they hoped would pay dividends in the future. Calling on organized labor to vote for Debs and socialism, the socialists sent organizers to strikes to take advantage of labor discontent.[68] Debs himself spoke extensively in the areas of Pennsylvania and West Virginia affected by the coal strike of 1900, and addressed record crowds in many towns. His old love, the railroaders, turned out wherever he went. "You railroad men are told that I am too radical, that I am dangerous, that as a leader I am a failure and a good many other things," he told one group after reminiscing over faded ARU cards, "but the time will come when you will know that from the first to the last I was true to you. . . . Time will tell and I can wait." [69]

How many labor organizations actually supported Debs in 1900 is unknown; the strongest labor support came from the Western Federation of Miners, whose membership ranged the Rockies and the mountain states of the West. There the rough rank-and-file mine workers were only too glad to vote for Debs and Harriman and the red banner. "Debs and Harriman come nearer representing the views of the WFM as expressed by its set of principles, and it is our duty, if we are sincere in our work, to vote for the men who represent the principles which we have already adopted," the union's official journal admonished its readers.[70] Scattered labor groups in the East supported Debs, but the socialists never won the support of the craft unions largely because the latter's leaders pursued a policy of caution and non-political action that clashed with the socialists.[71]

The lack of central direction in the socialist campaign in 1900 was in a sense a blessing, for it enabled local socialists to capitalize on local problems. Farmers, workers, even small businessmen, intellectuals and others were urged to vote for Debs. If the western radical socialists and Debs would not cooperate with reform elements, such was hardly the case in Milwaukee and elsewhere where "Slowcialists" were willing at least to soft pedal revolutionary slogans to win middle-class votes.[72]

Complexities of doctrine had no glamor for Debs as he swung through his crowded schedule. If he was repetitious, he was no less effective, and if socialism was too complex he made it simple; if comrades protested, he left it to them to untangle the knots afterwards.

By October the campaign was well underway. Even before that party officials of both groups eyed the progress of unity sentiment. Though the *Social Democratic Herald* did not recognize Harriman as the vice-presidential candidate until September 1, those who cared to read between the lines saw that unity would shortly be a fact. With refreshing dispatch and disregard for squabbles among leaders, state after state adopted the unity slate as the campaign progressed. Local socialists of all factions often met, talked, and generally agreed to unite for the campaign and to work for permanent unity after the contest was over. By late summer nearly every important state had adopted the unity ticket.[73] Officials at Springfield did their best to aid this movement, pointing out that once united for the campaign, the locals would hardly dissolve later.[74] It seemed obvious that unity would be accomplished by the end of the campaign.[75]

Job Harriman undertook an extensive tour to assist the unity movement, despite failing health that ultimately took him out of the race. In August he moved through the Middle West and parts of the East, trailing pleas for solidarity behind him. His meetings were successful, and many Debs-Harriman clubs remained behind him as testaments to the effectiveness of his kindly, soft-spoken manner. Sometimes, however, he met opposition, as when the DeLeonites held a mass meeting across the street from his platform.[76]

Harriman lived literally from hand to mouth during his tour, for he was a poor man, staying with local socialists and depending on collections for train fare and travel expenses. He received little but hope and encouragement from the national headquarters.

It was difficult to follow Debs, and the presidential candidate often angered Harriman and other Kangaroos by his posturing and posing. Perhaps Harriman envied the glamor and enthusiasm which accompanied Debs, and perhaps he tired of dingy hotel rooms and halfhearted crowds; or perhaps he was merely ill and tired. In any event, he often lashed out privately at his running mate. "He is a politician. He has a following in the west and if he goes out as an organizer, which he will, he will make us fight a little while yet," he wrote Morris Hillquit bitterly. "But his $100 a night fee will lead him into temptation and he will not work as hard at organizing as he will at making money. I am convinced that he is more of a coo-coo than a builder of nests." [77] Harriman's charges were basically untrue; if Debs worried about money it was because of his heavy expenses and the multitude of socialist causes he tried to support. Yet there was some justification for Harriman's criticisms. There was a strong streak of vanity in Debs that often irritated friend and foe alike. He loved the limelight; the applause of crowds was sweet music in his ears. He was a consummate actor, the ideal public figure, and he relished his radical role. He was not insincere, but he saw that he must fulfill this role to be effective. Had he failed to do so he would have been far less dynamic and far less effective. Harriman's irritation was doubtless the product of pique and exhaustion, but it signified that both sides had much to do before real unity could be accomplished.

This latent distrust was not confined to Harriman's personal letters alone; others too felt that it would be unwise to add to Debs' strength and popularity lest this give the Bergerites the whip hand in future negotiations. Butscher suggested that Debs and Harriman speak from the same platform as a show of unity, "but I wouldn't contribute one cent toward his expenses. Let the National Executive Board [of the SDP] pay that. It would be a peculiar situation anyway, wouldn't it? Debs representing one party, Harriman another. What a mess! Well, it will come out all right our way." [78] Fortunately for all concerned this last attitude increased as the campaign progressed.

Debs did his best to foster good will in every speech, but his larger mission was socialist propaganda. He preferred to spend his time and energy on recruiting converts rather than in exhorting socialists to mind one another's dogmas. The Middle West welcomed Debs several times during October. A strong socialist organization in Davenport, Iowa, produced a responsive crowd and outdid itself in preparations for his visit.[79]

In Chicago, socialists profited from some labor unrest and work among the immigrants. Resourceful and undeterred by lack of funds, the local socialists adopted effective and novel techniques in crowd pleasing. On Sunday evenings they migrated to the Salvation Army street corner meetings, waited for a crowd to collect, then mounted soap boxes and competed with drums and tambourines, not to say outraged protests, to harangue the assembled multitude. When one speaker was arrested another took his place until they filled the local jail, where presumably they continued their missionary work among their fellow inmates.[80]

Indiana, ever doubtful, swung between Democrats and

Republicans until the end of the campaign and some observers feared that Debs would swing his home state to Bryan by polling several thousand votes the Republicans could ill afford to lose.[81]

Farther east in Boston, Debs was accorded a warm welcome by local socialists who profited in numbers and enthusiasm by their earlier successes in Haverhill and other towns. Telling his audience, "It is a case of lead versus bread; which diet do you want?" Debs orated two and a half hours without even stopping for a drink of water.[82]

As Harriman's strength failed, Debs assumed more and more speaking engagements, but the two candidates appeared together in New York, where they packed Cooper Union's 9,000 seats, filled the aisles, and held overflow meetings outside on the sidewalk.[83] Back in Chicago on election eve the two again filled the Music Hall with counterblasts at capitalism.[84] As the campaign drew to a close, Debs took one last swipe at Bryan, whom he feared would draw some support from reform-minded socialists. "There is nothing in the platform, program or attitude of the Democratic party that points toward socialism," he stated emphatically.[85]

Many saw in the socialist campaign the early thunder of a promising movement; predictions flew that Debs would poll at least 100,000, possibly 250,000 votes, which in the face of President McKinley's assured re-election was no small total.[86] When the ballots were counted early in November, Debs' tally was 96,978 votes. To no one's surprise, McKinley triumphed over Bryan with 7,219,530 votes to the Commoner's 6,358,071. The socialist showing was strongest in New York, Illinois, Ohio, Indiana, Massachusetts, Wisconsin and California. Harriman had done much to raise the vote in the Golden State. The nearest minor group, the Prohibition Party, polled 209,166 votes, twice the socialist total. Clearly, the socialists had far to go before they realized their promise.

Debs himself was obviously disappointed by the vote. "The figures are smaller than most of us expected," he admitted frankly, "but we are satisfied [that] the showing, if not inspiring, has at least nothing discouraging in it." [87] He could not resist one final blast toward the enemy camp, however, and proclaimed, "This will be one of the last convulsions of capitalism before the social revolution sweeps it out of existence. . . . The next four years will witness the development of socialism to continental power and proportions." [88] Though full of his customary bombast and overstatement, the words expressed the devout belief of many socialists.

At the peak of their power the Populists had polled over a million votes for their presidential candidate. The socialists had far to go before they could rival that showing. Lack of news coverage, the refusal of many sympathizers to waste a vote on Debs, the failure to capture organized labor, confusion in socialist ranks, and inability to get on the ballot in some states explains much of the small vote. [89] It was not lack of energy or zeal that hampered the party. Many who sympathized took half the loaf, hoped, and voted for Bryan. [90]

Yet the picture was far from dark. All things considered, the party's maiden run was rewarding. In many areas the socialist vote rose considerably. In San Francisco the socialists polled ten times more votes than the Prohibitionists and one tenth of the Democratic total. [91]

In Chicago the socialist vote was ten times that of 1896, and the local party press was gratified not only by this but also by the spirit of cooperation that had characterized the entire campaign in that city. "This is certainly all that any reasonable thinking man could expect, and it should be a source of the greatest encouragement to every worker." [92]

Though the socialist vote in 1900 was insignificant in the total vote, it was important to the party. The organization had fulfilled its two key missions during the campaign —mass indoctrination and the drive for party unity. These two combined might make the party a formidable contender in the political ring in future contests. The vote came, for the most part, from sincere socialists who in the next two decades were the hard core of support behind Debs and other socialist politicians. The members enlisted in this campaign worked hard in years to come to establish and expand the party organization, press, and propaganda agencies. Though few in number, these dedicated souls were indeed the life of the party. [93]

The socialist campaign of 1900 also illustrated a deeper truth that was not lost on the political actionists in the party: When adapted to the American scene, socialist theory attracted many groups. By using American electoral techniques, and by appealing to local sentiment as well as to national sympathy, the socialists achieved a potentially powerful position. That was the great lesson of 1900 for Eugene Debs. It was not forgotten and in the years ahead the party perfected its propaganda machine and conducted constantly improving national campaigns.

The presidential candidate was bone weary, and he returned to Terre Haute to rest before resuming his lectures and writing. One morning, shortly after the election, an agitated Debs appeared on the doorstep of his friend, Stephen Reynolds. He seemed most anxious to talk and, after they had breakfasted, recounted a vivid dream he had experienced the night before. While walking through a swamp, he had seen a strange animal caught in a pool of mire. Rushing to its rescue he had worked frantically to free the beast, several times almost succeeding when it slid back into the mire again. Debs then hurried to a nearby village for help and, returning with Reynolds, worked harder than ever to release the animal. At day's end the beast was where it had been when they started. Then Debs had awakened.[94] It was a dream whose symbolism was to haunt Eugene Debs many times in the hectic years ahead.

III

The Rising Tide:
The Campaign of 1904

> *Viewed from any intelligent standpoint the outlook of the Socialist movement is full of promise to the workers of coming freedom.*
>
> Eugene V. Debs, 1904

Late in the summer of 1901, President William McKinley was shot by an anarchist at Buffalo. On September 14, the President died and Theodore Roosevelt inherited his mantle. The Rough Rider's rapid rise in national politics was but symptomatic of the times. McKinley's death marked the end of the old order in politics and presaged the rise of new forces, the sharpening of reform tendencies, and the development of a sentiment for change that permeated the entire fabric of American life. Clearly these were times in which socialism might prosper, borne upward on the appeal of its own doctrine and leaders while benefiting greatly from increased public interest in political, social and economic reform.

The socialists fulfilled the promise of unity which the campaign of 1900 had fostered in the early summer of 1901 when delegates from both the SDP and Kangaroo factions, as well as independent socialists, met in Indianapolis to found the new Socialist Party of America.[1] The resulting compromise party made DeLeon's SLP the only important socialist group in the country outside the new SPA.[2] Though the more optimistic claimed a membership of 12,000 in the new party, Morris Hillquit admitted that the figure was "born somewhat more of our enthusiasm than of actual fact."[3] At least half that number belonged, however, and the future promised more converts as the party perfected its organization and as progressive sentiment grew.

Though bound together by belief in the coming commonwealth, the new party held the seeds of factionalism which grew mighty in later years. The new constitution contained a liberalized set of "immediate demands" which satisfied the right wing, with statements on revolutionary socialism and radical labor organization which pacified the western left wing. Each group had surrendered part of its loaf in the name of unity. Berger and the conservatives fought hard for the independence of state organizations, which meant less central direction and more chances to disavow statements from the left wing.[4] Thus at the outset eastern and midwestern socialists separated themselves from their western comrades. But whatever the sources of present and future contention within the new party, its members were proud that they had joined forces and that the times were propitious for their work.

While the socialists' major concern was expansion and perfection of their party organization, they did not abandon their propaganda campaigns. Many socialists still clung to the belief that the AFL could be won and between 1901 and 1904 worked tirelessly within the organization. Many AFL members were socialists or sympathizers and it seemed for a time that the Federation might even en-

dorse socialism's ultimate aims. In the AFL convention of
1902 the socialists showed surprising influence and hope
quickened that the Federation might yet see the error
of its ways and join the party.[5] But socialist strength in
the Federation was deceptive, more apparent than real.
Debs was never convinced that the organization could be
won and favored establishment of a radical industrial
union. He summed up his own opinion when he said that
for all the good it did, the socialist could "orate to a lot
of wooden Indians as seek to change the controlling clique
of the [AFL] convention." [6]

Samuel Gompers, perpetual president of the AFL and
the leading craft unionist of his day, had supposedly
favored socialism early in his career; but by 1903 he
disavowed it thus: "I have kept close watch upon your
doctrines for thirty years; have been closely associated
with many of you and know how you think and what
you propose," he told the socialists at the Federation convention. "I know, too, what you have up your sleeve.
And I want to say that I am entirely at variance with
your philosophy. I declare it to you, I am not only at
variance with your doctrines, but with your philosophy.
Economically you are unsound; socially you are wrong;
industrially you are impossible." [7]

The socialists were split on the question of capturing
the AFL. The conservatives, though they did not like
craft unionism, tended to accept it as a fact and opposed
establishing rival unions. But in the West, which five
years later produced the ultra-radical Industrial Workers
of the World, a different sentiment prevailed. Debs condemned those who favored the AFL and charged them
with feeling that "it was wiser policy to curry favor with

numbers than to stand by principles." [8] He looked with favor upon the radical American Labor Union, whose core was the Western Federation of Miners; its avowed purpose was to fight the AFL, and Debs had favored that battle since 1894.

Politically the first three years of the party's work were full of promise. The congressional elections of 1902 brought surprising rewards and the socialist vote totalled almost 227,000, more than twice Debs' vote in 1900.[9] The vote was heaviest in Colorado, Indiana, Illinois, Massachusetts, New York, Ohio, Pennsylvania, and Wisconsin. In every case organizers worked to profit from the vote by establishing and strengthening locals. Every vote was a seed to be planted and carefully nourished for the future.[10] In April, 1904, Milwaukee elected nine socialist aldermen and several other local officials on a reformist platform, and Berger's strength was such that in the same year he received five votes for U.S. Senator in the state legislature.[11]

Fully as important as electoral success and growing membership was the budding socialist press. Private ownership and control gave it a flexibility and ease of growth that no other radical group commanded. Between 1900 and 1904 the socialists established a number of influential newspapers and magazines which carried their message to every part of the country. The rising group of muckrakers, most of whom were not formally socialists, were at least sympathetic toward much of the socialist program.[12]

In New York, California, Colorado, and several states of the Midwest, a variety of socialist newspapers sprang up, catering to local interests as well as national principles.

By 1904, eighteen weekly and seven monthly newspapers preached socialist doctrine in English, and few party organizers went to the field without subscription blanks and sample copies. In addition, papers in Yiddish, French, German, Bohemian, Italian, Norwegian, and Polish catered to the immigrant vote.[13] There were papers for the learned, the ignorant, the converted, the unconverted, the willing, and the unwilling. Few who could read at all could honestly claim that socialist literature was denied them.

By far the most influential socialist newspaper was the flamboyant *Appeal to Reason,* nicknamed "the Squeal of Treason" by critics, published in Girard, Kansas, by the shrewd Julius Wayland. Combining a flair for the colorful, a taste for the radical, and a deep appreciation of rising circulation figures and increasing profits, Wayland produced a cheaply-priced newspaper that caught on in the Midwest like wildfire. It was simply edited, devoid of formal socialist theory, full of intriguing news, arresting editorials, and combined the demand for socialism with money-making schemes and stock promotions that appealed to subscribers.[14] Curious as its jumbled attitudes were, the basic unifying strand was socialism of some kind, and its easy style and forceful format appealed to hundreds of thousands all over the country. For a decade and a half it reigned supreme as the leading socialist newspaper of the day and Debs himself was a contributing editor at one time.

Taking advantage of its growing press, the sentiment of progressivism, and the temper of the times, the party built up its organization as rapidly as possible. Zeal compensated for lack of funds and trained workers. In 1903,

22 organizers operated out of the national office; paid a mere $3 a day, they combined their talents with nearly a hundred regularly working soapbox orators who existed on their sales of literature and the charity of local socialists.[15] At one time the applications for party organizers exceeded the party's ability to pay, and thus many who would gladly have worked for the cause were turned away for lack of funds.[16] Debs himself paid tribute to these men and the organization which they were building, and he admired their work all the more because he had labored thus himself.[17]

Debs was far from idle. His own organizational and propaganda tours were perhaps the most important of all, for he was the best known socialist and a major drawing card at rallies and speeches. He defined his own techniques early and did not deviate from them later. He appealed frankly to the rank-and-file socialists, the half-convinced, and the sympathetic; to win them required color and a simple presentation, both of which he employed effectively. Debs was perpetually criticized for his easy use of socialist doctrine, but it did not deter him. Hairsplitting was not his forte. If the socialist commonwealth came it would come through agitation and political action, not through planning in a vacuum of socialist theory. He let others embroider the edges of theory; he carried a message to the people.[18]

Debs devoted most of his waking hours to the party's campaigns. He spent long and lonely weeks away from home on the lecture circuit, enduring bad food, lack of sleep, poor train travel, the exhausting formalities of the adulation accorded him, and all the other burdensome details of travel. But, spurred on by his beliefs, he seldom complained even though exhausted. He sat up all night many times after a grueling speech, talking with old ARU friends or fellow socialists. He visited the scene of nearly every major strike, urging strikers to join the socialist movement and to favor industrial unionism. Sessions lasting day and night consumed his time and energy when he was on the hustings. Once he admitted having had a talking marathon with strikers. "Last night," he told Ella Reeve Bloor, herself a famous strike organizer, "they were talking to me until pretty near morning and then when I was going to bed a fellow timidly knocked on my door. 'I thought,' he said, 'since you have got to get up at five anyway, we might as well spend the rest of the night talking.' " And so it went, week after week, in town after town.[19]

Although his wife, Kate, supported all Debs' efforts, it was no secret that she disliked his long absences from home. Though a gracious hostess when the occasion demanded, she did not always approve of the company he kept and many considered her cold. She had married Debs when he was relatively unknown and doubtless would have preferred what critics would have described as a middle-class existence, with assurance of social stature, a fixed income, and lack of notoriety. Childlessness may have contributed partially to their lack of home life together, which was aggravated further by Debs' constant restlessness. Nevertheless, he was exceedingly sentimental about his wife, and she was loyal to him, if not always understanding.

In the Far West, where logging camps and mining towns turned out to hear him attack capitalism, Debs received a boisterous welcome everywhere. Here was the real seedbed of American radicalism in his day and he exploited every advantage for socialism.) After speeches and picnics flavored more by alcohol than by food, Debs often held all night smoker sessions in his hotel room; pajama-clad, he discussed the coming revolution and the need for industrial unionism. Often as not he joined the drinking bouts, for he had a fondness for an occasional drink that he never tried to hide.[20] In New York and other large cities he often walked around the major squares at night, talking with hobos and bums, the flotsam and jetsam of the society he sought to renovate. "I get inspiration from them," he told a friend. "I can talk better at the meeting tonight." [21]

Although his approach was essentially lacking in doctrine, it was highly effective with the people he reached. If he was often sentimental and even maudlin, he touched the hearts of many. Whatever they said of his work, party leaders could not say that he was ineffective.

Thus it was with considerable pride and hope that the first national convention of the Socialist Party of America gathered on May 1, 1904, in Brand's Hall in Chicago. One hundred and eighty-three delegates, seven of them women, spoke for organizations in thirty-six states and territories. Their average age was 35 to 40, and most of them were from middle-class occupations, a trend that became dominant in a few years. One hundred and twenty were American born, which gave the lie to charges that the party was dominated by foreign elements; nineteen were German, and the rest came from various national backgrounds.[22]

While the delegates milled about talking, arguing and waiting for formal business to begin, the Socialist Singing

Society of Chicago entertained them with socialist songs. Festivity was in the air; success had marked their progress since 1901, and this would be a major year in their calendar.[23] The convention settled to its task, but, true to character, shortly bogged down in an argument over official party policy toward organized labor. The right wing opposed establishing new unions, while the left wing desired open condemnation of the AFL. A large bloc of center delegates, torn between socialism and realism, voted with the right and condemned dual unionism as a party policy.[24] It was the same old story, and many prominent socialists privately felt that the party had gone too far in its attacks on the AFL; Harriman himself suggested privately that Debs be passed over for the presidential nomination partly because his outspokenness had offended some labor support.[25]

When nominations were in order, however, the cry "Debs!" filled the air, and the impatient delegates would hear nothing else. His magnificent beard spilling down over an immaculate shirt and white tie, George Herron rose to nominate Debs and told the delegates what they wanted to hear. "Now, there is no man in America who more surely and faithfully incarnates the heartache and the protest and the struggle of labor for its emancipation, or more surely voices that struggle, than Eugene V. Debs." [26] The eager delegates could hardly wait for the speaker to finish before bursting into a tumultuous demonstration which clearly indicated that Debs could not repeat his coyness of 1900 and decline. Indeed, he did not. Making a rare appearance at a party convention, he proclaimed his acceptance. "In the councils of the Socialist Party the collective will is supreme. Personally, I could have wished to remain in the ranks to make my record, humble as it may be, fighting unnamed and unhonored, side by side with my comrades," he said with the modesty traditional in presidential candidates, be they capitalist or socialist. Attacking the old parties as corrupt and useless, he flayed their pretensions at reform. "Thomas Jefferson would scorn to enter a modern Democratic convention. He would have as little business there as Abraham Lincoln would have in a latter-day Republican convention. If they were alive today, they would be delegates to this convention." He promised a vivid campaign. "My controlling ambition shall be to bear the standard aloft where the battle waxes thickest. . . . I shall be heard in the coming campaign, as often, and as decidedly, and as emphatically, as revolutionarily, as uncompromisingly as my ability, my strength and my fidelity to the movement will allow." [27] Concluding with verbal fireworks, he received a standing ovation, repeated cheers, and a "tiger" from the enthusiastic delegates. In point of fact, Debs was not the least reluctant to run again; he had come to enjoy the campaign routine despite its rigors and he did not wish any other, more conservative socialist to represent the party.

To Debs' gratification the convention nominated Benjamin Hanford of New York for Vice-President. Hanford was widely known in socialist circles, having joined the party in New York where he carried its standard in gubernatorial races in 1900 and 1902. He was best known as a typographer and editor, creator of the lovable "Jimmie Higgins," the mythical rank-and-file party member who did all the work while others took all the credit. If there were leaflets to print, Jimmie Higgins did it; if there were tickets to sell, Jimmie Higgins did that too; and if Gene Debs came to town, Jimmie Higgins arranged for the auditorium and pasted placards all over town, but on the big night Jimmie Higgins didn't get to hear Debs because he was busy taking tickets at the door. Hanford's writings were popular with the socialists and he was well known in labor circles. Forty-six years old, he was a strong addition to the ticket.[28]

The candidates stood on a platform much like that of 1900, which combined a general call for radical socialism with immediate demands that satisfied the conservative socialists. Tempers flared during the debate on ways and means as conservatives attacked "impossibilists" and the latter sneered at "Slowcialists" and "parlor socialists," who never got out of the drawing room into the streets.[29] Acceptable resolutions were finally passed and the delegates sang the "Marseillaise," gave three cheers for the coming revolution, and left for home.[30]

As in 1900, many non-socialist commentators saw success for the socialists on the horizon. Discontent with the anti-trust program, labor dissatisfaction, and the intelligent character and wide appeal of the socialist ticket made the party's progress inevitable.[31] The Democrats seemed determined to help the socialists, for in July their convention passed over William Jennings Bryan and chose the ultra-conservative gold standard advocate, Judge Alton B. Parker of New York. It was obviously a move to counter the progressive trend toward Theodore Roosevelt and to cleanse the party of "Bryanism." President Roosevelt was duly renominated by a Republican Party eager to wear the other shoe for a change by capitalizing on his personal appeal and his supposedly liberal program.

It was an ironic campaign indeed, with the traditionally liberal Democrats running an avowed conservative, and the traditionally conservative Republicans running an avowed liberal. The socialists would profit much, it was said, from discontented Democrats who would swallow neither Parker nor Roosevelt.[32] Debs himself was aware of the discontent in American society and hoped that the party would profit from it. With typical flamboyance he asserted that "Slavery does not excite lofty aspirations nor inspire noble ideals. The tendency is to sodden ir-resolution and brutish inertia. But this very tendency nourishes the germ of resistance that ripens into the spirit of revolt." [33] He would capitalize on this "germ of re-sistance" to the fullest in the campaign ahead.

As in 1900, campaign funds were a major problem to the socialists. Though the party organization was solvent, its resources were limited. Several novel devices filled the gap in the emergency. By far the most productive and resourceful was the admission charge that eager listeners paid to hear Debs. It was ironic indeed that Americans should pay to listen to a presidential candidate, but Debs spoke to full houses everywhere. Lobbies in auditoriums were packed with socialist literature that produced revenue as well as converts for the campaign.

In addition, the ever resourceful staff of the *Appeal to Reason* printed lists of campaign donors, sent out coin cards to be filled with small change by the poorer faithful, and offered encouragement and prizes for specific sums.[34] The party urged members to donate half a day's pay to the campaign fund and to buy literature and send what funds they could to their local and national headquarters. They were expected, of course, to pay to hear Debs when he came to town.[35] All these were shrewd as well as practical moves for they identified the rank and file more closely with the campaign and with socialism by making success dependent on their help and contributions. All in all, a campaign fund of $32,700 was raised for Debs. It was an infinitesimal amount compared to the outlays from Republican and Democratic headquarters, but was nevertheless a source of pride to the socialists.[36]

While Debs rested, awaiting the fall campaign season, making occasional speeches and writing articles for the socialist press, local groups and national headquarters stimulated campaign preparations in every way possible. Distribution of literature and campaign paraphernalia had been unsystematic in 1900, but party unity and better help told a different story in 1904. The party press advertised a wide variety of campaign material before Debs began his tour, so that his path might be suitably paved. Campaign buttons, lithographs, ribbons, placards, lantern slides and other materials were available at bulk rates for organizers. There was even an elaborate gold and enamel Debs button which sold for a quarter by which the faithful could proclaim more than ordinary allegiance to the cause.[37] A talented socialist wrote a campaign song with Debs' picture on the cover, entitled "The Dawning Day," that supposedly left Girard by the carload. Its chorus, it was said, was "a hummer." [38]

A novel innovation in the campaign was the use of "little red stickers," the adhesive qualities of which were said to signify the permanence of the future commonwealth. Sold at a dollar a thousand, the *Appeal to Reason* suggested an unlimited number of uses for the stickers: they could be applied to chairs and walls while the boss wasn't looking; they could decorate menus, bars, hotels, trains, lamp posts, just about anything that would stick to glue. "The Little Red Stickers are good for the blind," the *Appeal* trumpeted. "They have loosened the scales on many an eye." [39] Gangs of small boys chanted Debs slogans as they decorated outhouses, barns and lamp posts with the stickers:

> The little red stickers keep going faster—
>   It's a chance that the boys are not going to miss;
> They're going to put the old earth in a plaster
>   oflittleredstickersasthicklyasthis.

Or so, at least, said the *Appeal to Reason*.[40] All the talents for circulation and propaganda that had made that paper successful were now placed at Debs' disposal.

In the major cities socialist newspapers in all languages advertised Debs' campaign, seeking to get out the vote. The *Appeal* outdid itself as cooler weather approached and thought nothing of issues of 400,000 copies; during the campaign several reached 700,000 and to the loud boasting of all concerned, one issue sold 1,000,000 copies.[41]

In an age when Americans took their political campaigns seriously, and when campaigning was both an art and a game, socialist rhetoric could match any mustered by the opposition. Socialists made the eagle scream, albeit in a different key, and outdid their opponents in flag waving, having both the red banner and the stars and stripes to display. The election organizers depended on the rank and file to do most of the routine work of campaigning and the membership did not fail. Still filled with belief in the promise of American socialism, they worked for a cause as well as a party; their candidate was a symbol as well as a man. National secretary William Mailly's injunction that the party needed more organizers and fewer writers did not fall on deaf ears, though his blunt remarks nettled many conservative socialists.[42]

State organizations bore the brunt of the campaign, combining their efforts with organizational work and the founding of new locals and strengthening of old ones. In Illinois, for example, the state organization kept forty-five speakers in the field and distributed 500,000 pieces of literature during the campaign.[43] Twenty-two paid organizers did their best to supplement state workers and Jimmie Higgins.[44] Chicago socialists ran a boat excursion to Michigan City one Sunday to raise funds and exhort the faithful.[45]

By 1904 the farmers' interest in socialism had risen enough to warrant exploitation, and socialist organizers mixed with farm encampments and visited rural Sunday schools and country fairs to teach socialist doctrine. Julius Wayland himself spent many evenings driving in the country around Girard, distributing leaflets and answering farmers' questions. During the campaign volunteer workers joined him and he often covered hundreds of miles a week in his buggy on lonely roads, talking socialism with farmers and hired hands, often savoring country food if his message appealed to the woman of the household.[46]

But, after all, the main event of the year for the socialists was Debs' campaign tour and as he steeled himself for the ordeal expectant socialists in cities and towns across the country awaited his arrival. His schedule called for appearances in the Far West in October, in the Midwest and on the East Coast in late October, and again in the Midwest in early November.[47] An early speech in Carnegie Hall, however, was a preview of what was to come, for that meeting was a flag-waving, foot-stamping socialist jamboree.[48]

Debs' speech in Chicago, from which he was to move westward, was awaited expectantly, and the socialist press warned readers to get their tickets early. "When the auditorium is packed and you have no seat, whose fault will it be?" asked one paper.[49] In mid-September, Debs spoke in the Midwest and parts of the South. Two thousand people filled the court house square in Pine Bluff, Arkansas, and he drew large crowds of miners in West Virginia as well.[50]

Moving west from Chicago, he lost no chance to benefit from western radicalism. While his train stopped in Albuquerque for repairs he mounted a baggage cart and treated a crowd of railroad workers, many of whom he knew, to a harangue on socialism and "the wage slave system." [51] In Colorado he drew crowds of miners from their work as he lashed out against company brutality in the mines and "government by militia and injunction" during mine strikes.[52] Once again the Western Federation of Miners endorsed him, urging its members to vote for him and to support socialism wherever possible. Dubbing Debs "labor's Cicero," the Federation's official papers and spokesmen did their best to insure support from the miners.[53]

In Los Angeles a large crowd ate up his words. "Mr. Debs paid respects to both the democrat and republican parties, but gave most attention to the republicans and to President Roosevelt." [54] Debs himself was highly gratified by his turnout in Los Angeles. "In all my experience there has been nothing to compare with it," he wrote back.[55] In San Francisco the story was the same as an audience of several thousand cheered his assault on capitalism. The city's usual labor troubles, especially in shipping, worked in his favor. Farther north in Tacoma, Washington, there was not even standing room in an auditorium littered with red rose petals thrown by cheering supporters.[56]

Debs set the tone of his campaign early by calling for "the overthrow of the capitalistic system and the emancipation of the working class from wage slavery." [57] Others might argue radical socialism versus conservative socialism, but there was no basic issue in the question for Debs; though he was never truly identified with the radical wing of the party, he called himself a radical socialist. He might disagree much with the elements that formed the IWW and later the Communist Party of America, but their methods and ideals still appealed more to him than those of Berger and Hillquit. He clearly did not favor anarchism or violence and repeatedly endorsed the ballot instead of the bullet. "Anarchy scorns the ballot and repudiates all politics as essentially corrupt and demoralizing. Socialism appeals to the ballot to express the untrammeled will of the people as the supreme law of society." [58] Nor did he adhere rigidly to any fixed poles of doctrine. While he never played loosely with his ideals and goals and never lowered his high hopes and ambitions for the Socialist Party, he felt that a politician must be flexible in expressing official policy. The same maxims and regulations did not apply to a farm audience and a worker audience and he generally tailored his talks to fit his listeners. In this respect Debs was not so different from other political leaders. He never forgot the wreckage that Daniel DeLeon's dogmatism had wrought and he had no desire to follow in that doctrinaire's footsteps.[59]

His favorite campaign sport was baiting the opposition. Insisting that the Democrats and Republicans were but "wings of the same old bird of prey," he denied interest in the "issues of the day." "The capitalists may have the tariff, finance, imperialism and other dust-covered and moth-eaten issues entirely to themselves," he said in his opening speech.[60] He shortly proved it by pointing out that planks in both old party platforms were interchangeable; by ridiculing Roosevelt's trust busting; and by telling his audiences that the President was merely a tool of the capitalists. "They know that his instincts, associations, tastes and desires are with them, that he is in fact one of them and that he has nothing in common with the working class." [61] As far as Roosevelt was concerned, the feeling was mutual; Debs was still the "undesirable citizen" he had been to Roosevelt at the time of the Pullman strike.[62] Debs let no chance to hit Roosevelt pass, for not only did he dislike him personally, but also feared that the popular President would win many reform-minded socialists. Recalling that Roosevelt had once praised Grover Cleveland, Debs thundered: "How impressive to see the Rough Rider embrace the Smooth Statesman! Oyster Bay and Buzzard's Bay! Two souls with but a single thought, two hearts that beat as one!" [63]

To dismiss Parker he had only to remind listeners of the time when that worthy had been an "Injunction Judge" in New York and was as conservative as possible. "The Democratic nominee for President was one of the Supreme Judges of the state of New York who declared the eight hour day unconstitutional and this is an index to his political character." [64] As though this was not enough, Debs dismissed Parker as "the proxy of Grover Cleveland, alias Wall Street . . ." and called the Democratic platform "a political omelet made chiefly of decayed eggs." [65] Though retired on the sidelines, Bryan was a potent force and took great pains to disassociate himself and his followers from socialism.[66]

Always anxious to win the labor vote, Debs appealed repeatedly to union and non-union men for their support. "O, workers of America, use your brains in your own interest instead of being satisfied with deforming your bodies to enrich your masters," he cried passionately to one group.[67] "The ballot of united labor expresses the people's will and the people's will is the supreme law of a free nation." [68] Knowing from bitter experience the cruelties of labor organizing and that the men would suffer for their work, he nonetheless appealed for their support and offered them his own in return. Though few labor unions officially endorsed Debs in 1904, he undoubtedly won the support of many workers.

Yet then, as later, American socialism could not win organized labor. Earlier in 1904, Senator Mark Hanna wrote words that may have been food for thought to many socialists. With shrewdness born of years in politics and industry, Hanna noted that socialism made little headway in unions and was not likely to succeed. He maintained that American workers were basically conservative, unlikely to be "led away from the straight road by hot headed members." [69]

New issues intruded during the campaign and Debs announced a stand on the Negro question. A tour through the South in 1903 and early in 1904 impressed him with the economic and social impoverishment of the Negro and aroused his anger at inequality and cruelty. "The history of the Negro in the United States is a history of crime without parallel," he thundered in print.[70] Though he condemned oppression of the Negro he admitted frankly that socialism had no specific cure for the problem except adoption of the cooperative commonwealth. "We have nothing special to offer the Negro, and we cannot make separate appeals to all races. The Socialist Party is the party of the working class, regardless of color—the whole working class of the whole world." [71] Discrimination did not entitle the Negro to special rights; it merely illustrated the brutalities of capitalism, which would be removed when socialism triumphed.

On this as on other issues the party was divided, many socialists justifiably deploring the use of Negroes as strike-breakers, some frankly racist. Yet to Eugene Debs this was a prime example of capitalist exploitation. In truth he had no solution for the problem except the adoption of socialism, and had but a vague understanding of the full ramifications of the problem in the South. The source of his anger was personal and humanitarian. He detested any inequality. He insisted that capitalists kept the Negro in bondage for use against organized labor and for economic exploitation.[72] His understanding, though vague, was not without perception.

Late in October, Debs headed east. In Boston's Faneuil Hall a respectful crowd stood during a long speech while several hundred curious and disappointed place seekers milled outside.[73] Admission charges and collection plates did not deter the faithful in the East any more than in the West, and they easily filled Carnegie Hall in New

York, with an estimated 6,000 turned away for lack of seating. At a nearby hall Senator Chauncey Depew of New York spoke to a small crowd, and many wondered if Depew, one of the best story-tellers of his day, noted his sparse turnout.[74] Doubtless many who came to hear Debs were not socialists—it was worth anybody's dime to see Eugene Debs—but many were, and many more were sympathizers who might vote for him on election day.

It was not all speechmaking, however, and Debs took breaks from his tight schedule whenever he could. A highlight of his eastern tour was a hurried visit to Walt Whitman's grave in Camden, New Jersey. Debs took five leaves from an elm tree that stood over the poet's grave and sent them to his wife, who dutifully pressed them in his scrapbook. Debs, who found much comfort in Whitman's rhapsodic poetry and democratic visions, wept unashamedly at the foot of the grave.[75] Even the stress of campaigning did not keep Debs from remembering his wedding anniversary and he dispatched sentiments to his wife between speeches.[76]

Back in the Middle West for the close of the campaign, Debs addressed an enthusiastic audience in Chicago, "men not from the effete and stunted classes of society, but men whose veins carried the red, unpolluted blood of the proletariat, full of eagerness for action as nature demands action." Sturdy socialists or merely curious workingmen, they gave him a rousing reception and parade. As he spoke, representatives of ninety-five unions sat behind him on the platform and though the membership they represented was often small, it was welcome.[77] In Rock Island, Illinois, the old story was repeated as crowds were turned away, admission charge or no admission charge. "The aisles were full of people. The seats were full of people. The halls were full of people. Outside the streets were full of people," the *Appeal* noted tersely.[78]

By now the strain was telling on Debs and he was glad that the ordeal was drawing to a close. He had visited almost every state and territory, sometimes in company with his brother Theodore or another helper, but often as not alone. The demands on his time and strength by local socialists were appalling and only his iron will saw him through.[79] Between October 17 and November 8, his friend Stephen Reynolds assisted him on his tour, but at other times he himself had to attend to such details as baggage, hotel accommodations, meals, schedules and correspondence.[80] Lack of funds complicated matters, but local comrades were understanding and the national office did its best. Debs had little sense of money; often as not he gave away his last dollar, watch, coat and anything else that would benefit someone poorer than he.

Debs closed his campaign with a speech to the people of his home town, Terre Haute.[81] There was one final call for comrades to sign up at local headquarters to take people to the polls and to act as poll watchers and one final burst of campaigning.[82] As the votes were counted exhausted party workers and officials congregated at smokers and celebrations to relax and congratulate themselves, sure that their work had not been in vain.[83] They were not disappointed, for Debs received 402,460 votes, four times his total in 1900. Roosevelt triumphed over Parker easily with 7,628,834 votes to the Democrat's 4,084,401.

The socialists were justly jubilant; at this rate they would be in power in a decade—they said. Illinois led the states with 69,225 votes for Debs, followed by New York, with 36,883; California, with 29,533; Wisconsin, with 28,220. The farm vote was rising and every major city reported an increase, which seemed to show that the labor vote was slowly being won.[84] Chicago returned 45,000 socialist votes; New York, 25,000; and Milwaukee, with Berger's machine in high gear, returned 17,000; in the West, San Francisco reported 7,000 votes for Debs.[85] Only in New England, where elected socialists disappointed those who put them in office, did the vote decline.[86] In Milwaukee, Debs ran well ahead of Parker and his campaign watered the tree that bore fruit for the socialists in the years to come.[87] In other areas of the Middle West, he also ran ahead of Parker and the Democrats.[88]

In the post mortem that followed the election many causes were assigned to the increased socialist vote. Undoubtedly Roosevelt had taken a considerable number of votes from them, yet their showing was still impressive.[89] The prediction that Democrats would abandon Parker for Debs came true and many Democrats, caught in Judge Parker's headlong rout, wondered if they might not now be endangered by the socialists.[90]

The most heartening aspect of the results was the party's coming of age as America's third party; significantly the socialists passed the Prohibitionists and left the Populists far behind.[91] Clearly there was a solid core of socialist support that insured a substantial election return and promised growth for the future.[92]

Yet there was a sobering side to the returns for the socialists and had they been more prescient and less optimistic they might have foreseen the fate of their movement. As the socialist vote rose the older parties moved closer and closer to their doctrine, adapting for their purposes the least radical portion of the socialist program. "As socialism gains headway one of the old parties takes its propaganda," a shrewd commentator noted, outlining the historic mission of minor parties in American history.[93]

The party's failure to win any substantial labor support was also significant. Ironically, many workers felt they could safely cast a protest vote for Debs because times were good and there was no risk of socialist victory.[94] Furthermore, ugly rifts lay beneath the surface of socialist unity.

Yet these realistic factors were hidden from most socialists, especially the rank-and-file membership who thought only in terms of proportions and election figures. Their hard work had paid handsome dividends; the future was full of promise; visions of success occupied their thoughts as they contemplated their quadrupled vote. And, all things considered, the party's future did look bright. An organization that could quadruple its vote in four years it would seem had much to hope for. Although it had failed to win labor's vote its influence there, and in the farm belt was rising. The party propaganda machine was expanding, reaching more and more people monthly. The endless chain of speeches and appearances, the transcontinental tours, the magazine articles were emphasizing and polishing Debs' position as a national figure and political leader. Contacting more and more people, he was acquiring the techniques of political action. Now more than ever he was the acknowledged popular spokesman for American socialism. If the party succeeded in the near future it would owe much to Eugene Debs.

IV

Red Special: The Campaign of 1908

> *Progress is born of agitation. It is agitation or stagnation. I have taken my choice.*
> Eugene V. Debs, 1908

Progressivism came into its own with Theodore Roosevelt's election in 1904, and the dynamic, colorful President stole much of the limelight from the socialists, although they profited greatly from the temper of the times. American socialism's golden age lay just ahead, in the years between 1910 and 1914, but internal troubles cast much of the party's work into the doldrums during the period 1904 to 1910. Yet they were times of slow growth and cautious reorganization. Having won footholds in many areas, the socialists now settled to consolidation and perfection of their organization in preparation for the great revolution which they confidently believed was just over the horizon.

The socialist propaganda machine ran more smoothly, sending forth an ever increasing stream of literature to ease the paths of organizers and speakers who extolled the virtues of the coming commonwealth. Moreover, the socialist press grew accordingly, capitalizing on the tenor of the times and the reflected glory of progressivism. The *Appeal to Reason,* the *International Socialist Review,* the New York *Call* and other publications filled many gaps in areas which had no socialist press of their own.[1]

While expanding its propaganda machine, the party welcomed dissidents from the professions and elsewhere, though its major appeal was still to the working class. By 1908 the socialists had begun a promising appeal to western and midwestern farmers.[2] Socialism was more and more a topic of discussion in the middle-class drawing room, the scholar's den, and the church pulpit. More ministers identified socialism with some form of Christianity.[3] A rising quantity of literature favorable to socialism, often written by non-socialists, paid tribute to the party's place in the progressive movement.[4]

The party also established several agencies to deal with special groups. Perhaps the two most influential were the Rand School of Social Science, established in New York with the aid of an endowment from George Herron and his wife, and the Intercollegiate Socialist Society, which owed much to Jack London and other young intellectuals.[5] Both organizations appealed to young people, hoping to educate them in socialism for the present and also for the future. Though their major influence came after 1908, the years between 1905 and 1908 saw a further growth.

By 1908 the party had made considerable progress toward fulfilling the promise it had shown in 1904. Politically the socialists gained strength on local levels in several areas. Although they just missed capturing the mayor's office in Milwaukee in 1906, their influence with the voters was strong enough to force the parties in power

"Debs has a face that looks like a death's head . . . he was bent at the hips like an old, old man, his eerie face peering up and out at the crowd like an old necromancer reading a charm"—observation by Los Angeles *Times* reporter. (*United Press International Photo*)

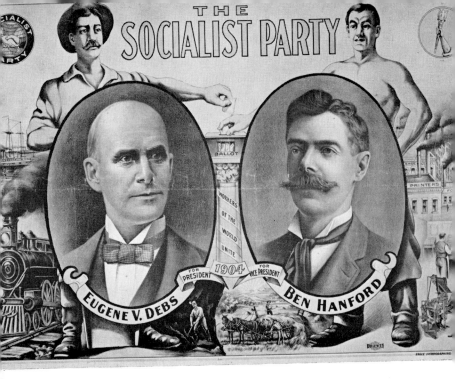

The official party campaign poster for 1904, depicting Debs and running mate Benjamin Hanford, the creator of the mythical rank-and-file party member, "Jimmie Higgins." (*Collections of the Library of Congress*)

"King Debs"—a cartoon appearing at the time of the Pullman Strike, in 1904. It insinuates that, despite Debs' stand against capitalism, he aspired to be monarch of the labor world and thus an indirect dictator in control of all industry. (*Collections of the Library of Congress*)

Debs campaigns vigorously to a sea of bowler hats—miners, railroaders and farm workers wearing their Sunday best. (*Brown Brothers*)

"Labor's Cicero," speaks vehemently, backed by a rostrum of typical socialists. (*United Press International Photo*)

Copyrighted 1908
by WILSHIRE'S MAGAZINE.

A formal portrait of Eugene V. Debs which was used in the campaign literature of 1908. (*Brown Brothers*)

Theodore Debs, upon whom his brother leaned heavily in many ways, here plays the role of secretary aboard the Red Special in 1908. (*Brown Brothers*)

The Debs brothers, Stephen M. Reynolds and Harry C. Parker, manager of the Red Special. Reynolds, was considered an eccentric intellectual. The flowing tie was a popular symbol of defiance. (*Brown Brothers*)

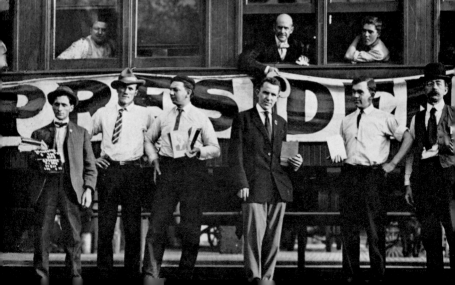

Cartoon published in *Harper's Weekly*, September 21, 1912, reflecting the clash of liberalisms between Debs, William Jennings Bryan and Theodore Roosevelt, and implying that the latter is stealing all the thunder. Bryan, nude in the bushes, is telling Debs, "he's hooked everything that belonged to me, and now he's gone off with yours."

Right: Debs' presidential running mate during the 1920 campaign, the more conservative Seymour Stedman. (*Duke University Library*)

Left: Debs leans out of the Red Special, while the crew displays campaign buttons and socialist literature. Second from the right is labor leader, Tom Mooney, who drew a death sentence, later commuted, as participant in the bomb killings during the San Francisco Preparedness Parade in 1916. (*Brown Brothers*)

Convict No. 9653, Atlanta Prison. A wearying Debs
clutches a bouquet of wilting carnations upon his
last presidential nomination in 1920. (*Brown
Brothers*)

to improve municipal government and public transporta-
tion. They also assisted other reform groups to combat
corruption.[6] The Wisconsin socialists elected some of their
number to the state legislature and to the Milwaukee city
council.[7] Elsewhere, socialist strength grew in New York,
Massachusetts, Pennsylvania and in several Midwestern
states.[8]

The party organization itself prospered as the times
reflected protest and reform. On January 1, 1907, the
socialists boasted organizations in 39 states, over 50
periodicals devoted to their cause, and growing political
strength in several states.[9] The sharp Panic of 1907,
growing social unrest, the socialist propaganda machine,
higher socialist electoral victories—all represented increasing socialist strength to fearful conservatives. Even
Theodore Roosevelt was worried and paid an indirect
compliment to the hard-working socialists when he said:
"I have felt that the growth of the socialist party in this
country was far more ominous than any populist or
similar movement in time past." [10]

Debs, as usual, devoted his time and energy to this
prospering organizational work, speaking, writing, appearing whenever and wherever possible. Aware that reform was the signal of the hour, he vigorously combated
the spread of what he called the "progressive heresy."
He found the notion that capitalism could be reformed
alien indeed. Panaceas of public control of the trusts,
even of public ownership, were false gods to him. "Every
hint at public ownership is now called socialism, without
regard to the fact that there can be no socialism, and
that public ownership means practically nothing, so long
as the capitalist class is in control of the national govern-

ment," he said during one attack on the progressives. "Government ownership of public ultilities means nothing for labor under capitalist ownership of the government." [11] Thus he quarreled continuously with the conservative socialists who felt that public office was in itself a valid socialist aim, and that public ownership and regulation of business were steps in the right direction.

Though his vision was constant, the flesh did tire. "I can hardly find it in my heart to cheer you on," he wrote one correspondent who wanted to take up lecturing. "There is so much to contend with and to overcome in the present condition of things that the undertaking is fraught with all that is calculated to make a man think a second and a third time before engaging in it. If you were a quack revivalist, or sensationalist or fantastic humbug of some sort, starting out to pander to the ignorance of the people, it would be different." [12] But exhausting, trying, and often disheartening as his work was, he persisted. Many times he refused flattering offers, such as lecture tours for large fees, because other duties consumed his time. [13]

Despite growing strength and seeming potential, the socialists posed no real threat to the political control of other parties. Those elected to office were usually moderates, pledged to reform rather than revolution, content to set their sights on a distant utopia. Inadvertently, the work they did helped other reform elements, and earned criticism from their revolutionary brethren. Debs himself grew increasingly wary of the right-wing socialists, but the great factional battles lay ahead and he spent more time praising socialism's progress than criticizing fellow socialists.

The radical socialists were an ever-present irritant to the AFL and persisted in "boring from within" in efforts to capture the Federation. By 1905, however, that hope failed and many left-wing socialists joined independent labor organizers to found the Industrial Workers of the World. Debs had long since abandoned attempts to win the AFL branding them "as wasteful of time as to spray a cesspool with attar of roses." [14] In 1905, he joined "Big Bill" Haywood and other labor leaders to form the IWW. Haywood, who had been a miner and who had lost an eye in an accident, knew the miners' problems firsthand.[15] Over the protests of conservative socialists who did not wish to antagonize the AFL, who disliked dual unionism, and above all who distrusted the elements to which the IWW appealed, Debs lent his voice and pen to the new cause.[16] He did so because he believed that the craft unionism symbolized by the AFL was divisive, corrupt, and harmful to the whole American labor movement. His ancient dream of industrial unionism never faded. "What we want today, above all things, is united economic and political action, and we can never have that while the working class are parcelled out among hundreds, aye, thousands of separate unions, that keep them divided for reasons, many of which readily suggest themselves." [17] Other socialist leaders shunned the IWW convention, but Debs appeared to support the cause of industrial unionism based on truly socialist principles.[18] The assembled radicals wildly cheered his speech but even then he counseled against radicalism and strongly favored gradual, efficient work and avoidance of violence.[19]

The IWW organization grew rapidly in the far western mining camps, fruit orchards, waterfronts and sawmills where its adherents worked. From its birth it bore the stigma of anarcho-syndicalism, a doctrine which was anathema to socialists as well as capitalists. The Socialist Party never supported the "Wobblies"—as members of the IWW were dubbed—and even Debs became disenchanted within a year; by 1906 he let his membership lapse, and though he defended many "Wobblies" long after that, he was no longer a member or champion of the organization. Especially dedicated to organizing the "unorganizable" workers of transient occupations, the "Wobblies" displayed both courage and color in their long but futile efforts. They were doomed to failure for lack of funds, ignorance among those they sought to help, and an increasing emphasis on violence, sabotage, and industrial unrest which made the organization an outcast in society. In time, with the advent of the World War, the IWW became the favorite whipping boy of the "one hundred percent Americans." [20]

It was not easy for Debs to disavow the IWW for he had worked hard and long for the principles it espoused. The fact that Gompers and other leaders castigated him for his work with the IWW hardly deterred him.[21] But as the developing organization turned from democratic methods and the ballot to industrial violence, his taste for it soured. Nevertheless, he vigorously defended Haywood and Charles Moyer, IWW leaders who were accused of killing former governor Frank Steunenberg of Idaho in 1905, protesting, "I know these men personally and truer men never drew a breath. They are as innocent as I of the crime charged against them. The law of the land and the common humanities have all been violated in dealing with these men whose only crime is that they are true to labor and the Mine Owners have not gold enough to debauch them. This incident has in it the elements of a national crisis. If these men are hanged without a fair trial it will be the crime of the century." [22] Thus spoke Debs, the humanitarian. But he disavowed formal connections with the IWW as an organization.[23] The "Wobbly" attitude toward political action repelled him. Asked if he favored votes for women, Haywood snapped: "Sure, and besides, they can have mine." [24] This frank cynicism toward the usefulness of the free ballot and other democratic means turned Debs and other liberals from the IWW.

Yet there was something more than mere dislike of the AFL behind Debs' move to found an industrial union with socialist goals. It was easy to condemn the socialists' idealism as impractical, and to praise the Federation's realism in demanding more economic benefits for labor. Yet the socialists at least had long-term ideals and a sense of social responsibility lacking in the materialistic craft union leaders. Indeed, the AFL policy of "half loaf materialism" was not very different from the idea of "getting ahead" that dominated the business interests of the day. The AFL's greatest failure, one which cost organized labor dearly, was its inability to rise above hand-to-mouth, day-to-day demands for more and more material rewards, and its lack of emphasis on long-range social goals.

For the socialists who bought their party newspapers, went to hear Eugene Debs, attended lyceum lectures on socialism, and studied tracts left at their doors, these were hopeful times. All concerned looked to the national campaign of 1908 to carry socialism a long stride forward to victory.

The delegates who converged on Chicago in May, 1908, for the Socialist Party convention had reason to be cheerful for they represented a party whose prospects had greatly improved since 1904. They spoke for more than 40,000 members, twice as many as in 1904, and represented an organization with nearly 3,000 locals—from almost every state and territory of the union. The dues and contributions paid into the national headquarters supported a propaganda machine operating day and night to spread the message of socialism. A number of full-time paid organizers as well as an estimated 4,000 unpaid stump speakers available on call worked for socialism the year around. More than 100 weekly newspapers were prosocialist, and the party boasted that its newspapers in Chicago and New York alone served 70,000 readers.[25] The *Appeal to Reason* reported an average circulation of 350,-000 copies per issue; and *Wilshire's Magazine* sold 270,-000 copies every month.[26] In other cities socialist and prosocialist newspapers reported rising circulation figures.[27]

Only seven years had passed since the foundation of the unified Socialist Party of America, but the membership had already undergone striking changes. These changes were reflected by the delegates who came to Chicago in 1908 to attend to party business and nominate a presidential ticket. Most of the founders of the party had been younger, engaged in radical pursuits within journalism, lecturing, labor work and the professions.[28] Many of their successors at the convention of 1908 bore testimony to the growing strength of the "parlor socialists" within the movement. Their watchword was orderly evolution toward state socialism; they rejected the class struggle and the need for revolution. They were usually ministers, lawyers, editors, professionals or small businessmen.[29]

The factional outlines in the party which finally crystallized in 1912 were plain in 1908. The "Slowcialists" were opposed within the party by a radical left wing and by a group of centrists who hoped to avoid violence but who called for forthright socialism. The more radical labor organizers, lecturers, writers, and figures like Eugene Debs either belonged openly to the left wing or flirted with it. The organization of the IWW in 1905 by this group and their continued talk of violence and revolution alarmed the conservatives and by 1908 lines were drawn between the groups for a struggle over control of the party machinery.[30]

The dragon's teeth of intra-party strife had been sown long before 1908, and it was evident to all who went to Chicago that the long-repressed intra-party dispute would flare. It soon did, in the debates over the party's official attitude toward organized labor, always an inflammatory question, and in the preliminary skirmishes over the platform for the coming campaign. Left-wing delegates again wanted open condemnation of the craft unions and a strong call for labor's support, with official recognition of the IWW's work. The right wing demanded a conciliatory resolution and no support for the "Wobblies." The inevitable compromise resolution called on labor to vote for socialism and appended a general statement on labor's importance.[31]

Factionalism again appeared when nominations for president were in order. Inevitably, Debs' name was before the convention. No figure in the party was so widely known and loved and the cheers that greeted his name were a tribute to his work for socialism. When the cheering died, John Spargo of New York, a conservative, rose to second the nomination but alluded to Debs' rumored poor health and his past mistakes—lack of attention to party doctrine, "inefficient" methods, and hinted egotism.[32] When Spargo finished, it seemed that the right and center groups might combine to defeat Debs, a telling blow to the radicals. The radicals did not help matters by whispering that if Debs failed or refused, Bill Haywood would accept.[33] Many delegates had heard rumors about Debs' supposed ill health and wondered if he was capable of another gruelling national campaign. Seymour Stedman of Chicago braved a chorus of boos and hisses from Debs' loyal followers to place in nomination the name of Algie Martin Simons, well-known moderate journalist.[34]

Then, while the convention hall buzzed with excitement and speculation, the slight figure of Benjamin Hanford rose in the New York delegation waving a piece of paper. Hanford's beloved "Jimmie Higgins" was fresh in everyone's mind; furthermore, Hanford was a friend of Debs. When the delegates quieted, Hanford revealed that the paper was a letter from Debs. Whatever doubts the delegates had entertained faded as Hanford read the letter. "My general health is about all that could be desired," Debs wrote. "So far as strength is concerned, I have never had more to my credit, if as much." The letter ended with a pledge of support for whoever was nominated and a tacit invitation for the nomination. "You need have no fear that I shall shirk my part in the coming campaign. I shall be in good condition, and I hope there will be no good cause for complaint when the fight is over." [35] Gone was the vacillation and coyness of the past; moreover, Debs had carefully insured his success by placing the letter with Hanford before the convention assembled. For once he left little to chance, for he knew that he need only denote his willingness to run in order to be nominated. The letter did not prevent further nominations, but Debs' assurances that he was physically fit to conduct another campaign together with his support among the rank and file made his selection inevitable. Clearly he was not willing to permit the nomination to go to the right wing without a fight; the significance of other nominations and the attacks from the right did not escape his notice nor that of his friends. The first ballot gave him 159 of the 198 votes cast. Hanford was chosen as his running mate to stand on the usual compromise platform. The left-wing delegates had some cause for cheer as they finished their business and returned home.

But others were less satisfied. There was a noticeable stiffening on all sides concerned which boded ill for the future. "I was surprised at the nominees," Job Harriman wrote Hillquit from the West where he was recovering his health. "It seems to me that a new set was more desirable. It looks as though the party had but one man in it." [36] Many right-wing members shared the thought and Debs' methods as well as his nomination rankled with some of them.

Ever anxious to avoid quarrels, Debs was in Girard writing copy for the *Appeal* while the convention decided his fate. He received the news of this third nomination there in his cramped office. He lost no time in beginning his campaign. Fred Warren, an *Appeal* staff member, suggested that he and Debs take a walk to the town square where a carnival was in progress. Anxious for a little exercise, Debs ageed. The "carnival" turned out to be a crowd waiting for Debs. Though somewhat surprised at Warren's subterfuge, the latter promptly launched into a characteristically biting attack on capitalism which set the tone of the whole campaign. He told the assembled townspeople and farmers that he hated capitalism because it was "a system in which labor is simply merchandise; in which the man who works the hardest and longest has the least to show for it." [37] To him the eternal issue was the many versus the few, want versus plenty, and he blamed all evil on capitalism. Unemployment and idle factories reminded voters of the Panic of 1907 and Debs exploited this theme to the fullest. "Nothing is more humiliating than to have to beg for work," he told his audience, "and a system in which any man has to beg for work stands condemned. No man can defend it." [38] He closed with his perpetual appeal for labor's support and asked his audience to join him in his attack on capitalism. "Progress is born of agitation. It is agitation or stagnation. I have taken my choice." [39]

The crowd responded, proving that Debs could still hold an audience. This was his first speech since a recent throat operation had sparked the ill-health rumors, but there was no sign of disability. At the beginning of his career, Debs was not considered a good speaker. Julius Wayland, peppery publisher of the *Appeal*, thought him only average; Art Young, a famous cartoonist of the day, compared him to a schoolboy elocutionist.[40] But by 1908, his two previous presidential campaigns and his incessant speaking tours had made their mark and he had become one of the most effective speakers of the day. There was little variety in his speeches but he poured the drama of his radicalism, the verve of his appeal, and a flair for the dramatic into vivid words and gestures that indelibly impressed the minds of his audiences. To see Eugene Debs once was to remember him always.

A few weeks after Debs' speech in Girard, the Republicans gathered in Chicago. President Roosevelt had assured the country in 1904 that he would not run again and in 1908 he advanced his Secretary of War, the genial and well-known William Howard Taft, for the Republican nomination. With Roosevelt's backing, Taft won easily on a platform that extolled Roosevelt's program and promised four more liberal years under Taft.[41] Though Taft himself was more cautious in his public utterances than Roosevelt desired, he had the President's full support during the campaign.

In July, the Democrats congregated at Denver to nominate their favorite, William Jennings Bryan, for a third time. Balder and more paunchy than in his golden days, Bryan still championed the common man, labor, and the farmer, and spoke for a variety of political liberals and reformers. Though he had twice failed to attain the Presidency he was still the most prominent Democrat and a powerful vote-getter. His platform called for a variety of reforms and in general was a more liberal document than the Republican platform.[42] The campaign promised to be a battle between personalities and between reform programs.

While the Republicans and Democrats nominated their candidates and drafted their platforms, the socialists busily organized their campaign. Once the ice was broken the campaign developed rapidly and it was soon apparent that Debs would have no rest until election day. Though he said he would rather write than speak, once nominated he entered the fray with all his legendary energy. By late summer he was speaking several times a day in New York and other eastern cities. Though admission was charged to defray campaign costs he spoke to full houses. Everywhere he inspired scenes of adulation and his receptions were often idolatrous. While he tried to quiet a crowd in New York a young woman leaped to her feet and cried out that Eugene Debs was "the living and not the missing link between God and man." [43] No matter how vast the audience, the listener felt that Debs spoke to him alone when the long, bony forefinger shot out and waggled up and down to emphasize a point, or when the fist smashed violently into the open palm. Thus, many identified with the tall, lanky, balding figure striding back and forth across the platform, his voice alternately scornful and soothing, rousing and hopeful, ironic and biting. He never spared an opponent but his audiences sensed no hatred or malice in his words, for even his harshest tone was softened by his intrinsic belief in the goodness of men. His quarrel was never with men but with the system that corrupted them. "When Debs speaks a harsh word," an admirer noted, "it is wet with tears." [44]

The flurry of activity around the socialist campaign and the success of Debs' early speeches aroused the curiosity of Lincoln Steffens, veteran journalist and muckraker. He asked Debs for an interview to question him about his own and his party's stand on the issues of the day. He met Debs in Milwaukee after attending a socialist picnic at which he estimated that 25,000 people bought admission tickets to hear Debs give a rousing speech. Steffens, Debs and Victor Berger went to the latter's home for an interview after the picnic. Debs gave some forthright answers to Steffens' questions. Asked what he would do with the trusts, he shrugged his shoulders and replied that he would confiscate them without compensation since the owners had been paid many times over. Berger, who was along for more than the ride, jumped to his feet. "No. No, you wouldn't. Not if I was there," he snapped at Debs. "And you shall not say it for the party. It is my party as much as it is your party, and I answer that we would offer to pay." [45] Conscious of the power of his carefully-built organization, Berger would not hazard the boomerang of a Debs epigram on confiscation and was as anxious as he was cautious that nothing radical come from the talk with Steffens.

If Debs and Berger disagreed on the confiscation of the trusts, they at least agreed that once capitalism was uprooted mankind could enter into an age of limitless progress. Berger also blamed all evils on capitalism, but he employed softer language and a smaller stick than Debs. He agreed with Debs, who argued that the trust owner, like the impoverished worker, was only a product of the system and that once the trusts were nationalized and operated for the benefit of all the people they would cease to be evil.[46]

The interchange between "the Bear" and the more radical Debs must have amused Steffens, who had seen more than one radical at close range.[47] The clash between the two socialists marked the differences between the wings of the party. Berger insisted that every day brought the ultimate revolution one day nearer, and that the cooperative commonwealth would be established without violence.

He and the conservatives for whom he spoke were anxious to attain political office to enact their immediate demands and they feared the publicity accorded their radical cohorts. They were content with evolution rather than revolution. "Next year, or ten years, or twenty years, or a hundred years from now, we shall still be working toward the completion of our civilization—toward Socialism," Berger told the delegates to the national convention that nominated Debs.[48] His conservative comrades could only nod in agreement.

Debs had as much faith as anybody in the coming revolution but he had less time. He felt that organized labor and political action were the keys to the socialist kingdom. There was often a wide gulf between his public statements and his private actions. In reality he was no more fond of violence than Berger, regardless of his sharp tongue and tall words, and he, too, believed that the revolution could be enacted without violence. He insisted, however, that American socialism would fail unless it was truly socialistic, based on the working class rather than the middle class. He watched the growing power of the conservatives within the party with alarm, and he undertook another national campaign in large part to check conservative tendencies and to make it clear to the right wing that the radicals were by no means beaten. To Berger's question: "Did you ever see an impossibilist do something?" Debs could answer that he had—at the Pullman barns in 1894, in his many tours of the West, and in his daily contacts with the people.[49]

Steffens said frankly that Debs did not seem to be presidential timber, and the socialist candidate readily agreed.

He answered that he campaigned for propaganda purposes, not for office, and that when socialism's day came he would gladly step aside in favor of a more qualified man. Debs realized as much as anyone that he was the evangelist, not the thinker or administrator of American socialism. He agitated frankly and used every means at his command to arouse enthusiasm. He preferred to speak and write in vivid metaphors that the people at large understood and remembered. A friend once told him that he simply could not accept some of the things that Debs said. "Well," Debs replied, "you have to give the workingmen something vigorous if you want to wake them up." [50] Steffens, for his part, left Milwaukee convinced that the socialists had chosen the proper man to bear their standard, for he later wrote Brand Whitlock, mayor of Toledo, to vote for Debs even though he couldn't win.[51]

While Debs toured the East and the Midwest speaking at rallies, picnics, parks, giving interviews and writing material for the party press, his campaign manager, J. Mahlon Barnes, had an inspiration. Why not rent a train and outfit it as a moving campaign headquarters? Debs could ride across the country speaking in every city and at every crossroads. What better way to advertise socialism and to reflect its growth as a national political force? Though most conservative socialists were skeptical, more willing to spend money on down-to-earth, door-to-door campaigning, Debs and others set to work raising funds. It was estimated that the train would cost $20,000; it ultimately came to $35,000.[52] Haywood conducted a series of meetings, asking for contributions; a corps of lesser socialists and sympathizers went fund-gathering and before long enough money was available to launch the "Red Special," as the train was immediately dubbed.

Chicago's LaSalle Street Station beheld a rare spectacle when the Red Special headed west on the morning of August 30, 1908. A large crowd came to see Debs and his party off and waved enthusiastically as the train departed with its red flags, bunting and streamers flapping in the breeze. Later that evening it arrived at Davenport, Iowa where Debs addressed a large crowd.[53] At each stop local socialists swarmed aboard, stumbling over piles of literature, boxes of buttons and red flags, all eager to shake Debs' hand and to pledge their support for the campaign. Though it seemed necessary to greet such party workers and admirers, they proved a great drain on Debs' time and strength. Often exhausted after a speech, he sank down in his chair, loosened his collar and smiled weakly after shaking hands, trying to say as little as possible to spare his throat for the next speech.

The Red Special comprised an engine, a combination sleeper, a diner, and a baggage car stuffed to the top with socialist literature. Accompanying Debs and his manager-brother, Theodore, was his friend, Stephen Reynolds, who was offered a berth in reward for his recent campaign biography. Sharing sleeping quarters with the Debs brothers may have been a doubtful privilege, however, for one newspaper commented:

> Mr. Debs and his brother sleep in one cot. It has never ceased to be a trial to Mr. Debs that the Pullman Company did not build a cot long enough to accommodate his six feet two. His brother is a six-footer, and Mr. Reynolds says it is little wonder that

he has been awakened not infrequently at 6.00 in the morning by a pillow fight in which the Debses were engaged, one or the other having encroached on his brother's side of the cot.[54]

Also to be accommodated aboard was a brass band to provide stirring music when the train pulled into a station.[55] Financially, the trip was hardly worth while for Debs, no matter what his opponents said, for he received a mere three dollars a day and limited secretarial help furnished by national headquarters.[56]

Even before the train was launched, Debs noted the enthusiasm that greeted his speeches and was sure that this was the year of fruition for socialism. "The meetings out here are big as all outdoors and red hot with enthusiasm," he wrote from Kansas a week before launching the Red Special. "The 'Red Special' is trump. The people are wild about it and the road will be lined with the cheering hosts of the proletarian revolution.[57] Once aboard the train, Debs praised it to the skies. "From the hour that it started it has made good a hundred-fold every inch of the way, and I am sure that not a comrade who has seen the train in action regrets having contributed to make it possible," he wrote. "The enthusiasm it inspires everywhere is a marvel to me. If nothing else it would be worth ten times its cost to the movement." [58]

Moving across the Midwest and West, Debs made a series of hard-hitting speeches to audiences of farmers, workers and miners. In Colorado he spoke to large crowds of miners who had not forgotten his long affiliation with organized labor. More than eighteen hundred people, half the population, jammed the largest hall in Grand Junction to hear him flay capitalism. The Red Special band gave a concert and Buffalo Bill called on Debs after the speech to pay his respects. In Leadville an estimated two thousand people stood in the street to hear Debs speak.[59]

The meetings on the West Coast surpassed even those of the Midwest. In Los Angeles on a hot September night, Debs addressed a sweating but enthusiastic crowd that filled the Shrine auditorium. In the course of the speech he condemned almost everyone and everything in sight—capitalism, Republicans, Democrats, Roosevelt, politicians—and called on his audience to adopt socialism. The Los Angeles *Times* reporter in the crowd was not impressed by Debs' logic but admired his flair for the dramatic. "Debs has a face that looks like a death's head . . . as the arch 'Red' talked he was bent at the hips like an old, old man, his eerie face peering up and out at the crowd like an old necromancer reading a charm." [60] Others in Los Angeles were glad to see Debs depart, fearing that his words would find fertile ground, however doubtful his logic. "He teaches [people] and teaches them wrong—possibly with malice; possibly because he too is a dreamer," wrote one *Times* staff member.[61]

Farther north Debs was refused the use of Stanford University's famous chapel, which did not surprise him when he reflected on the manner in which Leland Stanford had accumulated his fortune.[62] In Berkeley, he spoke in the Greek Theater on the campus of the University of California. Since a minor party candidate had already used the theater, university officials did not object.[63] The university administration did not permit the socialists to charge admission, however, so they set up large dinner pails at the entrances and exits into which spectators dropped their contributions. Debs entered to the strains of the "Marseillaise" and delivered a rousing speech to the assembled students and sensation seekers. After the speech, President Benjamin Ide Wheeler of the university shook hands with Debs.[64]

Another large crowd awaited Debs in the railroad station in Ashland, Oregon. Later that evening he addressed an estimated two thousand people at Medford and moved on to Portland where he was refused the use of the city armory for a rally.[65] In Spokane, Washington, three thousand people gathered at the railroad station and a larger number paid admission that evening to hear him speak.[66] His speech at Everett took on the air of a revival meeting in the early hours of the morning and the exhausted candidate had to face a determined audience that chanted: "We won't go home 'till morning." [67]

By this time the party on the Red Special had run out of funds and the train was threatened with being stranded on the West Coast. That would have been a blow at the whole socialist campaign and a very embarrassing situation indeed. Debs called a meeting and decided that they would have to proceed somehow. Edward Lewis of Portland offered to make a quick trip selling literature and guaranteed a return of eight hundred dollars. Appeals to the rank and file brought a flood of nickels and dimes into party headquarters. Contributions were taken at larger rallies and support from a few wealthy socialists in the East saved the day. The Red Special continued its journey.[68]

Debs' throat, a major concern among those around him, bothered him more and more. Incessant speaking kept it raw and the pressures of greeting people, appearing in public, tours, parades, and often rising in the middle of the night to wave to a crowd drained his strength and prevented recuperation. Sometimes his voice failed him completely in the middle of a speech and the audience waited patiently while one of the Red Special crew carried on until Debs could finish hoarsely. At many of the smaller stops, Debs' younger brother Theodore, who resembled him greatly, substituted for the exhausted candidate. The relief afforded by such measures restored some of Debs' strength and he finished the western tour on schedule.[69]

The Red Special left the West Coast and headed toward the Midwest facing an ambitious schedule in the population centers east of the Mississippi. Late in September the train was back in Chicago, its western tour finished. Debs had traveled 9,000 miles, made 187 speeches in twenty-five days in the Far West, and had spoken in every western state and territory.[70] An estimated 275,000 people had heard him.[71] On September 28 a large crowd met the train in Toledo, Ohio. Mayor Brand Whitlock, close friend of many reformers of the day and a famous municipal reformer himself, was in the crowd and seemed delighted to see Debs. He dropped five dollars into the collection hat as it passed him and later marched with Debs in a parade. That evening, 2,000 spectators heard Debs lambaste the masters of capital.[72]

The farmers showed increased interest in socialist politics and as the campaign developed in the Midwest and Southwest, Debs tailored more and more of his speeches for farm audiences. The Red Special combined the virtues of glamor, novelty, and practicality which greatly appealed to isolated farm families. As the train pulled into a rural station or paused momentarily at a country crossroads lined with buggies and wagons, red flags were put out, the band played a rousing socialist song, and members of the crew circulated in the crowd selling buttons, pictures, flags, ribbons and literature.[73] The whole idea, from the train itself to the glamor and publicity that accompanied its progress, was "trump" and had been partly designed to appeal to the spectacle-loving isolated farm families who might incline toward Debs. The entire socialist campaign of 1908 revealed this growing understanding of mass psychology and campaign techniques.

Socialist organizers in the South and Midwest prepared a special program for the farmers, the farm encampment. They set up tent villages and farmers from the surrounding countryside attended a combination Sunday school, picnic, and socialist indoctrination course. The farmers drove into the encampments in their buggies and wagons, each flying a red flag from the whip holder, and participated in meetings that lasted for days and often weeks. Local merchants, ironically, anticipated increased business and sometimes helped finance such encampments. When Oscar Ameringer, veteran socialist newspaperman and organizer, and his three sons were available, culture invaded the encampments in the form of a brass quartet (two trumpets, a tuba and a French horn) that played the music of Bach, Mozart, Wagner and Stephen Foster after Ameringer's short talks on the pleasures of music. Debs spoke at many such encampments during the campaign and often met former ARU members who had turned to farming after being blacklisted from railroad work.[74]

There was no rest for Debs and his stalwart crew on the Red Special. The train now moved east. In Boston he marched at the head of a ten-block long parade to Faneuil

Hall, which was packed with an expectant crowd. An over-flow meeting held outside on the sidewalk accommodated those who could not get in.[75] In Providence, Rhode Island, he spoke to 3,000 people in Infantry Hall and, after reviewing a labor parade, spoke again that night. In Haverhill, Massachusetts, scene of early socialist victories, he addressed a large crowd in the town square. The speech followed a parade of more than 2,000 people which disrupted traffic for some time. While troops paraded in honor of a new bridge in Hartford, Connecticut, Debs drew several thousand from the line of march to a nearby park where he lectured them on the evils of capitalism.[76]

Though the speeches elsewhere were impressive, the most spectacular meeting was held in the Hippodrome in New York City. When the Red Special pulled into the railroad station thousands of men, women and children surged forward, "eager to touch so much as the hem of his garment." [77] Almost 7,500 people paid admission for the Hippodrome speech and waited patiently for Debs' arrival, while 2,500 who could not get in awaited him in a nearby hall.[78] The managers had spared no pains and overlooked nothing to make this meeting the showpiece of the socialist campaign. Small squares of red cloth were sold for a nickel at the door and when Debs made a point that the audience liked the huge room became a sea of red as the listeners waved their small flags in agreement.[79] Backed by a rostrum of socialist dignitaries and officials, Debs gave the Hippodrome audience a long, earnest exposition of his reasons for opposing capitalism and for supporting socialism. When he hurriedly left the hall after the exhausting speech to avoid more tiring ceremonies, the crowd outside tried to carry his automobile to his hotel.

Later that evening at a dinner in his honor several women donated their jewels to the Red Special fund. They were added to the six hundred dollars already collected that day.[80]

Though Debs did not feel well during the New York speeches he appeared elsewhere in the city, touring the East Side on behalf of local socialist candidates. Gripped by colds and chills, and utterly fatigued, he had to force himself to finish his schedule. "The day I was on the East Side I was little more than a portable corpse," he wrote Morris Hillquit.[81] His chief problem was his manner of speaking; he spoke so vigorously and so long that he worked himself into a heated sweat which turned to chills and colds when he went outside.

Socialist plans for a giant rally in Philadelphia were thwarted when the management of the Opera House decided not to permit a socialist rally without a police permit. The permit was not forthcoming and Debs spoke twice in the same night in two smaller halls in the City of Brotherly Love.[82]

No speech passed without a biting attack on the old parties and their platforms, for Debs was always anxious to expose what he considered the hollowness of the regular party platforms. He spoke in Evansville, Indiana, the same evening that William Howard Taft spoke there, and many people who could have gone to hear Taft free preferred to pay to hear Debs.[83] Debs made great sport of Taft's pretensions to progressivism and ridiculed his past record. In reply to the question: "What is a man to do who is out of work in a financial panic and is starving?" Taft had supposedly said: "God knows!" If his remark was chaff to others, it was wheat to socialists and they promptly planted it, hoping to harvest discontent on election day from the unemployed.[84] For his part, Taft had no great love for the socialist candidate. Eugene Debs, he said, was a socialist "who would uproot existing institutions, destroy the right to private property and institute a new regime." [85] Debs agreed heartily with most of the charge.

Debs' campaign irritated President Roosevelt who was very much alive to socialist influence among liberals. The amazing energy of the Red Special tour showed that the socialists might take many progressive votes from Taft. Good politician that he was, Roosevelt did not underestimate the socialists and recognized them as a potentially powerful political force, despite his public dislike of their program.[86] He agreed that capitalism could stand a little reforming but labeled talk about "wage slavery" as "absurd." [87] He was aware of the influence of the socialist press, especially the *Appeal to Reason,* which he thought appealed more to hate than to reason.[88] He thought that Debs was destructive rather than constructive. "To praise and champion Debs, to condone his faults, is precisely like praising and championing Tweed and condoning Tweed's faults," he wrote a friend. He accused Debs' followers of preaching "mushy morality," a field in which he himself was a master, and labeled Debs' speeches "mere pieces of the literature of criminal violence." [89]

But the sword of criticism was double edged and Debs always had a quick reply. He called Roosevelt "the high priest of capitalism," [90] and insisted that he was merely another vessel containing the acids of capitalistic society and a willing tool of the financial interests who ran the government.[91] As for Bryan, his claims of representing both capital and labor were as impossible to Debs as riding two horses in opposite directions at the same time.[92] Bryan had cautiously advocated public ownership of the railroads after a world tour in 1906, but this was hardly an answer to society's ills in Debs' opinion. To him it was a half-measure designed to bolster rather than to weaken capitalism. Indeed, Bryan shunned socialism like the plague, reminding readers and audiences that "Socialism has grown because individualism has been abused and the friends of individualism owe it to themselves and to their cause to at once eradicate those abuses."[93] Throughout his campaign Debs aimed a steady fire of criticism at his opponents. When Taft declined to debate campaign issues with him, Debs excoriated him as a worthy tool of the capitalists.[94]

Debs especially disliked Roosevelt because of the popular President's influence with the "parlor socialists," and because he honestly believed that the President was merely trading on the progressive spirit of the times for votes. He ridiculed Taft's progressive pretensions by reading his judicial record and generally referred to him as "Injunction Bill Taft."

The campaign also brought sharp exchanges between Debs and President Samuel Gompers of the AFL. Debs and Gompers had quarreled before but seldom with such intensity. Long before the campaign began, he attacked Gompers for his cooperation with management. "President Gompers believes that the interests of labor and capital are identical or mutual. We do not," he wrote. "He believes that these interests can be harmonized and justice done to both. We do not. We believe that labor is entitled to all it produces and that labor must organize politically as well as economically to abolish the existing order. . . ." [95]

If he was baiting Gompers he got a quick reply. Irritated by Debs' whole attitude and especially by his work with the IWW,[96] Gompers snapped back and before long an impassable breach separated the two men. Debs attacked Gompers for "pleading" with management for a more lenient labor policy and for his work with the capitalist oriented National Civic Federation, demanding that the AFL leader turn the labor vote to the socialists.[97] Gompers in turn denounced Debs as "the Apostle of Failure" in the pages of the official AFL journal. He charged that Debs had never given labor anything but a black eye and echoed a rumor set afloat in the press that the Republicans were secretly financing the Red Special to frighten voters into playing safe with Taft.[98] When Debs angrily offered to debate the campaign issues, Gompers curtly refused.[99]

Debs and the socialists had good reason to attack Gompers in 1908, for, abandoning the Federation's long policy of non-political intervention, Gompers had endorsed Bryan. Hoping that the Commoner's election would benefit labor, he insisted that "a vote for the Socialist or Independent Party is one lost to the Democratic candidate." [100] Gompers himself conducted an extensive speaking tour for Bryan and the AFL issued and distributed hundreds of thousands of leaflets, supported speakers, and helped Bryan's cause in other ways despite irate condemnation from leading socialists and other union leaders.[101]

Debs was angered enough by Gompers' support of Bryan and by his continued defense of craft unionism, but he was stung most by charges that the Republicans were financing the Red Special. Debs knew only too well that nickels and dimes from the party rank and file paid for the train and for the whole socialist campaign. He made it clear at the beginning of the campaign that the party would publish all its campaign receipts and expenditures.[102] In a presidential campaign in which campaign funds were an issue, not even the socialists were spared an examination of their financial records. After Gompers made his charge the party's national headquarters published the names of everyone who had contributed to the campaign fund, together with the amount of their contribution. In point of fact, an estimated 200,000 people had contributed to the Red Special fund.[103] The press then charged that the party was dominated by foreign elements, a statement easily disproved when the party published its membership rolls, revealing that seventy per cent of the members had been born in the United States.[104]

The progress of the Red Special was such that the regular press could not ignore it and for the first time the socialists found themselves in the pages of some of the country's leading newspapers. The size of the crowds that greeted Debs and the vigor of the whole socialist campaign aroused fears in conservative circles that the socialist vote would rise sharply.[105] Ex-President Grover Cleveland, who died before the election, warned his countrymen that the socialists would poll a million votes.[106] The regular press thus could not ignore the news value of the Debs campaign and at the same time could not afford to give it added publicity. A nice compromise was struck in the back pages of many newspapers. The socialist press continued its impressive showing on behalf of

Debs and the *Appeal to Reason* distributed 22,000,000 copies of its regular and special issues in 1908.[107]

Arguments with Roosevelt and Gompers took second place in Debs' mind to spreading the message of socialism. During October he continued his speaking tour in the East and Midwest. Stephen Reynolds' campaign biography of Debs sold many copies along the route and the money from this and other literature sales was kept on the Red Special. In Duluth, staff members tried to deposit the money in a bank but could find none willing to accept a socialist deposit. The men carried the money, contained in several heavy canvas sacks, all over town and finally brought it all back to the Red Special, much to Debs' amusement.[108]

Debs was not without vigorous support on the local level during his campaign. Berger's organization outdid itself in efforts to capture the local scene and aid the national campaign. "From now until election day let no day pass without directing a stroke against capitalism," Berger exhorted his disciples. Every Sunday morning party workers made their rounds, fortified with pamphlets, literature, buttons, answers to questions and tireless feet. They carefully checked registration lists, sold newspaper subscriptions, won contributions and organized meetings.[109] The national campaign office distributed 3,000,000 pieces of literature and kept many speakers in the field.[110]

Debs made a special appeal for the Negro vote in 1908. Though he still had not devised a program for the Negro, he spoke in terms he thought the Negro could understand, asking him to adopt socialism to cure his ills. There was no appreciable Negro vote in the election, though Debs was trying to build one for the future. It was at best a token gesture in any event for had there been a Negro vote it would probably not have gone to the socialists. The Red Special stopped at Harpers Ferry where Debs saw the monument to John Brown, one of his heroes. He took the occasion to urge the Negroes to support socialism. "The Socialist Party is carrying on the work begun by John Brown," he said when asked for a statement.[111]

Toward the end of the campaign Debs returned to Woodstock, Illinois, where he had been imprisoned after the Pullman strike. His former jailer was among the five hundred well-wishers who greeted him at the jailhouse steps. Debs spoke briefly and went through the jail, this time as a tourist. A large crowd greeted him in Janesville, Wisconsin. The schools in the area had been closed and the railroad station was full of children of all ages, many of whom carried red flags. They were delighted by a handshake with Comrade Debs and a quick tour through the Red Special.[112]

The campaign drew to a close and Debs was glad, for the strain imposed on him by the innumerable speeches and appearances was greater than ever before. He gave his last speech from the Red Special to students at the University of Wisconsin. The campaign had added fifty thousand subscribers to the *Appeal*'s lists; and the St. Louis *Mirror* predicted a million and a half votes for Debs.[113]

On November 3, Debs and Bill Haywood marched at the head of a labor parade that extended more than two miles through Chicago's streets. Sixteen thousand people heard Debs speak that evening and the air was alive with red flags and choruses of approval. Despite intense fatigue he drew on his last reserves of strength for a rousing speech, appealing one final time for labor's vote. Again with Haywood, he closed the campaign with a speech to his Terre Haute neighbors and went home to await the returns.[114] He did not doubt that the campaign had greatly improved socialism's position across the country.

The arch-conservative Chicago *Tribune* expected Debs to poll a million votes.[115] The *International Socialist Review* predicted 676,500 votes for Debs,[116] but as the election returns ticked in socialist hopes sank. Neither Berger's confident prediction of a million and a half votes for Debs, nor Debs' own hopeful call for a million votes was realized.[117] The final tally gave Debs 420,793 votes, an increase of only 20,000 over the vote of 1904. The socialists retained their place as America's third party, showing greatest strength in the Far West and Midwest. Oklahoma, where farm encampments and hard work brought increased publicity to the socialist cause, and Pennsylvania, where the party had many sympathizers among the coal miners, reported slight increases over their 1904 totals.[118] Milwaukee, Berger's home town, elected six socialists to the state legislature but the bright spots were few and far between.[119]

What had happened? Why had the socialist total remained almost stationary despite the vigorous national campaign? Debs' appeal to the masses of sympathetic voters was obvious; great quantities of socialist literature had flooded promising areas; and hundreds of party members and workers followed in Debs' wake, preaching, teaching, exhorting the voters for Debs. Why had the vote increased so little?

The basic socialist miscalculation was reliance on the 1904 totals as a yardstick for their strength in 1908. In the former year, many Democrats, faced with the distasteful alternatives of Parker and Roosevelt, undoubtedly voted for Debs. These voters returned to Bryan in 1908.[120] Thus Debs reasoned that every socialist vote in 1908 was a pure socialist vote and that the seemingly small total was in fact a large increase in the party's strength. Taft's ample figure apparently fitted the mantle of progressivism passed on to him by Roosevelt and the President's support helped him during the campaign.[121]

An economic upswing turned many voters to the Republicans, who used the prosperity issue freely.[122] The socialists never overcame the American worker's fear of panaceas and experimentation in times of economic unrest; this was never better illustrated than in 1908, when the socialists logically should have benefited from economic disturbances.

Bryan captured the liberal Democratic vote; Taft won the progressive Republican vote; Samuel Gompers could not elect Bryan but turned many voters from Debs.[123] In addition, many workers lost their right to vote by leaving their precincts in search of work.[124] Such at least were the official socialist explanations for the small increase in their vote.

Whatever his comrades thought about the election results, Eugene Debs had little to regret, glad as he was to be back in the peace and quiet of Terre Haute. He looked back across the preceding months with satisfaction, feeling that the whole socialist campaign was another step toward the commonwealth. His primary aim during the campaign was to agitate for socialism and he had succeeded in this. There would be other campaigns, other speaking tours, countless chances in the years ahead to preach the coming revolution. His stand for socialism and his belief in the wisdom of the people remained unshaken. The people would know, in time, and when they did his dream would become reality. At the moment he was too tired to reflect on the campaign's deeper meanings. Before the votes were counted he had said that the socialist campaign had "expressed the true spirit of socialist comradeship, which is the making of our movement, and which will sustain it through every ordeal until it is finally triumphant." [125] He did not change his mind after the votes were counted.

V

The Harvest Year:
The Campaign of 1912

> *Let us make this our year! Let us make the
> numerals 1912 appear in flaming red in
> the calendar of the century.*
>   Eugene V. Debs, 1912

On a freezing March day in 1909, Theodore Roosevelt
handed the reins of government to his chosen successor,
William Howard Taft. The weather that greeted the new
chief executive was symbolic of the stormy times that lay
ahead for him and for America. The progressive sentiment that had gathered since the turn of the century rose
during Taft's administration to new heights, crashing
against many accepted institutions, leaving in its wake
changes that many thought impossible. In the years of
Taft's misfortune, with Theodore Roosevelt gone, the
Socialist Party profited more and more from his successor's mistakes and lack of color.

As Taft entered his administration full of hope and good
intentions, and as most Americans awaited the continua-
tion of political reform so closely identified with Roosevelt
and the Republican Party, all was not well with the American socialists. The party's poor showing in 1908 after so
spectacular an effort reflected what many feared was an

117

arrested growth. Party membership mounted slowly; the rank and file were depressed in many areas and for many reasons. Yet even as they counted their disappointments the socialists stood on the eve of their greatest success.

To their own surprise and gratification, the Milwaukee socialists elected Emil Seidel mayor in the municipal elections of 1910. Victor Berger himself was elected to Congress as the first socialist ever to sit in the national House of Representatives. When they had digested the surprise the socialists found that they had elected mayors in other cities and that the tide seemed to be running in their favor as never before.[1] The victory in Wisconsin was balm to Berger's irritation and he quickly pointed out that while his radical friends were involved in dreamy panaceas his own well-knit organization had captured important offices in state and nation.[2] The Milwaukee victory was indeed a morale builder, a tribute to the long years of hard work and efficient organization. Characteristically, the New York *Call* said of Seidel's victory: "That which has been cherished as a dream was beginning to look like reality." [3] To radicals and reformers in other camps the socialist victory was a highlight of the times, a preview of things to come.[4] Victories elsewhere gave the lie to predictions that socialism would decline.[5]

In municipal elections in 1911, the party won in other cities, and each victory stimulated the propaganda organization to greater efforts.[6] The party itself kept close watch on its electoral progress and digested and reprinted a great deal of information on the progress of socialist government across the country.[7] When the full returns of 1911 were in, socialists rejoiced at victories in thirty-three states, claiming 435 of their number in elective offices.[8]

While the victories were scattered, and usually minor in importance, each was a step toward the top of the political ladder and none was too insignificant to pass unnoticed in the party press or around the firesides of rank-and-file socialists. The regular press and social commentators paid more and more attention to the rising influence of socialism in politics.[9]

These local victories were as gratifying to the socialists as their few national successes for they signified the party's grass roots strength. By 1912, the socialists boasted that more than a thousand of their number occupied elective office in thirty-three states and 160 cities across the country.[10] The cities were the strongholds of socialism and the party registered its greatest success with the voters in municipal elections. The eleven states of the Midwest accounted for seventy per cent of the socialists in public office.[11]

Even these victories did not escape the taint of party factionalism, and they were a mixed blessing to many socialists, including Eugene Debs. The first victories came from conservative socialist strongholds, but success in more radical areas like Ohio, Pennsylvania, California, and the Far West indicated that the Bergerites were not the only ones who could win elections. Yet the Bergerites won the choicest posts and other conservatives carefully used their growing power in public affairs to insure their hold on the party machinery. Ever frightened that their radical brethren might endanger their success, they took no chances of losing their grip within the party. As their electoral progress increased, so did their determination to control party policy.

Debs had all this in mind when he warned his comrades

that their celebrations over election victories were perhaps premature. "Voting for socialism is not socialism any more than a menu is a meal," he said, noting that many socialist office-holders were little more than reformers. "The danger I see ahead is that the Socialist Party at this stage and under existing conditions, is apt to attract elements which it cannot assimilate, and that it may be either weighted down, or torn asunder with internal strife, or that it may become permeated and corrupted with the spirit of bourgeois reform to an extent that will practically destroy its virility and efficiency as a revolutionary organization." [12] He feared that vote-getting had become an end in itself with many socialists and that they might well forget their revolutionary program at the next election in order to retain their offices.[13]

Although socialists could well rejoice at their electoral successes, enemies pointed out that their power was scattered and concentrated in minor offices. The socialists elected to office were, as Debs rightly perceived, little more than reformers.[14] Their policies, personalities, and powers posed no threat to the established order. These socialist election victories were important to future work, party propaganda, and as bones of contention between radical and conservative socialists.

The conservatives rose to power in the party for several reasons. In part the radical socialists had only themselves to blame. Too often they concentrated their energies on local questions, and after 1905 they tended to concentrate on converting organized labor to socialism. They flirted consistently with the IWW and syndicalism, furnishing grist for the conservative mill in attacks on "impossibilists" and "revolutionary" positions. Though he could and did fight hard for his ideals, Debs himself did not demand or attain the leadership within the party that might have been his—partly because he disliked factional strife and partly because he preferred to remain above party and agitate among the people, a task for which his talents were far better suited.

But the conservatives could look to their own successes as well as the radicals' failures to explain their dominance within the party. As in most radical movements, thinkers rather than workers quickly dominated the Socialist Party of America. In this they were aided by better education and a more highly organized drive than the workers possessed. They generally made their livings as writers, professionals, lawyers or newspapermen and had more time to devote to party affairs. In addition to being better educated than their rivals they did not hesitate to use parliamentary methods to thwart their opponents. Aside from Debs, few radical socialists were well enough known among the rank and file to defeat such famous names as Victor Berger and Morris Hillquit. Furthermore, "Slowcialism" genuinely appealed to reform elements and the educated middle class and the conservatives were more and more successful in controlling the party machinery as their electoral success increased. The radicals scattered their strength in a multitude of causes and quarrels but the conservatives consolidated theirs in a concerted effort to dominate the party. Their electoral success gave them both publicity and respectability. A sizable portion of the socialist press was theirs and they used it ruthlessly to wage war against the radical elements which they felt were frightening away votes for the party.

Debs and other radicals worked hard to counteract this

conservative influence. Debs spoke in many strike areas, urging the miners to unite industrially and to adopt socialism.[15] Though he had abandoned the IWW he defended many individual "Wobblies," and proclaimed adherence to their ends if not their means. In 1910, when the Los Angeles *Times* plant was blown up, Debs rushed to the defense of the McNamara brothers who were charged. Their confession and imprisonment did not shake his belief in their innocence and their cause, though other socialists avoided the case for fear of being tarred with the brush of violence.[16]

The party organization grew with each victory and increased its efforts to organize and educate through the establishment of a lyceum bureau, which helped the Rand School and the Intercollegiate Socialist Society.[17] The entrenched socialist press continued its impressive showing, serving communities large and small.[18] New locals sprang up all over the country and beyond; there was even an incipient movement in Alaska, where members held regular meetings in a tightly chinked log cabin and warmed themselves at the fires of both wood and rhetoric.[19]

The First National Congress of the Socialist Party in 1910 was an arena of debate for the factions within the party. Labor unions, syndicalism, immigration, the farm problem, and a host of other questions were aired and the divisions among socialists were plain to see, though they compromised on their differences in the name of the coming commonwealth and party unity. Several of the issues touched Debs, but he waxed particularly eloquent on the immigration question. Though the conservatives held that the uneducated immigrants were fodder for capitalism's mill, Debs saw in them a source of radicalism on which the party could draw and consistently opposed all efforts to restrict immigration as un-socialistic.[20] The debates in the Party Congress illustrated the differences within the party. Clearly these were times of promise, and rewards made the struggles sharper with party leaders willing to risk division and discontent to make their own particular philosophies predominate.

Early in May, 1912, socialists from all over the country converged on Indianapolis to hammer out a national platform, to listen to "red" rhetoric, to select a presidential ticket and to exhort one another to work harder for the success that seemed imminent. The rising influence of the conservatives was symbolized by the delegates milling on the floor of the convention hall and engaging in animated debate during and after the sessions. Many famous socialists were there: Bill Haywood, "who sees enough with one eye"; Oscar Ameringer, "a man of gestures"; and Dan Hogan, "from Arkansas and proud of it." [21] It was rumored that the host city of Indianapolis had delegated a member to address the delegates in overalls, but he appeared at the appointed time clad in bourgeois pants. Job Harriman of California delighted the eyes of delegates and spectators alike as he moved about the floor and lobby clad in "a suit of vanilla ice cream color." And a delegate from Oklahoma, where socialism was still growing, wore a red flannel shirt which he never seemed to remove; it was rumored that he slept in it, so devoted was he to the coming revolution.[22] Yet there was something different about these delegates; they were too respectable. Their predecessors had been younger, more radical, full of a different philosophy, closer to the masses of the people. More than one old-timer noted sadly that he could talk to fewer and fewer people.[23]

Debs did not attend the convention because it promised from the first to be heated. Though he never refrained from attacking opponents, he had no stomach for intra-party warfare. In 1912 he preferred the lecture schedule to the pandemonium of the convention hall. The major bone of contention among the delegates was the work of the IWW socialists. The conservatives were determined to censure the "Wobblies" for their syndicalist views, and the radical socialists were equally determined to win of-ficial party support for the IWW. The radicals won early victories by seating Bill Haywood on the National Execu-tive Committee, by sending encouragement to western "Wobblies," and by a resolution seeming to favor indus-trial unionism. They were halted, however, when the con-servatives amended the party constitution to expel any socialists who favored industrial sabotage or syndicalism, and who renounced political agitation. The action was not taken without a free swinging floor fight in which more than words flew through the air. As a result many IWW socialists left the party and the wounds inflicted never fully healed.[24]

Debs was bitter at the outcome of the anti-sabotage amendment for he felt that Berger and Hillquit had steam-rollered the delegates. Even so, he could not support the "Wobblies." Before the convention began, he backtracked and re-stated his position on violence. "I am opposed to any tactics which involve stealth, secrecy, intrigue, and necessitate acts of individual violence for their execu-tion." [25] He frankly admitted that he obeyed capitalist laws only because he had to, but he did so because he feared that acts of violence would boomerang against the whole socialist movement and harm more than help the party. The "Wobblies" were not socialists but anarchists because they worked outside an organized group; their utopia was not the cooperative society envisaged by Eugene Debs.[26] Thus did he partially solve the ambivalence in his thinking over violence.

The crux of his dilemma was obvious. For years he had preached the overthrow of capitalism; he had defended men whose actions looked like revolution. Now at the crucial moment he denied that he advocated violence. At the same time he said he obeyed laws only because he had to. Many of his followers were frankly puzzled and found it difficult to reconcile some of his past statements with his present stand.

The truth of the matter was that he disliked any form of violence. He still insisted that the revolution would come through agitation and education. The revolution he had in mind transcended a limited program of industrial violence. He could not say with Berger that "Those who sing 'I'm a bum' should get out and form a bum party of their own. I can see anarchism under the cloak of the IWW and it is trying to fasten itself on the Socialist Party." [27] Debs still admired many "Wobblies" and liked their ideals; he was bitter in after years that so promising an organization had drifted into the wrong hands. Had it stayed on the proper path it might have brought to fruition his dreams of industrial unionism—so he thought.[28] Though many argued that the IWW had not abandoned political action, Debs was disenchanted. By the eve of World War One he saw that it was too late to revive the

IWW and condemned its leaders' failure to build a sound
organization.[29] Yet it was not easy to say goodbye to the
IWW, for the "Wobblies" took with them so much romantic color, so many fresh ideals, and a host of dreams
that had turned to dust in too short a time.

The party constitution amended, the delegates turned
to select a presidential slate. Berger, still hesitant about
Debs and his radical followers, hinted that the latter
might not run because of poor health. Some conservatives
had already questioned Debs' availability and his ability
as a political general, and were openly fearful that his
radicalism would hurt the party in its year of promise.[30]
The chairman of the day, Lewis Duncan of Montana, a
strong Debs man, declared emphatically that Debs would
run. Duncan said that Debs' friends knew what they were
talking about. "Do they?" queried Berger. "They do,"
answered the chairman with equal terseness.[31] Although
Debs did not actively seek the nomination his availability
was taken for granted; his reluctance in such matters
had faded years ago. The conservatives were not yet
beaten, however, and placed two more names in nomination, Emil Seidel of Milwaukee and Charles Edward
Russell, prominent New York muckraker. The outcome
was never seriously in doubt. The conservatives could
not unite behind a single candidate and it is doubtful
that they could have carried the day even if they had,
so great was Debs' popularity with the rank and file.
Someone started a chant for Debs and he received 156
votes to fifty-six for Seidel and fifty-four for Russell on
the first ballot. The right wing claimed a partial victory,
however, for the cautious Seidel won the vice-presidential
nomination.[32]

Once again, as in 1908, Debs accepted the nomination and responsibilities of another national campaign, his fourth, because he felt that the party had passed into the hands of men who were evolutionary rather than revolutionary. They denied the class struggle, radical propaganda and decried the dangers of what he felt was real socialism. Debs was anxious that workers rise in the party for he did not believe that lawyers, ministers, and doctors, regardless of their good intentions, adequately represented worker needs and views.

The convention had already adopted a compromise platform that savored of right-wing ideas, calling for cooperative organization of prisons, a national bureau of health, abolition of the United States Senate and the presidential veto, and a long list of progressive reform measures.[33] Their work accomplished, the delegates adjourned to prepare for the coming campaign.

Debs did not plan to begin active campaigning until late in the summer but the national campaign committee worked hard from the spring onwards. The party spent $66,000 on the campaign. Donations from party members in the form of one day's pay totaled $23,000. The sale of admission tickets and contributions taken at rallies yielded another $15,000 and literature sales added an additional $15,000.[34] Though the sum was insignificant in the total cost of the presidential campaign, it was a large amount for the socialists. Moreover, they got more than their money's worth from their slender resources because of the cooperative nature of their campaign work and their backlog of helpers willing to work without pay. As in previous campaigns, local and state organizations bore the brunt of the routine work. Thousands of party members and sympathizers volunteered their services as speakers, doorbell ringers and office workers during the campaign.

If the campaign committee was successful in raising funds, it was less happy in its choice of personnel to manage the effort. J. Mahlon Barnes, who had managed the campaign in 1908, was again chosen party manager, largely through the help of conservative socialist friends. The cooperation and friendliness with which he and Debs had worked in 1908 was gone in 1912. Even before the campaign got underway, many socialists attacked Barnes for his supposedly loose sexual morals. In the West some socialists labeled him "a moral cripple," and party headquarters received many protests at his selection; Debs himself opposed the choice, saying that he had not been consulted and did not approve of Barnes.[35] An official, but hush-hush, investigation did little but air the party's dirty linen, though Debs formally protested at one meeting.[36] The whole affair only widened the breach between radicals and conservatives. Debs' efforts to remove Barnes were vain and he remained during the campaign as testimony to the conservatives' strength within the party. Indeed, though he strongly disapproved of Barnes' private life, Debs' opposition was really aimed at the conservative men behind the campaign manager.

Undaunted, Debs simply decided to ignore the issue and have as little as possible to do with both the campaign manager and national headquarters; as in the past he would run his campaign the way he wanted to. But the issue died slowly and was one of many things that moved Victor Berger to say that Debs had "an unduly exaggerated ego," hinting that something would have to be done about it after the campaign.[37] Barnes himself walked softly during the campaign and distrusted the radicals. When the campaign left the national office with a small deficit, he bitterly accused the radicals of trying to use it to oust him.[38]

Debs originally had planned to rest and write during the hot summer months in preparation for his national tour during the fall. Progressive rumblings within Republican ranks and the increasing likelihood that the Democrats would nominate a liberal candidate, however, alarmed him and he began early. True to his fears, Taft's choice did not endear him to the Progressives who chose him in 1908, and, thwarted in receiving the regular Republican nomination from the President, Theodore Roosevelt returned to the political arena with a dynamic third party, the "Bull Moose" Progressive Party. The Democrats fulfilled predictions by choosing Governor Woodrow Wilson of New Jersey to bear their standard. The campaign promised to be the most sharply contested since 1896, and perhaps since 1860. Late in June, Debs opened his own campaign with a speech in St. Louis and began a slow tour across the country toward the Pacific Coast. From the beginning of the campaign he feared that Progressives and Democrats would siphon off socialist votes and he constantly ridiculed any idea that capitalism could be reformed or that the other parties were sincere. "The cause [of the present unrest] does not lie in a maladministration of present government, but in the very structure of society as at present constituted," he told an audience in Phoenix, Arizona early in the campaign. "And the remedy must be found in a reconstruction of all existing systems." [39]

Despite broiling heat and clouds of dust a large and enthusiastic crowd turned out in the copper mining center of Bisbee, Arizona to hear him assail capitalism. Socialists and IWW organizers were no strangers to these miners and their families. While members of the crowd, many sporting red neckties and bandanas, munched on peanuts and popcorn, Debs elaborated on a favorite theme, the problem of leadership. To the end of his life he feared the powers of leaders. Instead, he trusted in the education of the masses and had a firm belief in the innate goodness of man. "It would do no good for me to lead you to the promised land—Roosevelt would only come along and lead you out again." [40] Significantly, this was the traditional American answer to the need for reform. His reliance on self-help and mass education and a desire to avoid violence stamped Debs as a reformer firmly in the American tradition. He was first and foremost an American figure and the socialism he preached reflected American rather than Marxist or European ideals.

In Oakland, California, six thousand people heard him talk for more than an hour with all his old fire and vigor. His fist smashing into his open palm, his lean figure crouched dramatically, he roared out his hatred and defiance of capitalism and the society it produced.[41] In Portland, Oregon, he was vigorously applauded by eight thousand people who had patiently awaited his arrival despite a heavy thunderstorm. More than a hundred dollars in addition to admission charges was collected from the crowd.[42] Farther north he spoke to a large throng in Everett, Washington. His train had abruptly changed schedules and the crowd waited more than five hours, ardor undampened.[43] Everywhere in the West the story was the same. He had traveled this route before and recognized many familiar faces in the crowds. There were hundreds of hands to shake after every speech and countless times when he took the names of needy comrades for future reference. Favors, errands, reminiscences, greetings—all these interrupted the long hours of speaking, public appearances, and the monotony of campaigning.

His western tour ended, Debs returned to the East. The greatest meeting of the campaign was held in Madison Square Garden. Fifteen thousand tickets, costing from fifteen cents to a dollar each, were sold out weeks in advance and on the big night overflow meetings filled several adjacent halls to accommodate those who could not get into the Garden. Every seat in the huge auditorium was filled and large crowds stood in the aisles and in the back of the room. Girls in white aprons wearing red turbans and hair ribbons circulated in the crowd selling buttons, red flags and literature.[44]

While waiting for the speakers the crowd sang the "Marseillaise," and "International," both socialist favorites. Emil Seidel, the vice-presidential candidate, opened the meeting with an appeal for labor's vote and cited recent socialist victories as proof that the party was increasing daily in strength. "Only a year ago workingmen were throwing decayed vegetables and rotten eggs at us but now all is changed," he told the crowd. "Eggs are too high. There is a great giant growing up in this country that will someday take over the affairs of this nation. He is a little giant now but he is growing fast. The name of this little giant is socialism."[45]

The crowd cheered Seidel's words but that ovation was nothing compared to the bedlam that greeted Debs' carefully-timed appearance. The crowd stood up, cheered, and waved red flags for nearly thirty minutes. Looking immensely pleased, Debs acknowledged the ovation, quieted the crowd and launched into a vigorous exposition of socialism. He insisted that only the socialists represented labor; condemned "Injunction Bill Taft"; declared that Roosevelt was still a faker, even worse; and insisted that the Democrats, Progressives and Republicans alike were financed by the trusts. The only hope for America was socialism.[46] There was nothing new in the speech but the crowd loved it. Aside from his legendary reputation as a friend of labor, Debs' greatest contribution to socialism was his free swinging oratory. As one observer said: "The raging of Debs' fire is superbly spectacular." [47] Despite the admission charge, he spoke to full houses in 1912. Good politician that he was, he capitalized on every platform technique—voice, posture, vigor, and simple presentation—to capture the interest of his audience.

The socialist press greatly aided Debs and other candidates during the campaign. The regular press observed a conspiracy of silence on most events connected with the socialist campaign. By 1912 the loosely controlled but highly effective socialist press represented all shades of socialist opinion. In 1912, five English and eight foreign language dailies; 262 English and thirty-six foreign language weeklies; and ten English and two foreign language monthlies spoke for the Socialists.[48] In addition, some 400 union and independent papers carried information and bulletins sent them by the national party headquarters. In 1911 the party stationed a press representative in Washington, largely to publicize Berger's work.[49] The *Appeal* maintained its past record and served hundreds of thousands of new and old readers; its circulation rarely fell below the 500,000 mark.[50] Even before the campaign got underway, the national headquarters sent out 3,500,-000 pieces of literature, and during the campaign national headquarters kept close watch on all propaganda work.[51] The activity of the socialist press and careful attention to propaganda does much to explain Debs' success in 1912.

The campaign was strenuous for the candidate. In Philadelphia 18,000 people crowded into Convention Hall to hear him bait the masters of capital. It was a motley crowd, composed of hobos off the streets, professional politicians who had come to study the Debs technique, and plain curiosity seekers as well as the local faithful. The cry "Only a nickel!" persuaded more than one spectator to buy a small red flag, gaudy pamphlet, or campaign button from the red-and-white clad girls selling them.[52] Sales of literature added $300 to the money collected by the ushers, making a total of $2,700 collected that evening.[53]

Two thousand people greeted Debs' train in Muskogee, Oklahoma, and another five thousand met him in Indianapolis.[54] Despite pouring rain, an estimated ten thousand people paid admission to hear him speak in Pittsburgh.[55] The pattern was the same in other eastern and midwestern cities. Late in October he invaded New York's lower east side on behalf of Meyer London, who was running for Congress, and was greeted everywhere by large and enthusiastic crowds. All his speeches were sold out weeks in advance.[56]

While Debs crisscrossed the country, other socialists were also at work. After failing to win the presidential nomination, Charles Edward Russell ran for governor of New York. Early in November, a crowd of ten thousand gathered in New York City to hear him predict the coming triumph of socialism and the election of at least ten socialist congressmen on November 5.[57] Many famous socialists and labor organizers invaded New York on behalf of prominent socialists running for office.[58]

As he swung around the circle Debs returned time and again to the theme that Progressives and Democrats had stolen conservative socialist doctrine but lacked the courage to fashion a truly socialist program, which marked the hollowness of their pretensions. He commented acidly that for some at least the fluttering bandanas which greeted Theodore Roosevelt at the Bull Moose nominating convention had replaced the red flags of socialism.[59] Now more than ever he distrusted and feared Roosevelt, and attacked his labor record mercilessly in typical Debsian language. "To all those ragged and outraged workers, Roosevelt must appear as a charlatan, mountebank, and fraud, and his Progressive promises and pledges as the mouthings of a low and utterly unprincipled self seeker and demagogue." [60] No mean word artist himself, Roosevelt must have blanched if he saw the charge. Debs warned his followers that the Progressives would stop at nothing to win votes from the "parlor socialists." [61] Charging that Roosevelt had had himself photographed with a poverty-stricken family in the Pennsylvania coal fields only for publicity purposes, Debs denied that the Progressives were reformers. Noting that the new party was financed by George Perkins and other trust magnates, he ridiculed Roosevelt's pretensions to trust-busting. If the Progressives were financed by the trusts, how could they oppose the trusts? He dismissed out of hand any idea that the Colonel's followers were socialists in disguise. "When a spring chicken walks into your kitchen, lies on its back and begs to be picked and fried, then these pluto-crats will be for the Socialist ticket." [62] Roosevelt himself, be it noted, was at great pains to avoid any taint of socialism for fear "we would have been a rival to Debs. . . ." [63]

Still anxious for labor's votes, Debs appealed tirelessly for union backing and called on the workers to spurn Gompers' and other craft leaders' non-political dictum. "For the first time in the world's history a subject class has it within its own power to accomplish its own emanci-pation without an appeal to brute force." [64] Always in his speeches there was this belief that violence was un-necessary, that mercy and justice would triumph if only people would pause and hear what he had to say.

While Debs busily roused the faithful, Victor Berger waged a cautious campaign to retain his seat in Congress. However much Debs sneered at Berger's hesitant progress toward utopia, Berger was admittedly in a difficult posi-tion in 1912. He held the highest post ever occupied by an American socialist and felt that retaining his seat was the paramount objective of his campaign, not the estab-lishment of a new heaven. Debs still proclaimed himself a radical, as when he demanded confiscation of the trusts, but it was a different story to Berger. He soundly con-demned Debs' plan for confiscation and assured his prospective constituents that he stood for sensible, orderly socialism, not revolution. He denied that triumphant so-cialism would abolish private property. Rather, his scheme as outlined in a prominent magazine article, called for little more than the nationalization of certain basic industries. In such circumstances business would be operated "for use and not for profit." Such a program would evolve naturally out of the progressive movement. No violence was necessary. "Our sole objective in state and nation for the next few years is to elect a respectable minority of Socialists." [65]

Berger spoke for the now dominant right wing of the party and if he spoke for Debs' benefit his words fell on deaf ears. Debs would have none of it. To him any socialist program must be based first and last on the assumption that capitalism was evil and that there was a class struggle based on economics; until commonwealth replaced corporate wealth there could be no progress and no "respectable minority of Socialists."

Debs spoke five and six times a day for sixty-eight consecutive days, often with little rest and less sleep.[66] An immense correspondence followed him around the country, made doubly burdensome by his aversion to the typewriter; there were innumerable hands to shake; articles to write; friends to see; and all the petty details that go with a national speaking tour. He bore up through it all despite poor health and wearing nerves. He was more determined than ever to show that militant socialism still had a wide audience and to prove to the right wing of the party that their "sensible" approach to the issues of the day was not the only one to win votes.

Despite their growing respectability, socialists were often viewed with alarm and frequently harassed. Although he was subjected to fewer attacks than his colleagues, Debs did not entirely escape attempts to smear him. One evening, for instance, he returned to his hotel room to find it littered with women's lingerie. He calmly went downstairs and returned with witnesses who testified that the clothing had been planted.[67] When Roosevelt was shot by a fanatic in Milwaukee, long a socialist stronghold, the party headquarters issued a statement that the would-be assassin had never been a socialist.[68] Roosevelt himself privately paid Debs an indirect compliment by comparing the assassin to him.[69] Following a riot in New York City the courts ruled that socialists could use city parks for their meetings.[70] In Portland, Oregon, a group of socialists was arrested for making "derogatory and libellous remarks" about Theodore Roosevelt and his family. Arrests of socialists elsewhere on similar charges were not uncommon.[71] After considerable controversy, the New Jersey Supreme Court ruled that socialists could display the red flag since it was a legitimate party emblem.[72] All these incidents merely reflected the established order's growing concern over socialism's success with the voters. In reality every such arrest was a compliment to the influence the socialists had built up since 1900.

In Los Angeles, whose city fathers shed few tears over socialist problems, especially after the bombing of the *Times* plant in 1910, socialists were denied the use of city sidewalks and street corners for their meetings.[73] Perhaps in spite, but more probably because the opportunity was simply too good to miss, the socialists were ready for Governor Hiram Johnson of California, the Progressive Vice-Presidential candidate, when he came to Elizabeth, New Jersey. The Governor had barely begun his address when a local socialist set up a stand on the edge of the crowd and heckled and disputed with Johnson throughout his speech.[74]

The crucial nature of the contest of 1912, the high point of the long progressive groundswell, was sensed by all who watched the developing campaign. It was not long before the consensus eliminated Taft and narrowed the field to Wilson and Roosevelt. Despite heavy competition for liberal votes, most of which were conceded to Wilson, many still watched the socialists with alarm. The distinguished historian Albert Bushnell Hart warned that unless the Progressives were elected there would be a socialist administration in Washington in 16 years.[75]

His tour finished, a weary and exhausted Debs returned home to await the results. He himself was unable to vote because he was away during the registration period, so instead of going to the polls he stayed home to celebrate his fifty-seventh birthday.[76] The socialists had no special wire service. Instead, scouts in major population areas telegraphed results directly to the Debs home as soon as they were available.[77]

The final tally showed that Debs polled 897,011 votes of approximately 15,000,000 cast, an all-time high for the socialists to that date. The national campaign committee's confident prediction that Debs would receive two million votes and that twelve socialist congressmen would be elected proved illusory, for even Berger lost his seat in Milwaukee, where the opposition combined to beat him.[78] There were brighter spots in the total picture, however. The socialists outvoted the Republicans in Mississippi, which may not have been a major accomplishment, considering the state of the GOP in that area.

Eighteen new socialist legislators were elected in various local contests across the country.[79] Many local offices, ranging from road inspector to mayor were filled by socialists.

What strengths and weaknesses did the total returns indicate in the politics of American socialism? First, the center of socialist strength remained in the broad area west of the Mississippi, mainly in the great Mississippi Valley itself, the birthplace of so many radical movements in American history. The hard years of organizational work in that area consistently repaid the socialists in higher votes. Ohio led her sister states in the socialist column with 89,930 votes for Debs. She was followed by Pennsylvania, with 83,614; Illinois, with 81,249; California, with 79,201; and New York, with 63,381.[80] When the vote was tabulated proportionally, however, these states appeared further down the list. Agrarian Oklahoma, where socialists capitalized on poverty and general social unrest, tied with Nevada, each state giving Debs 16.61 per cent of its vote. They were followed by Montana, with 13.66; Arizona, with 13.33; Washington, with 12.43; and California, with 11.76.[81] In these Far Western states, scenes of so many labor troubles since 1900, the socialists registered their greatest proportional gains and showed their greatest grass roots strength. Socialist organizers in the mining and lumber camps of the Far West, not to forget cities like Spokane, San Francisco and Los Angeles, worked hard and gave Debs more votes than ever.

The returns also indicated that radical socialism seemed to be rising, for the areas dominated by the "Slowcialists" —New York, Massachusetts, Wisconsin and parts of the Midwest—gained less ground than the western states where Debs' brand of socialism found many sympathizers. In Pennsylvania and West Virginia, where the socialists worked among the miners, the vote was up as much as 300 per cent over the 1908 totals. If Roosevelt took socialist votes he seems to have taken them from the "parlor socialists," as Debs feared.[82] There was something to be said for the assertion, "For the first time in years the Socialist party vote was a clear-cut Socialist vote." [83]

For those who probed the results more deeply there were interesting sidelights. Those given to pure conjecture could note that if all the people who voted for Debs in California, Minnesota, Pennsylvania and Washington had voted instead for Wilson, the Democrats would have saved those states from the Progressive column. If, on the other hand, all the people who voted for Debs in Idaho, Illinois, Kansas, Montana, Nevada, North Dakota, and Oregon had voted instead for Roosevelt, the Rough Rider would have won those states from the Democrats. Thus Roosevelt could say with some heat that the socialists had fought him harder than the Democrats had.[84]

Although the vote was far below the predicted two million, the party's showing was significant. That the socialists did so well in the face of overwhelming liberal opposition indicates that there was not only a hard core of faithful to whom they could appeal but also that there was a considerable body of sympathetic Americans who would mark their ballots for Debs even when offered the liberalism of Wilson and Roosevelt. That he received nearly six per cent of the total presidential popular vote in 1912 is a mark of accomplishment for Debs and his hard-working followers. Unquestionably, Debs' candidacy was the greatest single factor in the socialist success. For a whole generation he had stood as the champion of the workers and the underprivileged of all classes. His popularity extended beyond the socialist party's membership rolls. While the party did not capture organized labor's vote, many workers voted for Debs.[85] Since the election of 1912 was the climax of the progressive movement the socialists naturally benefited from political unrest. Americans who distrusted Roosevelt and who were dissatisfied with Wilson voted for Debs.

Both radical and conservative socialists looked with pride on their organizational work to explain the vote. In such areas as Wisconsin and New York the conservatives had acquired a certain respectability and with it a certain amount of public trust. Their willingness to move beyond the Democrats and Progressives without adopting revolution impressed many voters. The radicals in turn had much of which to be proud. They had staged parades, taken advantage of strikes, preached, written, and organized among workers and farmers and their hard labor brought results. The whole socialist press was very active during the campaign and reached countless voters it had not served before.

The election returns showed that the socialists remained a force in American politics and that given time, funds, and the proper climate of opinion they could make an impressive showing. The campaign also showed that however unorthodox their dogma, their political tactics differed little from those of their opponents. The whole socialist campaign revealed a thorough understanding of mass psychology and the issues and tactics to which the American voter was most susceptible. George Harvey, an early Wilson backer and a shrewd political observer, was impressed by the socialist campaign and estimated that without Roosevelt's competition Debs would have received an additional half million votes.[86]

The socialists were indeed elated, filled with visions of success, anxious to continue in the path their gains outlined for them. But they never did so well again. They never captured the vote of labor, and their grass roots strength dwindled with the years. Debs ran for President once more, this time from jail in 1920. His total vote that year was higher than in 1912, but the percentage was almost cut in half. The World War and Russian revolution were destined to dye the socialists in deepest red for the average American. The stresses and strains introduced by the Russian revolution into the party structure already weakened by factionalism and decline were the final straws that broke it. The socialist victory celebrations of 1912 were not unjustified, however. Party membership had increased; the party press was stimulated; Debs had made wider contacts than ever before. The returns indicated areas where special efforts might be exerted. There was every hope in socialist ranks for even greater success in 1916 and 1920. Neither Debs nor his followers could have recognized that this was the harvest year, the summertime of American socialism, and that only winter lay ahead.

VI

American Socialism's Time of Troubles: 1913-1920

I am opposed to every war but one; I am for that war heart and soul, and that is the world-wide revolution.

Eugene V. Debs, 1915

If any American socialists cheered Woodrow Wilson's inauguration in March, 1913, they had bitter recollections of it in a few short years, for this man possessed of such dynamic plans and motivated by such exalted visions became in time a scourge of socialist dreams. The New Freedom which he implemented robbed the socialists of much of their inspiration and program and drew followers from their ranks with each passing month. His every success was a debit in the socialist ledger. The World War and the repressive controls against free speech and the free press of his second administration shattered what socialist visions of success remained. In the ranks of socialist opponents, none cut a larger figure than he who would make the world safe for democracy.

Wilson's administration and the world situation were not alone responsible for the decline and fragmentation of socialist influence in the decade after the success of 1912. All was far from well within the party itself, and in all

143

too many instances socialist was pitted against socialist in struggles over doctrine and control of the party machinery that inevitably weakened the movement's impetus and success.

The shouts of victory after the election of 1912 had hardly subsided before factional dissension threatened party unity. The ill feelings that lurked beneath the surface of united party efforts and which periodically rose to threaten the movement's success, focused in 1913 on the figure of Bill Haywood. Haywood had been chosen a member of the party's National Executive Committee, and after struggles in the convention of 1912, was duly seated; it was a victory that sent cheers ringing through radical ranks. This, plus the seeming growth of radical socialism reflected by the election of 1912, and Debs' apparently reviving leadership filled the radicals with optimism.

Their hope was short lived, however, for the conservatives carefully bided their time, using their press, personalities, and grasp of parliamentary procedure to censure and ultimately to oust Haywood, thus removing the most potent symbol of left-wing authority from the party. Fearing that the forces he represented threatened the further progress of constructive socialism, the conservatives determined to remove him and his following from a voice in party affairs. As Victor Berger had said before, they could get out and form a party of their own.

During the campaign of 1912, Haywood's insistent adherence to syndicalism and radical labor activities drew concerted fire from the conservatives and gave Debs himself more than one bad moment. Together with the Barnes affair, Haywood and his followers were a major bone of contention during the campaign. The conservatives were ready to remove that bone once the campaign and the need for party unity were over. Haywood's colorful, unorthodox, and successful work in the great Lawrence, Massachusetts, textile strike of 1912, where he implemented much IWW doctrine, was gall and wormwood to the socialist right wing. They labeled his success syndicalism and denied that he favored political action or that he was a socialist.[1] The charge was not without an element of truth; Haywood did not have the faith of many socialists in the ballot. He had seen too much of life, knew too much of his opposition, and gauged his role far too well to believe that he could enact all his goals with the ballot. To those who had no ballot he appealed with other and less cautious means. Yet he had served political action and socialist politicians well in the past, well enough to be rankled by the stream of charges from the right that he did not favor political action.[2]

Whatever Haywood's real attitude toward political action and socialist doctrine, he was manifestly out of place in the party now controlled by "Slowcialists." The latter now urged a party referendum on his recall from the National Executive Committee on grounds that he had violated the party constitution by favoring industrial sabotage and opposing political action. Early in March, 1913, he was recalled from the Committee; it was a major victory for the right wing.[3]

To the conservatives, Haywood's ouster meant control of the party; the recall lessened their fears that radicals would frighten reform elements from socialism and impede their forward motion. To the radicals it meant something else. Many left the party in disgust not only at the ouster of radicals, but at the means by which it was done. On the eve of the National Convention in 1912, party membership hovered at 150,000; throughout that year it averaged 118,000 per month; in 1913, it was listed at 113,371.[4] Whatever else it did, Haywood's ouster drove many radicals from the party. The conservatives gained their control at a price, though it was a price they deemed worthwhile.

Despite growing tension in the party and the polarization of factions, socialism continued on the path outlined in 1912. Much to Roosevelt's disgust the socialists in Chicago polled as many votes as the Progressives in the city elections.[5] That they could survive even in the glow of New Freedom reforms indicated something. In 1913, the party claimed 41 members in 9 different state legislatures, and attributed 141 separate pieces of state legislation to socialist members.[6] In the congressional elections of 1914 the party mounted an old-fashioned crusade. Meyer London won his House seat from New York and once again the party had a spokesman in Congress.[7] At the beginning of 1915, thirty-one socialists sat in state legislatures between Massachusetts and Ohio.[8]

The socialist press continued its vigorous fight, expressing its lack of sympathy toward the popular President Wilson. The *Appeal* worked harder than ever to counteract waning public interest in socialism and the tend toward Wilsonian democracy,[9] despite the setback it suffered at the loss of its editor. For, bereaved by the recent death of his wife, and the target of a smear attempt to brand him immoral, Julius Wayland had ended his own life with the words, "The struggle under the capitalist system isn't worth the effort. Let it pass."[10] Socialism had lost a valiant member and Debs a good friend. But the *Appeal* struggled on and Roosevelt could once more lament that the socialist press was doing damage—though his hopes that it might perish were fulfilled in all too few years.[11]

In an effort to revivify the party membership and to regain a solid base of popular support, the party created special foreign language federations which, though semi-independent, worked with national headquarters and for socialism all over the country.[12] But these were troubled times for Debs and for many socialists, radical and conservative alike. Sensing that their cause lost more and more each passing day to the forces of reform and reaction alike, they felt that shadows did indeed follow the high noon of 1912. Perceiving his own estrangement from both the leadership of the party and the trends of the times, Debs issued a special plea for solidarity early in 1914, calling on his comrades to return to the inspirations which first gave impetus to their movement and which had impelled them to hazard so much for so long. They must not jeopardize their work now. "I appeal to all Socialist comrades . . . to join in harmonizing the various elements of the revolutionary movement," he wrote from the vantage point of elder statesman and harmonizer, roles he assumed with more and more willingness and less and less effect in the troubled years ahead. "If this be done, a new glorious era will dawn for the working class in the United States."[13] Somehow it sounded old-fashioned, unrealistic, and the guns of the Marne shortly drowned what he and other socialists had to say as America's interest turned to events in Europe.

The World War struck the American socialists with all the force of a body blow; if the conflict was closer to their European comrades, its ramifications were no less real to them. For one frightening moment all their doubts focused, all their confident belief that the tide of history bore them to inevitable success faded. The defection of their European socialist comrades to the causes of war and nationalism shook them badly. "When the war broke out I was struck dumb," Haywood recalled in bitter, incredulous words the feelings that most socialists shared. "For weeks I could scarcely talk." [14]

In December, 1915, two days after taking office, Meyer London introduced a peace resolution, asking the President to summon an international peace congress.[15] For the moment personal considerations fell away and the war brought temporary unity to the party as members high and low decried the conflict and the European socialists who supported it. In 1915, the party membership overwhelmingly endorsed a referendum expelling any socialist official who voted for war credits or for war.[16] Party leaders like Morris Hillquit urged Americans not to take sides in the conflict lest their country be drawn into the war; their best hope was the exhaustion and collapse of the old order, from which socialism would rise.[17] In war their dreams, ironically, might yet be fulfilled.

Yet it was a long-range idea and at best a visionary approach. Debs' call for unity had but a temporary effect on the party. The socialists were, after all, Americans too; like most of their countrymen they were from the first inclined toward the Allies, though Berger and many German socialists were accused of pro-German leanings. As American intervention and entanglement drew closer and closer, more and more prominent socialists turned to the Allied camp.

Thus confused, disheartened, and anxious, hoping against hope, yet weakened by doubt and division, the American socialists faced the presidential election of 1916. As in the past, the national campaign vitalized the party and served for a moment, like the shot at Sarajevo, to unify discordant elements, to call forth promises of aid, and to add luster to the predictions of the coming commonwealth. Four times Eugene Debs had run for President; four times he had faced seas of people, had spoken in far corners and distant cities, had given his time and health and energy to the cause, but in 1916 he positively declined to be a candidate. He made it known at once that he would not accept a fifth nomination. He had done more than his share, more than other men, to advance the party's cause; he was older, tired, unwell; they could not ask him to run again, to face the barrage of criticism, the mounting tide of unrest centered on the issue of foreign policy which he detested most—war and possible American intervention.

Accordingly, the party turned elsewhere. To save money and avoid conflict, no national convention met to nominate the presidential ticket. Instead, a referendum chose Allan Benson, veteran newspaperman and socialist organizer, for President and George Kirkpatrick, also a newspaperman, for Vice-President.[18] Debs' refusal to run robbed the socialists of their chief orator and they counted on the candidates' writing skills to compensate for this loss. Benson was not a novice and understood fully that he trod in large footsteps in trailing Debs. Born in 1871 in Michigan, he had edited the Detroit *Times* and the Washington *Times,* and was the author of several standard socialist books and tracts. He had assisted in numerous campaigns in the past and was a suitable compromise for the party factions.

The platform on which Benson ran was concerned chiefly with the Wilson administration's efforts to prepare the country for self defense. To the socialists as to many other Americans, this was the first step toward armed intervention, and the cry "He kept us out of war!" meant nothing but hypocrisy to them. Official party doctrine called for pacifism and non-intervention; entanglement with nationalism and armaments had brought European socialists to ruin and their American counterparts were not willing to fall into the same trap.[19] Benson himself vigorously opposed the war and preparedness, but like more and more party members he favored the Allied cause once the conflict was underway on the assumption that Germany's defeat would spell the beginning of a new social era in Europe.[20]

Benson made his stand clear and like Debs employed hard language in condemning the conflict. "If ever there was a need of devotion to a just cause, it is now," he said in accepting the nomination. "If ever there was a time when our philosophy should be convincing it is now. Yesterday we were dismissed as unpleasant theorists, today Europe is writing in letters of fire and blood athwart her midnight skies: 'This war was caused by the greeds and hatreds engendered by the capitalist system.' "[21] The socialist presidential candidate appeared before the House Committee on Naval Affairs as an anti-preparedness witness and outraged the Committee by attacking Wilson and the whole defense movement. Several representatives vigorously pounded the table and shouted at Benson, disrupting the proceedings. The candidate was pleased; he got little publicity and this was indeed a plum. Benson held his ground, accused the President of fomenting hysteria, and insisted that the European war posed no threat to the United States.[22]

Thus the issues of the socialist campaign were set at the first. In many ways it was an unfortunate time to stand inflexibly for unpopular principles. Already tarred with the brush of radicalism, suspected of less than "100 percent Americanism," decried on every hand for their lack of enthusiasm for America's slowly emerging war effort, the socialists were caught in many crossfires. In one sense, by emphasizing anti-preparedness as the paramount issue of the day, Benson played into the hands of the preparedness supporters, who now used him as a scapegoat.[23]

The formal socialist campaign was late in starting and when it did begin combated the twin problems of lethargy in the party ranks and public apathy.[24] By autumn the campaign was in motion, and though the socialists struggled against hostility they still mustered sizable crowds. Ten thousand eager watchers assembled under the auspices of the New York socialists to cheer local candidates and to hear speeches by Benson, Kirkpatrick, London, and others. Red flags and enthusiasm lifted the effort for a moment from the humdrum routine of politics.[25]

In his early speeches Benson set the tone for the socialist campaign everywhere. "I think if we Socialists can speak only one word in this campaign that word should be peace." [26] Thus he hoped to catch liberal votes and votes from those who were disenchanted both with Wilson and the Republican candidate, Charles Evans Hughes. Hughes' dignity and long judicial record may have impressed others, but he was fully as distasteful to the socialists as Wilson. He had been connected with reform in New York; he was a judge; his stand on preparedness and intervention was unclear; and his bent of mind was leagues away from socialism of any kind.

Though Benson early fired his "first shot in the war on war," as he called his opening speech, his reception by the faithful was far from incendiary. He was not Debs and everyone knew it. He lacked the color, the fire, the long tradition of protest that surrounded Debs with glamor and impetus, and he was a poor speaker in a movement that savored oratory. "He proved to be a rather quiet speaker, and probably a hundred of his audience, who possibly expected a more impassioned appeal, left before he had finished," a newspaper reported of his first major address.[27] Yet the socialists supported him as best they could, attending rallies, listening to local candidates, distributing the mass of literature that compensated somewhat for the lack of a vivid candidate.

On May Day, an estimated 100,000 people marched in an orderly labor parade in New York. Parks and street corners were filled with speakers, and one group heard August Claessens say: "We Socialists are going to answer all of this preparedness talk with a slogan that is short and sweet. It is this: 'To hell with preparedness!' "[28] Though the attitude and the speakers did not endear themselves to local authorities, police reported that the parade was a normal affair.

Elsewhere prominent socialists elaborated old themes in opposing the trend toward war. "Hideous as they are, the horrors of the far-stretched battlefield of the old world are dwarfed by the evil results of the capitalistic system, even in normal times," the party stated officially.[29]

If Debs hoped to rest during this campaign he was sorely disappointed, for his Indiana comrades nominated him for Congress, and his strenuous protests availed nothing. The regular press promptly cried opportunism. "Eugene V. Debs did not run as the Socialist candidate for president this year, because he thought he saw a chance to be elected to Congress from Indiana," the New York *Times* sneered. "His chances are very doubtful." [30]

Debs cared little for what anyone else thought about his motives and less about what they said. Once in the campaign he devoted himself to the cause with all his old verve. His hopes for rest were dashed as his local campaign took on national significance. Like Benson, but with even greater scorn, he lambasted the Wilson administration's movement toward intervention and denied that America had any quarrel abroad.[31] In an article widely distributed in 1916 he stated his own belief that the destruction of capitalism, not victory for the Allies, would bring peace. "Permanent peace, however, peace based upon social justice, will never prevail until national industrial despotism has been supplanted by international industrial democracy. The end of the profit and plunder among nations will also mean the end of war and the dawning of the era of 'Peace on earth and good will among men.' " [32]

In two weeks, Debs spoke more than fifty times in his district, traveling rough country roads in a Model T touring car, speaking to crowds at crossroads and in town squares. Often he hopped on the hood of the car if the crowd was too big. In many places the socialists sold small red feathers bearing the legend: "Feather your nest. Vote for Debs." [33]

To counterbalance their lack of speakers the socialists distributed an immense quantity of literature. More than 22,000,000 written pieces went out on Benson's behalf, some of it written by the candidate himself.[34] Total cost of the literature to the national office was nearly eight thousand dollars and receipts from its sales lagged considerably behind the cost.[35] In addition, campaign headquarters distributed $2,500 worth of buttons, pencil clips, pennants, posters and watch fobs which the faithful and the curious alike were expected to wear, carry, or use.[36] Hampered by lack of funds and trained workers, the campaign managers tried their best to follow in the Debs tradition. But contributions taken at rallies did not match expenses, and admission charges were down; only five personal contributions during the campaign totaled more than one hundred dollars each.[37]

Other organizations lent their strength to the campaign. The Young Peoples' Socialist League, founded in 1913, continued its organizational growth and propaganda, appealing to young people who would have to fight if war came.[38] The Intercollegiate Socialist Society did its part also. Such prominent socialists as Rose Pastor Stokes, and John Spargo spoke on college campuses; an estimated 30,000 students and 12,000 other interested spectators heard them.[39]

In Milwaukee the party ran true to form in the mayoralty contest, using all the efficient techniques that had brought it success in the past.[40] As the campaign drew to its close party leaders predicted a fifty to one hundred per cent rise in their vote. Their three strongest areas were Oklahoma, New York and Wisconsin. Meyer London seemed a walk-in in his race for re-election in New York and many socialists expected to win the electoral votes of Oklahoma.[41] Benson, himself, after a whirlwind tour across the country which did not revive lagging spirits, predicted Wilson's election because Hughes was tied too closely to the business interests.[42] Though often colorful and intensive, the campaign was far from the spectacle of older days when Debs had crossed the country not once but many times in the course of a national campaign. Benson spoke at sixty meetings; Kirkpatrick spoke at sixty-one. But they lacked the passion, the flair, the sense of hope and expectation which characterized Debs' best efforts. Somehow it was not the same, somehow everyone knew before the votes were counted what the result would be.[43]

Socialists were indeed disappointed at the final tally, for Benson fell far below Debs' total of 1912, receiving only 585,113 votes. As before, the far western states of Nevada, Washington, Arizona, Montana, and the southern states of Oklahoma and Texas gave the party the highest proportional vote.[44]

Debs himself lost his contest in Indiana, despite a vigorous final burst of campaigning lighted by flaming torches and red flags. "Blessed are they who expect nothing, for they shall not be disappointed," was his only comment on the outcome.[45]

The election was a double disappointment to the socialists for they had hoped by their race not only to win votes for socialism but to awaken their countrymen to the peril of intervention which they felt lay ahead. "The campaign of 1916 proved in many ways a disappointment," the party said officially four years later; that disappointment was all the more real in 1916 for Wilson's endorsement meant continued trends toward war and the destruction of socialist ideals.[46]

Wilson had barely been inaugurated a second time when the socialists' bitterest fears were realized; on April 6, 1917, America entered the war and the European conflict became world wide. American entry took many of the socialists by surprise for they had not expected it so soon. In a hastily called emergency convention in St. Louis, held early in April, they vigorously condemned American intervention, an action which the party membership overwhelmingly endorsed. Sensing the coming chaos and persecution the assembled socialists hopefully wired Wilson urging that the administration not restrict traditional civil liberties and freedom of speech and press.[47] For the moment the party closed ranks and, as in 1914, war gave the organization temporary unity and purpose.

Yet even in this there was division, for adoption of the majority report opposing the war was opposed by prominent socialists. Most could agree with the demand that no excess taxes be levied or money borrowed to fight the war: "We demand that the capitalist class, which is responsible for the war, pay its cost. Let those who kindled the fire furnish the fuel." [48] But other prominent socialists could not condemn intervention; adoption of the anti-war stand forced many to leave the party to agitate for the war effort or to sit idly by while others did.[49] William R. Gaylord of Wisconsin, prominent right-wing socialist, put his finger on many a sore spot when he told the delegates to the special convention: "I am voting against the majority report on war because it is not only non-Socialist but it is anti-Socialist in doctrine: it contradicts the historical facts; it condemns no national government except that of the United States, therein being pro-European and peculiarly un-American; it misses by a mile the big constructive opportunity of the Socialist Party in this war, it crystallizes needlessly the ignorant and vicious anti-Socialist prejudices, and it gives reckless occasion for those rantings by the capitalist press which will most effectively close the public mind completely for many months to the effective and constructive Socialist propaganda—if nothing worse." [50] Thus did one clear-sighted socialist see the dark pattern of the months ahead.

If some socialists condoned the war and justified their stand on the basis of Americanism, such was not the case with Eugene Debs. He traveled a different road. From the outbreak of the war in Europe he had opposed the trend toward American intervention; he had based his own campaign of 1916 against preparedness; he had opposed Wilson's every move to help the Allies. He sent a telegram to the emergency convention stating his anti-war position, though he refused to attend the meeting because he felt his stand was well known; appeals and a special motorcade of the faithful from St. Louis did not move him to go to the convention.[51] It would be carrying coals to Newcastle.

Their anti-war stand taken, plain for all to see, the American socialists entered a time of troubles such as they had never seen before, even in the days of their stormy beginnings. Caught in the grip of war, subjected to manu-factured patriotism and suppression, the socialists became the butt of all "true Americans," subjects of lynching, riots, and disgraceful prejudice in every corner of the land.

As bond drives enveloped the country, as George Creel's propaganda machine crushed out opposition, as the Justice Department enforced special repressive legislation, socialist influence declined. Despite their best efforts to the contrary the socialists were often confused with communists in the public mind. The Russian Revolutions of 1917, which the socialists greeted with unaccustomed unity, turned the public mind even further from the party. The fact that many veteran socialists opposed the emerging Soviet state was lost on the American public who equated them with the red specters and bloody revolution that wafted across the seas from Russia. "Socialism," the Detroit *Journal* trumpeted, "is Bolshevism with a shave." [52]

Accordingly, local and national authorities closely watched socialist meetings and organizations. The party seemed to do nothing right: it opposed the war, favored Russia, objected to the Administration's repression. Detectives and special agents were thick at socialist meetings. At one such gathering the evening's speaker calmly announced: "All Secret Service men are invited to the platform so that they may see and hear better." [53] Many socialists agreed with Morris Hillquit when he said: "The air was infested with spying, denunciations, and false accusations. No person suspected of radical or pacifist opinions was safe. The spirit of heresy hunting and witch burning had come back to America in the year of our Lord, 1918." [54] Socialist organizers were heckled, followed, hounded by official and semi-official agencies and agents. [55] The actions of the government and local organizations against the socialists were bad enough for party work, but even more devastating were the snubs and lack of interest displayed by former sympathizers. Art Young's experience was repeated countless times: "Men and women whom I had counted as friends found it convenient to pass me on the street without speaking, or were brief and impersonal in their conversations." [56]

The *American Socialist,* the New York *Call,* and other party newspapers lost mail privileges or fourth class privileges.[57] In September, 1917, federal agents raided the party headquarters in Chicago. Indiana and other states reported that offices were raided, files seized and membership lists checked.[58] Berger and other socialist leaders were indicted under the Espionage Act for opposition to the war effort; in November, 1918, despite his pending case, Berger was elected to Congress. Denied his seat, he was re-elected at a special election in 1919; again refused his seat, his case was left pending until 1920 when a fusion candidate in Milwaukee defeated him.[59]

Of all the groups subjected to persecution and the demand for conformity and support of the war, none suffered more than the IWW. To many the "Wobblies" were "canker sores on the body politic," and in the national emergency and public demand for patriotism, many saw their chance to destroy the IWW once and for all.[60] The press, law enforcement agencies, business interests and many other labor groups joined or permitted the concerted effort to destroy the already weak IWW.[61] In San Francisco, a group of uniformed soldiers raided "Wobbly" headquarters, destroyed records and furniture, and broke as many "Wobbly" noses as possible.[62] The story was the same elsewhere as super-patriots rallied against the common enemy, the radicalism symbolized by the IWW. Haywood and dozens of other IWW leaders were imprisoned and heavily fined by federal courts.[63] The remainder of the once potent organization was ground to dust in the mills of war.

Debs' sense of justice and individualism was outraged by the treatment accorded the IWW and though he still disliked their methods he defended many of them. "Everything that happens nowadays that the ruling classes do not like and everything that does not happen that they do like is laid at the door of the I.W.W. Its name is anathema wherever capitalism wields the lash and drains the veins of its exploited victims." [64] The problem was made doubly bitter for him by AFL support of the war effort, an added reason for his dislike of craft unionism and "Gompersism."

Yet, harassed and persecuted as many of them were, the socialists refused to perish quietly. They would at least go down fighting and the stubbornness that had brought them earlier success now saved many of them from destruction. To everyone's surprise, Morris Hillquit made an excellent showing in New York's mayoralty race in the fall of 1917, running third in a four-man race and polling nearly 150,000 votes. Roosevelt, Hughes, Clarence Darrow and other prominent leaders from all camps opposed him and demanded unity for the war effort, but he polled four times as many votes as the socialist candidate in 1912 had received.[65] The elections sent ten socialist assemblymen to Albany, seven aldermen to the city council, and Jacob Panken to the city bench for a ten-year term.[66] The socialist vote was up in Cleveland, Toledo, Sandusky, and smaller towns in the West and Midwest.[67] The results startled war advocates and supporters of the Wilson administration. Theodore Roosevelt called the socialist victories "rather ominous." [68]

But it was more a protest vote than a socialist vote. Many were dissatisfied with the Wilson administration's conduct of the war and its enforcement of repressive legislation. Moreover, the party profited from agitation among immigrant groups in the cities with whom the war was unpopular. Whatever the trend might have seemed to be on the surface, the deeper one was that of protest instead of socialism. In point of fact, the party's membership rolls told the story of its decline far better than temporary election victories. In 1916, 83,284 members held party cards; in 1917, 80,379; in 1918, due to the specially-created foreign language federations, the figure rose to 104,822, only to plummet to 26,766 after the great purges of 1918–1920. In 1921 a mere 13,484 members held cards.[69] The golden age of American socialism was over, a victim of war and faction.

All of this was profoundly disturbing to Eugene Debs. He had worked too hard and too long in too relatively free an atmosphere to accept hysteria and repression in silence. Through 1917 he pursued a vacillating position, stating his convictions yet not acting on them. In part he was waiting to see the full outlines of the government's policy. "I cannot yet believe that they will ever dare to send you to prison for exercising your constitutional rights of free speech," he wrote Kate Richards O'Hare, then under indictment for violating the Espionage Act. "But if they do . . . I shall feel guilty to be at large." [70] As the pressures mounted and as the threat to the socialist movement crystallized, Debs realized at last that he must exert the leadership that was rightly his. He would speak out, risk prosecution and imprisonment if necessary. In mid-June, 1918, Debs boarded a train and headed for Canton, Ohio; the time for indecision was past. He would now speak his mind for all to hear, would repeat his life-long adherence to radicalism and would attack the injustice abroad in the land. He did not choose Ohio accidentally; the state had long been a radical stronghold and already a number of Ohio socialists had been arrested.

On June 18, 1918, addressing a crowd in Canton, Debs uttered the words that sent him to prison for a second time. His speech was a catalogue of socialist persecutions, a cry against injustice, and a reaffirmation of his radical principles. It was in effect a challenge to the federal government; did it dare arrest so prominent an American radical as Eugene Debs? His speech contained little that was new, nothing that he had not said before, and much that was not incendiary. The federal government and state authorities felt, however, that his words assisted those evading the draft, and that his tone and the content of the speech in general gave aid and comfort to those opposing the war effort. Washington hesitated, however, for the case might be difficult and it would be embarrassing and perhaps fatal to weaken the Espionage Act by failing to secure a conviction. While the Justice Department wavered, federal officials in Ohio secured the indictment.[71]

Debs was impatient to be arrested. Feeling that his place was in jail with other socialists, he was angered by the government's delay and even fearful that he might not be arrested. On June 30, 1918, his wish was fulfilled. As he prepared to address a socialist picnic in Cleveland he was taken into custody, booked in the federal building, and jailed.[72] He spent the day and night in prison because he could not post bond. Later in the day a group of comrades brought him an armload of red roses; within a matter of hours a thousand dollar defense fund had been raised at the picnic he was to address. While incarcerated he heard that he had been nominated for Congress by his home district, an honor which he could for once decline. The following day a ten thousand dollar bond was posted by friends and he was freed.[73]

The whole apparatus of socialist propaganda moved into motion on his behalf. A national figure, he was an ideal pole around which dissident elements in all parties could rally to oppose the Wilson administration's repression of civil liberties. Prominent party members and organizers dropped their work to raise funds; the national office sent out information and appeals for aid; Debs himself never had any money, and his family relied on friends for support during much of the crisis. Awaiting his trial, Debs had some uneasy moments with "pure Americans" in Terre Haute but violence never touched him.[74]

In September, 1918, Debs was duly tried for sedition. It was obvious to those who knew him that he welcomed conviction and imprisonment; thus could he end his historic role as a prophet of discontent; thus could he aid his party and his country best. He did nothing to impede the prosecution's case; indeed, he often verified its facts. Twice he held the court in attentive silence as he outlined his utopia and uttered the famous words: "While there is a lower class, I am in it, while there is a criminal element, I am of it, while there is a soul in prison, I am not free." For a time the old fire flashed, the doubts and shadows that had beset him fled and he stood as he had stood before, preeminently as a champion of the cause of individual freedom and rights. "I never so clearly comprehended as now the great struggle between the powers of greed and exploitation on the one hand and upon the other the rising hosts of industrial freedom and social justice." [75] He would not recant, he would not restate, he would not take back what he had said, whatever the cost.

In view of his age and ill-health, the cost was high, for he was sentenced to ten years in federal prison. Debs' conviction constituted "perhaps the highest point reached by the government in its efforts to punish violators of [the Espionage Act]." [76] When the Supreme Court upheld his conviction, Debs called the justices "begowned, bewhiskered, bepowdered old fossils." Two weeks later when the mayor of Toledo refused to permit a mass demonstration on Debs' behalf, local socialists chanted "To hell with the Mayor!" [77]

Debs entered federal prison at Moundsville, West Virginia in April, 1919. As he entered the prison gates he cast back one more epigram for the faithful, "I enter the prison doors a flaming revolutionist, my head erect, my spirit untamed, my soul unconquerable." [78] Life at Moundsville was not grueling. Assigned a light hospital job, he enjoyed a good deal of personal freedom. "Really, this place is not bad," he later told Clarence Darrow in discussing prison life. "I look at that garden of flowers. There are bars in front, I know—but I never see the bars." [79]

The easy existence at Moundsville was rudely interrupted in June, 1919, when he was transferred to the federal prison at Atlanta to finish his term. Already, the party and many sympathizers worked for his release. That he entered prison after the war was over and when acts for which he was judged a criminal had ceased to be crimes drew many to his cause. A host of celebrities besieged President Wilson, visited Debs, agitated for his release, and met with considerable success everywhere but at the White House. Wilson in the end was immovable in his stubborn conviction that Debs was guilty of treason and must be punished as an example as well as for his actions.[80]

While Debs served his prison term, sure that in the end he would be proved right, all was far from well with his party. Indeed, its troubles had only begun and those who hoped that the end of the war would mean the end of persecution and dissension were badly disappointed. Prison life was trying, but at least it was quiet and orderly; such was hardly the case with those socialists still free. There were times when many wished to join Debs to escape the madhouse that the world had become in the wake of war and revolution.

The final phase of socialist disaster was now at hand, for the end of the war brought the great "Palmer raids" of 1919, in which many socialists were unceremoniously bundled out of the country and otherwise silenced by a government in no mood to define radicalism.

The basic divisive question among socialists now was the status of the new communist state in Russia. The revolutions of 1917 struck most American socialists with the force of divine revelation; now, out of the horrors of war, had come at last a sign that the new age was at hand. "To millions of persons in all lands it seemed that the age-long dream of a reign of reason and justice was about to come true," Morris Hillquit remembered.[81] It is difficult now to recapture the fervor that gripped many American socialists but from their point of view the kingdom was at hand; the war in Europe had brought down the repressive monarchies; labor was restless everywhere, the communist experiment in Russia seemed destined to live and grow.[82]

With this fervor the radical socialists demanded that the party adapt itself to the new era and fashion a truly revolutionary program to capitalize on the discontent of the day. With optimism and naivete born of hope the radicals assumed that the tottering socialist party could miraculously rally the workers to its standard in America. The right wing was in no mood to argue. In the summer of 1919 they began expelling radical members. The months after the revolution in Russia took the scales from some socialist eyes and more and more the right wing of the American party moved away from endorsement of the Soviet state. "The Bolshevists do not favor representative government," Berger declared. "They preach 'direct action' and the 'dictatorship of the proletariat.'"[83] Finding that they could neither convert nor dominate the Socialist Party, the radicals under the leadership of romantic rebels like John Reed, deserted socialism and gladly founded what became the Communist Party of America and various other leftist groups.[84] The regular socialists took no nonsense from the radicals and ruthlessly expelled them, suppressed their words and works, and denied them access to party information.[85] They had faced quite enough outside trouble without pandering to impossible radicals within the party. It was a sad spectacle for Debs who, though isolated in prison, keenly felt the collapse and destruction of the party whose banner he had borne for twenty-five years. "It has been the fate of our movement from the beginning, especially in this country, to split," he sadly wrote his brother. "About the time we get in shape to do something we have to split up and waste our energy in factional strife. We preach unity everlastingly, but we ourselves keep splitting apart." [86]

Debs' sympathies were naturally with the Bolshevik revolutionary forces who overturned the Czar, and he wished them godspeed in their formation of a new order. "From the crown of my head to the soles of my feet I am a Bolshevik, and proud of it. 'The day of the People has arrived!'" he proclaimed as he entered prison.[87] But as he studied the emerging communist state, his disenchantment was obvious. Lack of information and a fervent desire to stay neutral to form a symbol around which all socialists might unite made Debs carefully refrain from making his position clear. He condemned the murder of the Czar's family by the communists and in other ways clearly objected to what he considered unnecessary violence and bloodshed in Russia.[88] Debs may have flirted with the new American communist movement; he knew and admired many of its members; and he may secretly have cherished the hope that it might bring to fruition the dreams that had withered in other hands. In fact, he knew little of the true situation in Russia, but he knew enough to fear its full ramifications and to know that such methods could never make headway in his own country or with men who, even while radicals, cherished the freedom and individualism that allowed them to be radical. Debs was torn between the desire to recognize the good in communism and awareness that it was basically evil and could not be transplanted to the United States. He could never go all the way in his radicalism; he could never turn the wheel, no matter how much he favored some of the ideology of communism; he could never abandon his American heritage.[89]

Thus did the war leave the American socialists divided and depressed; the full impact of that historic conflict had shaken the party to its very foundations. As David Karsner so succinctly put it years later: "The World War proved that Socialists are victims of the same emotions and prejudices that ensnare us all." [90] Divided, weakened in numbers and impetus, its once proud press a feeble echo of itself, its leaders in prison or under indictment, its strength diluted, with rival organizations threatening it on every hand, and most of all, with the progressive climate in which it had flourished now overcast by the gloom and cynicism that was war's legacy, the party emerged from the second decade of the twentieth century. Thus did it stand on the eve of its most curious, and in many ways, its most striking presidential campaign.

VII

Convict Number 9653 for President: The Campaign of 1920

While there is a lower class, I am in it, while there is a criminal element, I am of it, while there is a soul in prison, I am not free.

Eugene V. Debs, 1918

America in 1919 and 1920 was a nation at peace with everyone except itself. The war it fought for democracy had come and gone and though the peace it brought was the great issue in the campaign of 1920, that peace was already hollow. Bitter disillusionment with the fruits of war and victory alike filled many with apathy. They took unkindly, with much justification, any talk of crusades and moral chimeras. It was a poor climate for socialism. The forces of change triggered by the war and its accompanying hysteria still operated in many parts of the land. If the German menace had been overcome, fear of anarchism, communism and radicalism of any kind had not, and countless Americans who had fought for democracy abroad now perverted it at home. It was but fitting, and somehow symbolic of the times, that the socialist presidential candidate ran from a prison cell.

Debs' name was in the presidential arena long before the socialists met in New York early in May, 1920, to nominate him. As he went to prison, Debs had left the door ajar for his nomination in 1920, while protesting, as often before, that he was unworthy and did not desire it. "There is better timber in the woods than I," he told David Karsner. "Let me see. The presidential campaign is two years away. Why, in two years I'll be the best swabber of floors or the best prison clerk in Mounds-ville!" [1] Debs held a commanding position in the party and his presence in jail made him all the more intriguing as a presidential candidate. He had lost his rights of citizenship but as he himself said: "The government has made me a citizen of the world." [2] This was the role which the party needed and which he so admirably filled in the campaign.

There was another and far more important reason in Debs' own mind for accepting a fifth presidential nomination, even if it involved the incongruity of running from prison. He had sadly surveyed the wreckage of party unity after the purges and communist splits of 1919 and hoped that, as before, he might rise above faction and provide party cohesion—even from jail.[3] With this in mind he had pleaded for unity but his words had fallen by the wayside as the party battled out its principles and purged its membership in 1919 and 1920.[4] So Debs hopefully permitted the use of his name as a presidential candidate as early as March, 1920.[5]

In view of the dissension and ill-feeling within the party many felt that Debs' followers grasped at straws in thinking that he could unite the failing organization. Even his faithful brother Theodore was uncertain. "But I am not so sure, as the *Call* seems to believe, that his nomination will bring a unification of the socialist forces. The wounds are deep and past experience has taught me that healing processes are not . . . speedy. . . ." [6]

Even with these doubts about Debs' ability to unite the party, everyone acknowledged his coming nomination.[7] Before the convention met, crowds cheered his name and parades and meetings were staged in his honor. In Newark, New Jersey, 4,000 people shouted their greetings to him and there were some 100 cars. Police turned away many who could not enter the auditorium where a testimonial meeting was held.[8] Six thousand people rang the rafters of Madison Square Garden with his name before the party had officially nominated him.[9] As the convention delegates gathered for the first session, one thing was sure: Eugene Debs in prison was a better socialist nominee than many men outside. "It is doubtful if ever before a political convention met with its mind so united and riveted upon accomplishing one aim as the Socialist convention that has just nominated Debs," a spectator noted.[10]

May 8, 1920, brought 143 socialist delegates from twenty-six states to New York for the party convention. The meeting opened with the usual flutter of socialist excitement. The delegates took their seats to the tune of the traditional "Marseillaise" and "International." When the music ended, amid a dramatic hush, the curtains on the stage parted to reveal a life-sized portrait of Debs on the platform. Each mention of his name brought thunderous cheers from the crowd.[11] The delegates themselves ran true to form but in this year of troubles displayed surprising outspokenness; persecution and dismemberment seemed to bring all the latent protest to the fore and even

Morris Hillquit seemed more radical than anyone could remember.[12] Spurred on by communist competition, a presidential candidate in jail, disaffection in their ranks and persecution elsewhere, the remaining socialists seemed determined to retain a portion of their thunder by presenting an old-fashioned radical platform.

But they were not so radical as to endorse communism or to permit the communists to dominate what remained of the party, or to reverse the well-known tactic of boring from within. As debates unfolded, three groups emerged, each stabilizing around an attitude toward the newly formed Third International. The question was whether or not the party should enter the International and on what terms. Moscow demanded conformity to rules; the left-wing American socialists agreed; the center wing favored entrance on their own terms; the right wing wanted nothing to do with Moscow.[13] Morris Hillquit was chosen chairman for the first day, a clear victory for the right. From then on the conservatives held the convention in their hands. As of old, if the party delegates were radical, the party leadership was not. Resolutions favoring union with the International on compromise terms ultimately triumphed, but the issue died when Moscow later refused to admit the Americans unless they conformed to the famous 21 Points, which they did not do.

The left-wing socialists raised their voices loudest when the platform was discussed. They wanted frank recognition of gains made by Russia; a more liberally organized party structure; a frankly revolutionary platform to fit Debs' prison candidacy; and other statements of principle which the conservatives thought unwise. On the surface the delegates, as usual, were with the radicals, but as in former conventions the conservatives rallied support and under Hillquit's leadership triumphed. The right wing that had freely expelled communists and radical language federations would not permit the remaining radical socialists to dictate party strategy in 1920. The resulting platform, which Debs frankly criticized, was a compromise "designed to catch votes," as some critics said. "The Socialist party had put its Right side forward" in the platform, said the New York *Times*.[14]

The business which all delegates savored was not doctrine or even communist influence, but Debs' nomination. On May 13, 1920, Edward Henry of Indiana, a long-time friend of Debs, rose to nominate him for the fifth time. Characterizing Debs "the Lincoln of the Wabash," the tall, slow-speaking Henry placed Debs' name before the convention. The dense crowd cheered his words for nearly thirty minutes. Morris Hillquit seconded the nomination. "We nominate him because he has always been the embodiment of all the militant working class spirit . . . Debs is a challenge to all who stand for repression." [15]

When Hillquit finished pandemonium reigned on the convention floor as red streamers poured down from the balconies on the jubilant delegates. Choruses of "We Want Debs!" punctuated the proceedings and Hillquit and other staid figures led their comrades in a snake dance around the floor. "Is there any further nomination?" the smiling chairman asked even as his gavel fell; there was not and Debs received a unanimous nomination as delegates piled red roses before his picture on the stage.[16] There was still some of the old flame left, and the shadows of Debs' former fire seemed to flicker on the walls for a time as banners waved and the scent of roses filled the air. Delegates cheered and snake danced at the mention of his name. But they were aging delegates, a little incongruous despite their gallant efforts, and weariness was undisguised in many faces.[17]

The party nominated no stranger, for Debs' radicalism had increased, if anything, since his imprisonment. "Personally, I am a radical," he said on hearing of his nomination. "My only fear has always been that I might not be radical enough. In my own party I always led a minority, but I hope to lead a united Socialist Party to the polls this year." [18] His fifth nomination was a fitting climax to his long career, the inevitable apex of his political agitation. "The nomination of the prisoner of Atlanta, Convict No. 9653, was not only a tribute of love for the aged warrior, but a challenge to the reactionary powers that held him captive as a prisoner of war almost two years after the armistice," Hillquit recalled. "It was unanimous and was acclaimed with fervid enthusiasm." [19]

The delegates passed to other business. There was strong sympathy for Kate Richards O'Hare for the vice-presidential nomination. Mrs. O'Hare was also in prison for her socialist agitation and the prospect of a whole slate in jail appealed to many socialists. But wiser heads prevailed and on the assumption that at least one candidate should be free to campaign, Seymour Stedman was named vice-presidential candidate. Stedman, a friend of Debs despite his conservative leanings, and a well-known writer and speaker, was a suitable compromise.[20]

Money, as usual, was a major problem and the party had fewer resources and places to which to turn than ever before. Expensive lawsuits had cost individuals and the organization a great deal; receipts from literature sales and other sources were practically nothing; contributions were difficult to obtain, for most sympathizers had turned from the party during the war and after. But the delegates to the national convention did their best. At a special fund-raising dinner, while the speaker of the evening read mock telegrams from Harding, Wilson and other national figures, the delegates pledged $2,500 for the campaign.[21] The session which nominated Debs raised some $2,000 and pledged several thousand dollars more.[22] Amid laughter and general applause the spokesman of the Soviet of Newspapermen, a Russian group in the audience, rose to donate 29,000,000 rubles or six dollars, to the Debs fund.[23] It was a small beginning which grew little during the campaign but it was at least a beginning.

The platform was more radical than some of its predecessors, despite the conservatives' work with it. Some of the planks had a Debsian ring as the party called for trade and diplomatic relations with Russia, cancellation of war debts, abandonment of the League of Nations in favor of an international democratic parliament, freedom of speech and press, and release of political prisoners. Demands for the nationalization of industry, direct election of the president, and curtailment of the powers of the courts and government in civil liberties added socialistic and reform tones to the document.[24]

Under deft guidance from Hillquit and others, the convention passed resolutions opposing communist efforts to dominate the Socialist Party and condemned acts of violence and bloodshed in Russia.[25] The reconstituted socialist party, while sending fraternal greetings and best wishes to the Russian people, moved steadily away from anything approaching communism or identification with bolshevism.

A committee was appointed to tour Russia and report its findings but its mission failed in 1921.[26]

On the last day of the convention cheering delegates adjourned and staged a demonstration in Washington on Debs' behalf. They marched four abreast from the train station to their meeting hall and later a delegation presented Debs' views at the White House.[27] Interviewed on his nomination and its incongruity, Debs laughed and told reporters: "I will be a candidate at home in seclusion. It will be much less tiresome and my managers and opponents can always locate me."[28] America had seen more than one "front porch campaign," but this was its first "front cell campaign."

Late in May the formal socialist notification committee journeyed to Atlanta to inform Debs of his nomination and to hear his acceptance. It was surely the strangest such ceremony in American history; in place of frock coats and high collars there were faded denims and prison stripes against a background of prison walls. The warden permitted the ceremony without much delay and Debs received the committee while sitting at one end of a long table in the warden's office. He listened intently to the message of notification and read a careful statement in which he disapproved of the tone of the platform but accepted it. "We can breathe the spirit of revolution into any platform." He favored a vigorous campaign, a forgiving and cooperative attitude toward the newly-formed communist groups, and entrance into the Third International with reservations. After the ceremony, Debs embraced and kissed each member of the committee and held a large bouquet of roses while the group was photographed for the benefit of movies, newspapers and magazines.

Spying a Debs button, the candidate flashed with puckish humor: "Better take that off. They'll put you in the penitentiary for wearing that!" [29] The performance over, he bade his well-wishers goodbye and returned to his cell. For him the campaign was under way.

Debs deprived of his voice was a strange Debs indeed; he who had spellbound millions, whose chosen medium was the public platform, must now be silent while others spoke for him. He talked freely with his visitors, however, and long before the campaign began in earnest he lashed out at his opponents, proving that prison had cost him none of his old fervor.[30] Since he could not speak publicly he relied heavily on statements and press releases. The New York *Call* republished his former writings and speeches to compensate for the lack of fresh material and many tracts and pamphlets used in the campaign were reprints of his more famous statements.[31]

In September, the Justice Department permitted Debs to send out statements at the rate of 500 words per week.[32] Debs wrote these statements in his cell, passed them on to prison officials for approval, then forwarded them to Terre Haute where they were transcribed and sent to party headquarters in Chicago for general release and distribution.[33] He received no special favors from the government, which was still anxious to guard his utterances and whose officials had a keen eye for "treason." Only pressure from the wire services, especially the United Press, moved the government to act at all and Debs' statements were restricted; he could not write articles for magazines nor could he extend his correspondence beyond its normal limits.[34] There was some question that he was eligible for the nomination since his rights of citizenship had been revoked. Shrewd lawyers assured the candidate that the issue could be settled when and if he was elected. He was perhaps the only presidential candidate in American history who was prevented from taking his case to the people.

Poor prospects, lack of funds and public apathy did not deter the socialists from attempting to mount an old-fashioned crusade. "The Socialist Party enters the campaign of 1920 confident in the ultimate success of Socialism," one official trumpeted. "It has nominated candidates of the working class for the national and state offices; it is carrying on propaganda; it is working as never before. THE PEOPLE MUST BE TAUGHT FURTHER THE NECESSITY OF MARXIAN SOCIALISM. The great vote will liberate Debs and thousands of others unjustly imprisoned, and will serve notice on the capitalist class that the workers demand the nation for themselves." [35] Some socialists even convinced themselves that they would top their vote of 1912 and that the amnesty issue and suppression of speech and the press would bring hundreds of thousands to their banner in protest against the Wilson administration.[36]

It all sounded very well and there were grains of logic in every socialist hope, but the party had never been in a poorer position, not even in 1900. There were few brass bands, no trains, no blankets of literature, no vocal party press, few torchlight parades. In truth, "Debs' personality is doing most of the Socialist Party campaigning," said one journal.[37] Though the socialist ticket ran on ballots in almost every state, the campaign could not cover them all and managers and organizers realized from the first that they could do little to improve the party's organization; they would do well to spread socialism and Debs' message at all.[38]

The party established campaign headquarters in Atlanta to keep in touch with Debs and to capitalize on his martyrdom.[39] For the first time in his life the candidate found the campaign restful; no grueling speeches, no hands to shake, only occasional statements to write. He received boxes of fruit, candy and tobacco from socialists and sympathizers, most of which he gave to other inmates. He devoted his idle hours to reading, exercise and light prison duties.[40]

If Debs rested for once his running mate did not. Stedman, "Steddie" to Debs, emphasized the party's basic Americanism, its past record and future hopes, and its concern with immediate as well as long-run issues in accepting his nomination.[41] He suffered from no illusions; he knew only too well that it was a bad year for socialism, that he could not fill Debs' shoes, and that the campaign would be exhausting. But he was an old campaigner, alive to the possibilities as well as the drawbacks of a campaign and he fell to his work with a will. "The old parties are sterile, their candidates funny manikins," he said in true Debsian fashion as he began his crusade.[42]

He might well sneer at his opposition, for it was indeed a bleak year for presidential choices. Wilson, old, embittered, with but a few years to live as a semi-invalid, could not dictate the Democratic choice, which fell to Governor James Cox of Ohio; the vice-presidential candidate was Franklin D. Roosevelt of New York. To counter Tweedledum for Tweedledee, the Republicans chose the genial Senator Warren G. Harding of Ohio to bear their banner.

Neither candidate touched upon basic issues and the campaign, which supposedly centered on the League of Nations, in fact centered on little but America's desire to return to the "normalcy" which Harding outlined from the safety of his front porch.

Speaking on the "Nine Steps to a New Age," Stedman hammered home a socialist message to the crowds he faced. Asking for nationalization of basic industries, no deportation of aliens, individual freedom, a world parliament, and other progressive measures, he reflected the party's disgust with the times and the opposition. "We enter the conflict with the call 'From the dungeon to liberty,' 'From the white walls of Atlanta's bastille to the White House of Washington,' " he said in accepting his nomination.[43] Though they were alone most of the time, a few minor groups endorsed the socialists.[44] Stedman's speeches were models of their kind, though he lacked Debs' dynamic personality, and he persuaded many fence-sitters to listen to him if not to vote for him. The times were still such that many prepared to hear him incognito and he received at least one letter from a self-confessed "Coward," who wished him well but refused to sign his name.[45] In San Francisco, Stedman drew a larger crowd than Debs faced in 1912. Upton Sinclair worked for socialism in California and scattered old-time reformers and party workers rallied to the cause across the country.[46]

Stedman was not alone in his campaign. In addition to the organizers and volunteer speakers, Kate Richards O'Hare was an unexpected but welcome addition to the ranks of famous socialists on the stump during the campaign. Released from prison by President Wilson on May 29, she entered the fray at once, combining a drive for funds with an appeal for prison reform and socialism that was effective in many enthusiastic meetings. Clad in an astonishing dress of purple, black, green and blue stripes given her upon her release from prison, she addressed sizable crowds in the East and Midwest during September and October. "My Christmas dress," as she called her costume, drew as many people as her message, for the party press used it as a symbol as much as Debs' own faded denim.[47]

It was not all silence for Debs. He made the most of the space and time allotted him, repeating in different guises the tenets of his career. He appealed to workers and intelligent voters to think, discuss the issues, weigh the alternatives before voting, for only intelligent votes could solve America's problems. "I would rather have a man think and vote against me than give me his vote like a sheep."[48] He was all too aware of the formidable opposition which he and his cause faced in 1920, and knew full well that there were many miles yet to travel on the road to utopia. "If by some miracle we should attain national power, would not the ignorance, prejudice and apathy of the people destroy it? Are we not rather engaged in the task of educating the workers of America to the point where they will see that they must adopt our Socialist program if they would not be devoured by capitalism?"[49] Thus he ended where he began; belief in education, agitation, and understanding among the electorate would in time bring socialism to America without the bloodshed and violence of the Russian revolution.

The old ardor flashed occasionally. President-baiting was his favorite sport and he could not resist attacks on the opposition. "There is no fundamental difference between the Republicans or the Democrats. They are wings of the same old bird of prey," he said when nominated.[50] Late in August he blasted his opponents with some accuracy. "Senator Harding and Governor Cox remind me of two humpty dumpties," he said. "They are stuffed people, not real. They have not a single idea for a man who is alive. They get their inspiration from the tombs. The whole performance is artificial." [51]

Nor could he pass by without a stab at his old labor foes. "The labor leaders of the land referred to are all for Cox and Harding, that is to say, for capitalism and wage slavery," he snapped, contemptuously dismissing Gompers and his friends.[52] The war veterans who came home with expectations of peace and prosperity found little of either; their discontent was a major factor in the election. It was left to Debs to sum up many of the soldiers' complaints when he said: "They were told they were heroes, and found they were hoboes." [53]

All of this was grist for his familiar mill but he did not ignore the popular issues of the day or deny that socialism had a remedy for them as well as for the long-range ills of society. He condemned the administration's handling of the coal shortage and blamed inflation on the forces that had caused the war and which had profited from it. He saw the inevitable postwar depression as a familiar phase of capitalism.[54]

Socialists elsewhere were busy as Debs led the charge as best he could. Four thousand people attended a socialist picnic in New York. No speeches enlivened the proceedings but liberal quantities of beer loosened many tongues and worked wonders for the cause.[55] At campaign headquarters the limited staff was busy. "Mail pours in like water over a dam," Debs' brother wrote.[56] A temporary flurry of publicity aided Hillquit and the socialists as newspapers condemned his earlier statement that once in power the party would feel justified in using force to maintain its position. The statement was hardly new and was nothing but accepted legal belief that a government may resist revolution, but the newspapers made the most of every straw in their attack on socialism.[57]

As though the campaign was not dramatic enough the party in Toledo employed four airplanes to drop socialist literature over the city. Each piece of literature which fluttered down over the city on the appointed day, was stamped with a letter of the alphabet. Finders of pieces with the letters D E B S won cash prizes.[58] All things considered, the party showed amazing energy. Five million leaflets were readied; organizers and volunteer workers were set; even paintings of Debs were sold.[59]

Carried away by prospects of ladies at the polls for the first time, one militant suffragette reported that the ghost of Susan B. Anthony had appeared to her and advised that she vote for Debs. Debs and Miss Anthony had been friends, which added a small element of truth to the visitation; but the medium was Mrs. Charles Edward Russell, wife of the prominent socialist, which detracted somewhat from her claims.[60]

The campaigning had its effect and many conservatives again feared that Debs would receive a large protest vote. The New York *Times* attacked the socialists for using appeals to emotion, as thought this were a socialist innovation in politics, and condemned the cheers that greeted Debs' be-striped appearance on movie screens. "Few who are responsive to the appeal of the dramatic, whose hearts are sensitive to the pathos of old age in distress, can stifle a responsive emotion." [61] That was exactly what the socialists hoped.

Money was still a major problem and sources dwindled as needs arose. By October some 60,000 people had reportedly donated to the party campaign fund. The largest source of funds was still donations and contributions taken at rallies. In fact, some $60,000 was available for the campaign and the party emerged in debt, though not due solely to the campaign. Funds were there, though hard to gather, and many socialists were grateful that they did as well as they did. Party headquarters stoutly denied that the socialists had received any Russian funds.[62]

The demand for political amnesty ran through the Debs campaign like a bright thread and few socialists lost an opportunity to represent Debs as a martyr of Democratic persecution. The hope of catching votes from the other parties on this issue spurred many socialists, and they worked hard to spread their demand for release of political prisoners. The party slogan was "From the Prison to the White House," and few forgot that the liberal Wilson had put Debs in prison.[63] Throughout the campaign the socialists and other groups worked for Debs' release, but the candidate himself stubbornly refused special favors. He felt that as long as any political prisoners were behind bars he deserved to remain too. "I wish no special consideration and I wish to fare no better than my comrades," he told visitors. "As long as they are held criminals and convicts my place is here. My comrades will therefore understand that they can serve me best by bringing their influence to bear on behalf of all." [64] Though he disliked

Wilson intensely, Debs recognized that in many ways the President was a victim of the forces of the time.[65]

All this did not deter Debs' fellow inmates at Atlanta in their zeal to elect him President. Debs was immensely popular with the inmates, most of whom he believed were there because of the capitalistic system. They assiduously divided the cell blocks into precincts and assured Debs that he would sweep the penitentiary and that neither Cox nor Harding would win a single prison electoral vote.[66]

Though the persecution of radicals had abated somewhat, the socialists faced grim opposition in many places. In Connecticut and elsewhere speakers and socialist organizers were arrested by police and harassed by townspeople.[67] "In America the workers are denied not only the full product of their labor but even the right of free speech, free press, right of assemblage and the right of representation," a party spokesman noted bitterly.[68]

To the socialists the presidential campaign had significance for the party's future as well as its present. Debs had accepted the nomination in large measure to help unify the party and had consistently refrained from entering into the destructive strife that so weakened the organization during and after the war. "For myself, I have no stomach for factional quarreling and I refuse to be consumed in it," he wrote shortly before his nomination in 1920. "If it has to be done others will have to do it. I can fight capitalists but not comrades." [69] He trod lightly on the thin ice of party discontent, carefully phrasing his public statements, refusing to be used by any group, anxious to remain above the din of faction. He saw no reason for disunity; believed that a united effort during the campaign would help the party; and he denied that the party rank and file had anything to do with the endless dissension.[70] Debs' attitude toward party faction was characteristic of the man; loathing dissension and discussion, he turned his back on it, hoping that it would go away, and thereby refusing the full leadership that was his because of the factional responsibility such leadership implied. Many men who devoted their time and energy to holding the party together were irritated by Debs' often self-righteous vagueness on the subject; for one who had been in the socialist battle as long as he, he seemed to show remarkably little willingness to understand the sources of factionalism within the party.

The conservative elements in the party did not miss the chance to lambaste their communist opponents during the campaign. "The achievements of the Russian Revolution, and the great increase of foreign-speaking members in the Socialist Party led to the denunciation of the party organization as lacking in revolutionary fervor and failing to adhere to revolutionary Socialist principles by a noisy group of people, most of whom had joined the party after the end of the war," the official campaign handbook said drily of the opposition.[71]

The newly formed Communist Party of America was anxious to win Debs, for his name would add luster and publicity to its cause. But Debs was at best reluctant to consort with the communists. Reversing a former stand he told a visiting group that the socialists could never enter the Third International without reservations because that body was too autocratic.[72] His sympathy toward Russia displayed in 1917 and 1918 was not dead, however, and many times he justified acts of violence in Russia on the grounds that the revolution was being consolidated.[73] He objected to violence but could sympathize with the elements that destroyed the Czarist government. "All along the track of the ages, wherever a government has been overthrown by force and violence that government had been maintained by force and violence." [74]

The glamor of this explanation rapidly faded, however, and Debs shortly sang a different song. He shrewdly perceived the heart of the matter. "It seems to me that outside of the fact that Russia has achieved a social revolutionary triumph, she has at the same time actually swapped dictators," he told a friend later.[75] Arguing that it was not a true workers' revolution since intellectuals were at the helm, Debs in time turned entirely against the Soviet revolution.

The American communists did their best to sway Debs. A special delegation visited him and offered their support in the campaign if he would repudiate Berger and the right wing. Without ceremony, Debs refused.[76] Many of Debs' friends and family attacked the communists then and later for not helping agitate for his release.[77] Ironically, earlier in the year Debs was named President of the Soviet Republic of the United States by a secret session of the International Communist Congress in Moscow.[78] If he knew of his election he said nothing; doubtless he preferred to risk his chances with the other duly-chosen American presidential aspirants.

Failing to win Debs, individual communists alternated between scorn and contempt for him publicly. His acceptance of the Socialist Party nomination brought stinging rebukes from the communists, with the injunction that "Between the Communist party and the Socialist party there can be no compromise." [79] It was exactly this philosophy that prevented Debs from endorsing communism.

As the campaign closed the socialists made one last bid for votes. They circulated more literature, put their last speakers into the field, played on the dissension of the times and urged everyone opposed to the administration to vote for Debs. Julius Gerber, executive secretary of the New York party, predicted a total vote of 3,000,000 in the country and the election of at least five socialist congressmen and thirteen socialist assemblymen in New York. Other observers felt that the socialist vote would rise considerably because of protest against Debs' imprisonment.[80]

But Gerber and others who predicted a great increase in the socialist vote were whistling in the dark. For all their bravado, the socialists knew they were waging a losing battle. The war and government repression had hampered their organization and cut their popularity with many segments of the population. Their candidate was in prison, their press was ineffective, they had little money, their organization was in decline. Hillquit and other party spokesmen appealed for liberal votes but this was a stopgap; in other days Debs would have repudiated such support. The socialists hoped that many women, voting for the first time, would vote for Debs and liberty. But all this was morale-building. Few but die-hards really anticipated any socialist upsurge.

Debs himself had no illusions. As the returns ticked in, Warden Zerbst relayed them to him in his office and Debs, wearing prison garb, looked over the figures before conceding defeat to Harding. He was neither disappointed nor surprised, joked a while with Zerbst and others, predicted that 1924 would be socialism's year, and went to bed. "In the next hour I was in dreamland sailing the seven seas in quest of new worlds to conquer." The same could not be said of his fellow inmates, who were bitterly disappointed that Debs had not been elected; they assumed that once safely in office he would pardon them for their loyalty and hard intramural work on his behalf.[81] Yet even Debs' usual optimism could not hide the note of discouragement in his voice. "In my maturer years I no longer permit myself to be either disappointed or discouraged. I hope for everything and expect nothing. The people can have anything they want. The trouble is they do not want anything. At least they vote that way on election day." [82]

Debs received 3.5 per cent of the total vote, slightly more than half his 1912 total, with 919,000 votes. New York led his column with an impressive 204,146 votes, followed by Wisconsin, with 70,021; California, with 64,-076; Minnesota, with 56,106; and Colorado, with 47,-316.[83] Careful work, public dislike of the Wilson administration, and sound socialist tactics explained the large vote in New York. Significantly, the old radical strongholds of the Far West were almost gone; the biggest socialist vote came from the East and conservative Midwest.

For the party the returns meant American repudiation of Wilson.[84] In this at least they savored the flavor of victory, for the departure of the hated schoolmaster in apparent public disfavor was to them a victory of great proportions. Even Harding would be better, for he was at least a nonentity. Who knew but that they would find greater favor under an amiable conservative than a harsh liberal? They rejoiced at the nearly million votes, congratulated themselves on the fact that they had so many sympathizers. But they were not fooled; in their heart of hearts they knew that socialism had nowhere to go but down.[85] "The relatively big vote was the last flicker of the dying candle and did not deceive the Socialists," Hillquit remembered.[86]

To Debs it did not matter; he knew only too well that the party's future, if it were to have one, would rest on hard work, slow work, the kind of dogged, persistent work that had brought it to third place in American politics. His illusions concerning socialism's future had vanished long ago and he sometimes scorned the appellation "Grand Old Man" and longed to return to the organizational work that was his forte, for he knew how long and hard the road ahead would be.

He was tired, old, sick; many predicted that he would not live to be pardoned, if that was the new administration's intention. He neared the end of the road physically and otherwise. More than a tinge of bitterness had pervaded him now, framing in pessimism his reflections on the past and his hopes for the future. "The people can have anything they want," he had said. "The trouble is they do not want anything."

But those who predicted his demise were a trifle premature, for one further effort lay ahead of him, the fulfillment of his long role as American socialism's pacifier, evangelizer, and organizer. Once free he could pursue that goal. His last campaign now concluded, his friends turned to the problem of freeing him with greater force and conviction than ever before, for they knew that his time was short.

VIII

The Final Years: 1921-1926

> *I did not start out expecting gratitude and*
> *I have never been disappointed. To be*
> *true to my principles and my ideals*
> *and to have my place in the ranks with*
> *the Comrades who share them has been*
> *more than sufficient, and everything*
> *that has come to me in return has been*
> *for my good and has added to my compen-*
> *sation.*
>
> Eugene V. Debs, 1922

The shadows seemed to lift in Washington and across the land in the spring of 1921 when the affable Warren G. Harding took the oath of office as President and ended the eventful eight-year administration of Woodrow Wilson. A gala inaugural ball greeted the new President's guests; he opened the White House to the public; he lifted many petty restrictions and encumbrances, indicating that he and his administration would depart markedly from the harshness of Wilson's latter years. Hopes rose that he would also undo much of the harm done to civil liberties. In this climate, amid returning prosperity and "normalcy," the drive for Debs' release from prison took on added life. Success was all but assured; it was merely a matter of time.

President Harding doubtless knew little of the details of the Debs case, but he inclined toward release of political prisoners. Anxious to remedy the Wilson administration's repressive legislation, he was also personally kind. But he moved cautiously, good politician that he was, testing the ground and public opinion before acting in the case.

He did not lack advice. Scarcely a day passed that did not bring a delegation to the White House urging Debs' release. Famous men like Lincoln Steffens, Debs' old enemy Samuel Gompers, Meyer London, and a host of others interviewed Harding and his Attorney-General.[1] A month after his inauguration, Harding faced a group of labor leaders and liberals who asked for Debs' freedom; the President smiled, as was his wont, but was noncommittal.[2] Socialists were not always sanguine about Debs' prospects. The comparative freedom accorded him while he was a presidential candidate was now withdrawn and he was less accessible than usual.[3]

Yet many factors worked in Debs' favor. The pressures from varying sources, Harding's desire to free him, the impressive socialist vote of 1920, the prisoner's age and ill-health, and the manifest injustice of keeping him in prison moved Harding's administration to recommend clemency.[4] Accordingly, the President ordered Debs' release, together with several other political prisoners, on Christmas Day, 1921. After a day in Washington and a short talk with Harding, which both men seemed to appreciate, Debs journeyed home to Terre Haute.

The air of freedom tasted good to Debs even though his welcome in Terre Haute exhausted him, but he left many friends behind in prison. He recalled with a touch of pride and gratitude the deference accorded him by the other inmates, and remembered with emotion how they had beat against their prison walls and shouted goodbyes as he waved to them on his departure.[5] He did not forget them and spent much of his time in the next few years working for prison reform and for the final release of all remaining political prisoners.[6] The socialists were jubilant and crowds of well-wishers welcomed him back to freedom. Tired, physically exhausted and ill from his incarceration, old and worried by the party's and the world's future, Debs barely survived the reception. "I could stand going to the penitentiary again, yes! But I couldn't endure another release," he wrote a friend.[7]

The petty problems that he had escaped in prison now closed in on him remorselessly. Groups on every side tugged at him, claiming his allegiance and attempting to convince him of the soundness of their positions. Russia was foremost on everyone's list and while those who knew him realized that Debs' attitude on the Soviet state had changed, many radicals and former comrades begged him to endorse communism at home and abroad to revive the flagging radicalism of the Socialist Party. Steffens and others interviewed him before and after his release, asking his allegiance to the new Russia. Debs listened carefully, digested information and weighed alternatives. As always, his sympathies lay with the Russian people as they struggled to fashion a new order from the ashes of the old.[8] But he was disturbed by the dogmatic tone that emanated from Moscow and disliked Soviet efforts to dictate to socialist parties elsewhere.[9] In the end it came to the question of violence and he had not changed. "When the people of Russia aspire toward freedom I'm all for them, but I detest the terror which the Bolsheviks imposed to wrest and hold power. I still have, and always will have, a profound faith in the efficacy of the ballot," he told a friend. "There's nothing in our United States government that it can't remedy . . . I'm not ready to go with those who've lost faith in the process of democracy. But men must learn how to use the ballot!" [10] In 1922 he cabled a protest to Lenin against Soviet execution of political opponents; in this and other ways he showed that his first inclinations toward communism had long since vanished.[11]

Just as he disliked Soviet methods abroad, so he disliked communist methods at home and the American communists got no more sympathy from him when he left prison than when they approached him in 1920. He condemned the communist trend toward violence and underground activity as foolish and suicidal.[12] Many did not understand Debs' unwillingness to endorse communism after his release. Many felt with Ella Reeve Bloor that "when he came out of prison, sixty-eight years old, and in broken health, he permitted the socialist leaders to use him as a figurehead and failed to take the step that would have been the logical fulfillment of his life as a great revolutionist." [13] They did not realize that Debs had taken all the steps in his career and that to endorse communism or bolshevism would have repudiated his whole past. However radical he may have been, his radicalism never accepted dictation or control from foreign sources; in this he was as American as the things he criticized. A socialist he could be, but never a communist.[14]

The Socialist Party to which he returned and which now claimed his attention had indeed fallen on evil days. The sword of faction had opened many wounds and sundered many a socialist friendship; the climate of opinion in the age of "normalcy" was not conducive to socialism; membership was down and funds were scarce; the party press was a thing of the past.[15] "It is lost in the wilderness, and knows not which way to turn," a commentator said of the party.[16] The Midwest, former socialist stronghold, reported steadily declining membership and activity, if it reported at all.[17] More than one veteran socialist withdrew in sadness and by 1924 one of Debs' closest friends could say of the party: "It is a political ghost stalking in the graveyard of current events seeking respectable burial." [18]

Both the leaders and the rank and file now saw Debs as the new Moses to guide a path from this wilderness; the old magic might yet revive the faithful again as it had in the past. The bitterest factional fights had passed Debs by in prison, but everyone knew how demoralizing they were; calls now for unity fell on deaf ears.[19] As he rested, gathering his strength for coming battles, Debs still declined to side with any faction. "He has kept himself aloof from all factional strife until he could gather strength enough to take his position, hold his ground and justify himself," his brother wrote. "He is perfectly right, I am sure, in not permitting himself to be drawn into some of these vicious snarls at a time when he is struggling for breath and life." [20]

When he did comment on factionalism, Debs was harsh, as in the past, for he had neither taste nor patience for such quarreling. "When I entered prison the party was united and when I was released it was torn into warring factions," he said in 1922. "All this could in my opinion and should have been avoided. There has been no difference of which I have any knowledge that could not I believe have been settled within the party and without dismembering it and turning it into impotent quarreling fragments." Pleading ill-health, but promising future work, he still sympathized with those who had favored a more radical Socialist Party. "The many thousands who lost confidence [in the socialist party] as a revolutionary party of the working class and deserted its ranks could not have done so without reason." [21] It was easy for Debs to take so strong a position against the great divisions of 1919 because he was not involved; prison had at least removed him from that arena. In fairness to the conservative socialists, they believed that purges of communists presaged a better fate than the party's capture by Moscow. Yet there was but one alternative for Debs; he could not desert the party with which he had been so intimately associated since 1897. By October, 1922, he clearly stated that he would not leave the Socialist Party for any other organization.[22]

Party leaders, anxious for Debs' voice, blocked out an ambitious organizational tour for him in 1923, oblivious to his doctors' pleas. Debs himself was eager to return to the fray at whatever cost to life and limb.[23] "I am stronger in spirit than ever but lacking in physical strength and have to keep quiet for a considerable time, if that be possible," he wrote Tom Mooney. "Otherwise you know I should be at my post again without delay." [24]

In 1923, Debs undertook a series of exhausting speeches, attempting to breathe life into the dying party organization. For a time the grandeur of other days surrounded his progress as he faced immense crowds and packed receptions in major cities.[25] Though often opposed by local authorities and patriotic organizations, they did not prevent his progress and he addressed large groups wherever he went.[26] For Debs it was grueling. "To tell you the truth it was a terrible strain, especially as I was still in a convalescent state," he admitted privately of his efforts, "and I was glad enough to get away with my sanity." [27] Fifty-three speeches raised funds, drew the curious and the faithful, but in the end it all failed; Debs collapsed and returned home to rest and for a series of cures at a sanitarium. The party could not follow up his work and thus lost most of the momentum he gave it.[28] Those who surveyed the scene logically knew the worst; American socialism was all but dead.

Debs had stated positively that he would not run for President again, and as the election of 1924 approached those Americans anxious to form a third party turned to a more logical and more willing candidate, Senator Robert M. La Follette of Wisconsin.[29] Facing facts, many socialists called on the party to support La Follette and his new Progressive Party.[30] Though he had always opposed fusion, Debs now supported endorsing La Follette on the simple grounds that there was nothing else to do. In July, 1924, the socialist convention endorsed the Senator after heated debate. Debs, now serving for the first time as a party official, National Chairman of the Socialist Party, agreed. "I think it wise for our party to make no nominations under the circumstances, but at the same time to hold the Socialist Party intact, adhere rigidly to its principles, and keep the red flag flying. I hope above all there will be no division but that all will unite loyally in carrying out the program adopted by the Convention." [31]

In the campaign which followed many socialists loyally

supported La Follette, following Deb's advice as sincerely as possible. Socialist candidates withdrew from many state contests; the party press supported the Senator; many socialist groups did their best for him during the campaign.[32] Charges from the communist camp that the socialists had turned bourgeois drew sharp answers from Debs. "You may be right in your position and I may be wrong, as I have been before," he snapped at William Z. Foster. "Having no Vatican in Moscow to guide me I must follow the light I have, and this I have done in the present instance."[33] La Follette undoubtedly benefited in many places from socialist support and he owed many of the five million votes he received to the party's work.[34]

For the socialists themselves the election was neither a triumph nor a disappointment, for they had expected little. Berger was elected to congress again but his steady drift to the right had taken him far from the ranks of old-line socialists.[35] Some socialist strongholds had been indifferent and many former party members openly laughed at their comrades' pretensions and hopes. The party organization emerged from the campaign in dire straits; the low membership was falling lower and badly needed funds had been spent on the campaign.[36]

Debs was disappointed at the election results and called for a new socialism and no further combination with reform movements.[37] Early in 1925 a group of radicals attempted to revive the Conference for Progressive Political Action, which had formed La Follette's party, but no one worked under any illusions. The Senator may have received five million votes but he could not buck the tide of Coolidge prosperity; the days of genuine radicalism would have to wait. As Hillquit said of the delegates to the last meeting of the Conference, they had "come to bury Caesar, not to praise him." [38]

Debs himself was convalescing and by carefully husbanding his strength he maintained a light schedule of party work. He attended a meeting of the National Executive Committee in Washington in December, 1924, and kept up his writing and correspondence with old friends and workers.[39] To laments that socialism was dead, never to rise again, he lashed back with some of his old fire.[40]

But Debs waged a losing fight and he knew it. He had come too far too long not to know that the end was at hand. On October 20, 1926, after a long illness, Debs died at Lindlahr Sanitarium in Elmhurst, Illinois. From New York to Los Angeles, in memorial meetings, silent parades, and black bordered editorials the socialists eulogized the man who had been their symbol for so many years. Although their paths had hardly crossed, it seems fitting that the funeral orator was none other than Norman Thomas, who was to succeed Debs as the leader of the Socialist Party.[41]

Thus ended the long career of Debs as a socialist and American radical, a career as varied as his personality and as effective as his presentation could make it, a career marked by failures and successes, by hopes and half-realized dreams. Debs was not so remarkable for the way he worked, in which he differed little from many contemporaries, as for the effectiveness with which he preached socialism. If his means differed little from those of other politicians of his day, his goals did, and that he persuaded nearly six per cent of the voting Americans in 1912 to mark their ballots for him was no small accomplishment.

Yet, because they recognized his basic Americanism and because he was at such pains to disavow the more extreme socialist tendencies even if it displeased his comrades, the Americans who voted for him did not fear him. His belief in the goodness of man, and his personal sentimentality tempered whatever edge of violence remained on the doctrines he spoke. Knowing little of formal socialist logic he was indebted to no theorizer or dogmatist for his doctrines.

This in part explains his remarkable effectiveness with the voting public of his day, for he cast doctrine and theory aside, like most good politicians, and fitted his remarks and his program into the mainstream of the time. He appealed to many different groups successfully because he realized that to be effective any political doctrine, even idealistic socialism, must be understood by its audience. Thus he avoided extended philosophical discussions, preferring the concrete realities of the life around him to sophistry.

However wise this may have been in terms of gathering votes and followers, it is one measure of Debs' weakness as a leader that he did not fully grasp the elements of socialist theory and use them in his leadership. He was not, strictly speaking, a socialist party leader yet he was the most famous socialist of his day. Characteristically, he preferred to leave control of the party, with all its bitter dissension and routine labor, to others while he himself used his talents to rally popular opinion for what he considered the party program. From his point of view it was wise to remain above faction that he might be a true leader above the battle to whom all socialists could look for leadership. Yet in doing so he permitted the party organization to drift into the firm control of men with whom he disagreed, while he could not wholeheartedly join the men with whom he agreed. Thus, like many radical leaders, he was perpetually between two fires, radical socialism and evolutionary socialism. Had he chosen to exercise the power represented by his following he no doubt could have dominated the party, yet by doing so he would have risked his neutral position and the formation of yet another faction. The loosely organized party, composed of varied elements prone to disagreement, was hard to govern at best and Debs disliked the formality and procedures of such rule as much as the methods of obtaining them.

If he did not fully exercise his talents for leadership within the party he did so outside the party organization. As the best-known socialist of his day, and recognizing his role as the prophet and evangelizer of socialism, he lent his talents to spreading the meaning if not the formal doctrines of American socialism. His career was varied, though it flowed from the same central source; he worked as a labor organizer, protest leader, socialist propagandizer, and as a symbol of freedom in a time of oppression. In his role as a presidential candidate he brought to bear all his understanding of the temper of the times, of human nature, and of the political system in which he worked. His idealism did not prevent him from being a shrewd judge of character and men, and he understood mass psychology as well as or better than any other political leader of his day. Debs' political career illustrates the curious blending of intellectual and emotional idealism and practical realism so common to liberal politics in America. On the one hand he sincerely believed in the utopian idealism he preached; on the other hand he knew full well that his new order could be attained only by working within the existing system. This was a wise and profound understanding on his part, and it is the measure of his familiarity with the political habits of his countrymen. Thus he eschewed violence not only because he himself could not justify it but because he knew it would ruin his chances of success with the American people.

Debs' presidential campaigns were important to the Socialist Party for they focused the strength of socialism every four years. Furthermore, Debs' evangelizing and his popularity with the sympathetic masses to whom he appealed added new members to the rolls, stimulated the party press, brought others to work for socialism and illustrated to those in doubt the vigor of the movement. Debs, acutely aware of this, missed no chance to add to the party strength by appealing to labor, seeking members, and doing organizational work.

The Socialist Party greatly benefited from the progressive temper in the years between 1901 and 1914, but it also profited from its own hard work with the masses. It had a genuine appeal to the educated middle class, and though Debs himself deplored the middle-class trend in the party after 1908, he could do little to arrest it. In fact, organized labor did not vote the socialist ticket except when it knew that socialism had no chance of winning; this in turn drove many socialists to the middle class for support. The failure to win organized labor sealed socialism's doom as a growing political force in America.[42]

The socialism movement as a whole suffered from many more defects than its failure to win organized labor.

Its loose organization, while a blessing to much of the membership, prevented the discipline and unity of European socialist parties. Debs himself would have been the last to sanction such discipline and though he perpetually called for socialist unity he based that unity on principles, rather than organizational discipline. The internal factions which arose in the party in its golden age contributed greatly to its decline, yet in the end were only part of a multitude of factors working against its success.

In the last analysis, the American socialist movement failed to conquer capitalism and its society for deeper reasons than internal strife. The unexpected vitality of capitalism, the immovable middle-class psychology of the workers, the truly basic American belief in individual rather than cooperative effort, the conservative constitutional features of the political system, and the anti-socialism of organized labor which prevented a broadly-based coalition labor party—these deeply woven threads in the fabric of American life prevented socialism's triumph.[43]

Yet American socialism's ultimate failure is not so impressive as its temporary success. The people who voted for Debs five times apparently believed in many of his ideals; the party elevated several hundred of its members to office; undeniably socialism influenced the older parties in their search for reform measures. The mere fact that socialism flourished indicated to Republicans and Democrats that reform was necessary. Thus the party fulfilled the historic role of third parties in the American system— it attained enough success with the people to force older parties to steal its thunder. Despite its idealism and seemingly un-American approach to the problems of the day, the Socialist Party gained more success with the voters than any other recent third party except the Populists.

Many condemned socialism's idealism, pointing out that the American electorate traditionally opposed impractical solutions. But in the end, American socialism suffered not so much from its ideals as from its illusions. The idea that capitalism was not flexible enough to adapt to the demands for reform and change, that Americans were deeply dissatisfied with their political system, that man was basically logical rather than emotional, that industry would never cooperate with organized labor, that the older parties would never reform—these were the illusions which, together with the passing of the public demand for reform, the World War, and the final onrush of party factionalism, ended the socialist dream of triumph in America.

Yet the solid body of past achievement remains an instructive lesson in the degree and manner of socialist success. However limited it was, it was nonetheless a monument to the best efforts of men like Eugene Debs during the age when America boasted a powerful socialist movement.

None gave more to that movement than Eugene Victor Debs. If he was often beset by doubts, if he often vacillated on momentous issues, if he partially failed in his role as a leader within the Socialist Party, and if his thinking was indeed shallow, he was no less effective. He appealed frankly to the people whom he understood in terms they understood and let others in the movement explain the fine points. Though he wore his romantic idealism like a crusading knight capitalizing on every gain to be made from the dramatic role, his sincerity was above question. He did in truth believe that socialism was inevitable, and that its inauguration would mean the rule of reason and love on earth. He suffered for his beliefs, yet did not abandon them. Twice imprisoned, once as an old man, he nonetheless clung to his ideals. "I do not consider that I have made any sacrifice whatever," he said early in his career, "no man does, unless he violates his conscience." [44] At the end of the road he might well have repeated that phrase, for indeed he had not violated his own.

Bibliographical Note

A note on sources will interest readers and students. The basic printed bibliography for the American socialist movement is volume II of *Socialism and American Life* (Princeton: Princeton University Press, 1952), edited by Donald Drew Egbert and Stow S. Persons.

Manuscripts have been of secondary importance in this study. Socialist opinions were public property and the scattered letters that survive seldom throw light or revelation upon the broader problems with which they deal. Debs kept no copies of correspondence, and was effusive and repetitious in much of his correspondence. The basic manuscript collection for the Socialist Party is the Socialist Party Collection at Duke University, Durham, North Carolina. Though voluminous, much of the collection is of little use and the bulk of the papers dates subsequent to 1920. In the Manuscripts Division of the Library of Congress the papers of Charles Edward Russell, William J. Ghent, Woodrow Wilson, William Jennings Bryan and others are of some value. The David Karsner papers at the New York Public Library contain a good many late Debs letters. The Library also has a large collection of socialist pamphlets. The Tamiment Institute in New York, formerly the Rand School of Social Science, has a large collection of Debs material chiefly clippings in the Debs Scrapbooks and a few scattered items of correspondence which were of use in this study. The Tom Mooney papers in the Bancroft Library at the University of California at Berkeley have several late Debs letters, The State Historical Society of Wisconsin in Madison has the papers of Morris Hillquit, Seymour Stedman, Daniel DeLeon, Henry D. Lloyd, and Algie Martin Simons, which were of some use. There is a considerable number of Debs letters, dating largely from the 1880's and 1890's in the Debs-Holl collection at the Barker History Center of the University of Texas at Austin, which were of interest, though largely peripheral to this study.

The basic biography of Debs is Ray Ginger, *The Bending Cross* (New Brunswick, New Jersey: Rutgers University Press, 1949). Of the older studies, McAllister Coleman, *Eugene V. Debs: A Man Unafraid* (New York: Greenberg Publishers, 1930), is useful. The extensive bibliography in Ginger's work is of great interest to Debs scholars. Debs' writings and speeches have been collected twice, in 1908 and again in 1948, and are a basic source. Files of socialist newspapers are also a primary source for his activities and for the history of American socialism in general.

Three excellent studies of the Socialist Party have appeared in recent years. Howard Quint, *The Forging of American Socialism* (Columbia, South Carolina: University of South Carolina Press, 1953), carries American socialism from its inception to the establishment of the Socialist Party of America in 1901 and is in every respect an excellent and judicious account. Ira Kipnis, *The American Socialist Movement 1897–1912* (New York: Columbia University Press, 1952), is the only detailed account of the party in its golden age and is an extremely valuable book for its information. I have not always, however, agreed with its thesis or presentation. David A. Shannon, *The Socialist Party of America* (New York: Macmillan and Company, 1955), is the only full history of the party and though it lacks detailed coverage it contains many valuable facts and insights. The extensive bibliography in Kipnis' book and the valuable bibliographic essay in Shannon's work are also helpful.

I have used a great many general works and older histories

not cited in the notes but easily available. The sources for the study of American socialism and for Eugene Debs' life are scattered and often disappointing, but their study brings to life the character and progress of a fascinating movement and of a colorful and important figure in the history of American radicalism.

Notes to Chapters

Chapter I

1. Debs to David Karsner, December 26, 1924, David Karsner papers, New York Public Library.
2. Ray Ginger, *The Bending Cross: A Biography of Eugene Victor Debs* (New Brunswick, N.J.: Rutgers University Press, 1949), pp. 12ff. Cited hereafter as Ginger, *The Bending Cross*.
3. *Ibid.*, pp. 42–43.
4. *The Writings and Speeches of Eugene V. Debs* (New York: Hermitage Press, 1948), p. 44. Cited hereafter as Debs, *Writings and Speeches*.
5. David A. Shannon, "Eugene V. Debs: Conservative Labor Editor," *Indiana Magazine of History,* 47 (December, 1951), 357–66.
6. "Self-Made Men," *Locomotive Firemen's Magazine,* 17 (April, 1893), 267–71.
7. "Editorial: Jay Gould," *ibid.,* 17 (February, 1893), 103–108.
8. "The Pulpit and Socialism," *ibid.,* 17 (September, 1893), 740–41.
9. "Editorial: Eighteen Hundred and Ninety-Three," *ibid.,* 17 (January, 1893), 4.
10. The workers themselves were not sanguine about their chances of winning the strike. See Almont Lindsay, *The Pullman Strike* (Chicago: University of Chicago Press, 1942), p. 126.
11. *Ibid.,* pp. 124–25.

12. Debs never forgot nor forgave the failure of the craft union leaders to come to his aid in 1894. See David Karsner, *Talks With Debs in Terre Haute* (New York: The New York Call, 1922), pp. 60–61. Cited hereafter as Karsner, *Talks With Debs.*

13. See Allan Nevins (ed.), *Letters of Grover Cleveland* (New York: Houghton-Mifflin Company, 1933), pp. 357ff, for the exchange between the two men.

14. Debs, *Writings and Speeches*, p. 7.

15. *Ibid.*, p. 45.

16. See Clarence Darrow, *The Story of My Life* (New York: Charles Scribner's Sons, 1932), p. 61.

17. *Appeal to Reason,* January 18, March 14, July 18, 1896. See Debs to F. X. Holl, October 3, 1894, Debs papers, Barker History Center, University of Texas, Austin.

18. *Appeal to Reason,* February 1, 1896.

19. Social Democratic Party, *Social Democracy Red Book* (Terre Haute, 1900), p. 54.

20. Henry D. Lloyd, "The Populists at St. Louis," *Review of Reviews,* 14 (September, 1896), 299.

21. Debs to Bryan, July 27, 1896, William Jennings Bryan papers, Library of Congress. Also reprinted in James A. Barnes, *John G. Carlisle: Financial Statesman* (New York: Dodd-Mead Company, 1931), pp. 463–64.

22. The Populists were hardly socialists. "Socialism would only replace one master by another; the monopolist by the community, substitute one slavery for another," a Populist publication said. "All the systems of anarchy and socialism are based upon a supposed quality innate in man, which history from the earliest moment of his existence has disproved." See Howard Quint, *The Forging of American Socialism* (Columbia, S.C.: University of South Carolina Press, 1953), p. 211. See also Debs to Henry D. Lloyd, February 1, 1896, Henry D. Lloyd papers, State Historical Society of Wisconsin, Madison.

23. See *Cleveland Leader*, October 22, 28, 1896.

24. It is interesting to note, however, that Debs' hatred of Cleveland moved him to say that "I would far rather see McKinley elected than have another [regular] Democratic administration." Canton, Ohio, *Repository*, August 18, 1896.

25. See Quint, *The Forging of American Socialism*, pp. 281ff.

26. Morris Hillquit, *Loose Leaves From a Busy Life* (New York: Macmillan and Company, 1934), p. 324; *American Labor Yearbook 1916*, p. 89.

27. Morris Hillquit, *History of Socialism in the United States* (New York: Funk and Wagnalls Company, fifth rev. ed., 1910), p. 242. Cited hereafter as Hillquit, *History of Socialism*.

28. *Ibid.*, pp. 204ff.

29. *Ibid.*, pp. 249ff.

30. *Ibid.*, p. 359.

31. Hillel Rogoff, *An East Side Epic* (New York: The Vanguard Press, 1930), p. 15.

32. Art Young, *Art Young: His Life and Times* (New York: Sheridan House, 1939), p. 158. Cited hereafter as Young, *Life and Times*.

33. See Arnold Petersen, *Daniel DeLeon: Social Architect*, 2 vols. (New York: New York Labor News Company, 1942); Marc Karson, *American Labor Unions and Politics 1900–1918* (Carbondale, Illinois: Southern Illinois University Press, 1958), pp. 28ff.

34. William D. Haywood, *Bill Haywood's Book* (New York: International Publishers, 1929), pp. 183–84.

35. For the background and success of the Berger movement in Wisconsin, see Marvin Wachman, *History of the Social-Democratic Party of Milwaukee 1897–1910* (Urbana, Illinois: University of Illinois Press, 1945).

36. *Social Democrat*, July 15, 1897.

37. New York *Journal*, May 30, 1897. At the time of the June, 1897 convention, Debs naively sent John D. Rockefeller an

outline of the scheme and asked his support. Rockefeller did not reply. Chicago *Tribune,* June 20, 1897.

38. Quoted in Ginger, *The Bending Cross,* p. 196.

39. *Social Democrat,* June 16, 1898; Quint, *The Forging of American Socialism,* pp. 314–15. At the convention's start he took a typically Debsian stand, advocating both political action and colonization, but by the time of the bolt he was convinced that colonization would fail.

40. *Social Democratic Herald,* September 3, 1898.

41. For a general analysis of Debs' social theory see H. Wayne Morgan, "The Utopia of Eugene V. Debs," *American Quarterly,* 11 (Summer, 1959), 120–35.

42. Debs, *Writings and Speeches,* p. 119.

43. Karsner, *Talks With Debs,* p. 42.

44. Debs, *Writings and Speeches,* p. 32.

45. *Workers' Call,* March 10, 1900.

46. Debs, *Writings and Speeches,* p. 11.

47. Eugene V. Debs, "Socialist Ideals," *The Arena,* 40 (November, 1908), 433–34.

48. Karsner, *Talks With Debs,* p. 20.

49. See Daniel Bell, "The Background and Development of Marxian Socialism in the United States," in Donald Drew Egbert and Stow Persons (eds.), *Socialism and American Life,* 2 vols. (Princeton, New Jersey: Princeton University Press, 1952), I, 273.

Chapter II

1. See Ira Kipnis, *The American Socialist Movement 1897–1912* (New York: Columbia University Press, 1952), pp. 32ff; Quint, *The Forging of American Socialism,* pp. 335ff.

2. New York *Daily Tribune,* July 10–14, 1899.

3. Hillquit, *History of Socialism,* pp. 299–301.

4. McAlister Coleman, *Eugene V. Debs: A Man Unafraid* (New York: Greenberg Publishers, 1930), pp. 199–204. Hereafter cited as Coleman, *Eugene V. Debs.*

5. *Social Democrat,* October 21, 1897.
6. *Social Democratic Herald,* June 11, March 17, 1900.
7. See *Social Democracy Red Book,* p. 60.
8. *Ibid.*
9. Calvin M. Clark, "A Socialist Mayor in Haverhill, Mass.," *The Independent,* 50 (December 29, 1898), pp. 1926–1927; "The Socialist Mayors in Massachusetts," *The Outlook,* 64 (February 17, 1900), p. 412.
10. *Appeal to Reason,* December 24, 1898.
11. *Social Democratic Herald,* March 17, 1900.
12. *Social Democracy Red Book,* p. 60.
13. *Social Democratic Herald,* October 22, November 12, 16, December 17, 1898; Kipnis, *American Socialist Movement,* p. 80.
14. *Social Democratic Herald,* January 20, 1900.
15. Negotiations for unity between the two groups are extremely complex and can be followed best in Kipnis, *American Socialist Movement,* pp. 81–106; and Quint, *The Forging of American Socialism,* pp. 335–75.
16. *Social Democracy Red Book,* pp. 72–73.
17. *Social Democratic Herald,* February 10, 1900.
18. *Ibid.,* March 17, 1900.
19. *Ibid.*
20. Ginger, *The Bending Cross,* p. 209.
21. Quint, *The Forging of American Socialism,* pp. 348–49.
22. *Social Democratic Herald,* April 7, 1900.
23. Ginger, *The Bending Cross,* p. 209.
24. Coleman, *Eugene V. Debs,* p. 205.
25. See Quint, *The Forging of American Socialism,* p. 349.
26. Social Democratic Party, *Socialist Campaign Book 1900* (Chicago, 1900), p. 151; Eugene V. Debs, "The Social Democratic Party," *The Independent,* 52 (August 23, 1900), 2018–2021.
27. Ginger, *The Bending Cross,* p. 209.
28. *Social Democratic Herald,* April 7, 1900; Quint, *The Forging of American Socialism,* p. 352.

29. *Social Democratic Herald,* April 28, 1900. Debs himself declined to enter the quarrel over doctrinal purity, stating only that the Social Democratic Party was a revolutionary socialist party. "It refused to be flattered, bribed, stampeded or otherwise deflected from the straight course mapped out for it by Marx and Engels, its founders." *Ibid.,* June 9, 1900.

30. *Social Democratic Herald,* May 12, 1900. Kipnis, the *American Socialist Movement,* p. 93, n46 questions the validity of the published returns.

31. William Mailly to Morris Hillquit, April 10, 1900, Hillquit papers, State Historical Society of Wisconsin, Madison.

32. John Chase to Hillquit, July 24, 1900, *ibid.*

33. Debs never trusted DeLeon. Berger had suggested earlier in the year that the SDP might cooperate locally with some SLP groups and drew fire from Debs. "There are hundreds of perfectly straight 'Kangaroo' Socialists who will be disgusted and enraged by one of our leading papers supporting DeLeon. Nor do I agree with you that it would hurt the socialist movement to vote against such a black-hearted scoundrel as DeLeon . . . I also disagree with you when you say you have nothing against DeLeon . . . Have we nothing against the arch-enemies of the socialist movement? Are you unconcerned about the slimy slander to your colleagues and yourself in this *official* capacity? I *have* something against DeLeon and every other enemy of my party. . . ." Ginger, *The Bending Cross,* p. 210.

34. Kipnis, *American Socialist Movement,* p. 92; *Social Democratic Herald,* April 21, 1900.

35. *Workers' Call,* April 21, 1900.

36. *Ibid.,* July 28, 1900.

37. Quint, *The Forging of American Socialism,* pp. 366–67.

38. Job Harriman to Hillquit, June 13, 1900, Hillquit papers.

39. *Workers' Call,* August 11, 1900. Harriman had accepted his vice-presidential nomination with alacrity.

40. Quint, *The Forging of American Socialism,* p. 367.

41. William Butscher to C. Heydrick, August 7, 1900, Socialist Party Papers, Duke University, Durham, North Carolina. Hereafter cited as SPP Duke. See also Butscher to Harriman, August 7, 1900, *ibid.;* Butscher to Hillquit, August 11, 1900, Hillquit papers.

42. *Workers' Call,* May 5, 1900; *The Public,* 3 (May 5, 1900), 57.

43. Butscher to Harry D. Thomas, August 16, 1900, SPP Duke.

44. Butscher to *The Volkszeitung,* August 7, 1800, *ibid.*

45. *Workers' Call,* July 21, 1900.

46. Kipnis, *American Socialist Movement,* p. 97.

47. Butscher to Theodore Kochler, August 6, 1900, SPP Duke.

48. Debs, *Writings and Speeches,* p. 35.

49. Butscher to G. W. Poague, September 5, 1900, SPP Duke; *Social Democratic Herald,* December 1, 1900; *The Workers' Call,* October 20, 1900.

50. Debs apparently corresponded little, if at all, with the Springfield office, and that group depended on Harriman for the inner details of the campaign. See Butscher to H. S. Thomas, August 23, 1900, SPP Duke.

51. *The Public,* 3 (August 11, 1900), 282.

52. Debs, *Writings and Speeches,* pp. 34–40.

53. *Social Democratic Herald,* September 29, 1900; William Butscher to James Carey, August 10, 1900, SPP Duke.

54. *Workers' Call,* October 20, 1900.

55. Quint, *The Forging of American Socialism,* p. 369; *Workers' Call,* October 6, 1900.

56. Art Young, *On My Way* (New York: Horace Liveright, 1928), pp. 160–61.

57. Social Democratic Party, *Socialist Campaign Book 1900,* p. 44.

58. *Ibid.,* pp. 143–44.

59. Debs, *Writings and Speeches,* p. 39.

60. Coleman, *Eugene V. Debs,* p. 219.

61. *Workers' Call,* October 13, 1900.

62. Kipnis, *American Socialist Movement,* pp. 62–65; *Social Democratic Herald,* June 24, 1899.

63. Social Democratic Party, *Socialist Campaign Book 1900,* pp. 31–32.

64. *Ibid.,* pp. 40–41.

65. *Workers' Call,* October 6, 1900.

66. It is interesting to note that the socialists, like the Populists, looked backward to a golden age of rustic simplicity and human virtue before industrialization blighted the earth. Like Jefferson, the socialists believed in the innate goodness of the common man. "But the working class is also the source of all progress, intellectual and spiritual. It is this class that stands close to nature, wrenches from her the means of existence, and in this struggle learns nature's life giving secrets. The individuals of this class are forced shoulder to shoulder, and in close contact with each other without the barriers of cast or conventionality, learn to know the human heart and develop the feelings of human kinship, without which true progress is impossible. It is in the experiences of this close struggle with nature and man that the forces of success and progress are found. In this struggle only does evolution produce types of real value to mankind." Social Democratic Party, *Socialist Campaign Book 1900,* p. 7.

67. *Ibid.,* p. 104.

68. *Ibid.,* p. 21; Kipnis, *American Socialist Movement,* pp. 98–99.

69. Coleman, *Eugene V. Debs,* pp. 209–10.

70. "The Coming Election," *The Miners' Magazine,* 1 (November, 1900), 7.

71. In addition to the WFM, Debs and Harriman were endorsed by the International Typographical Union, the New York Central Labor Federation, the St. Louis Trades and Labor Council, the Milwaukee Federated Trades Council, and scattered local groups. Quint, *The Forging of American Socialism,* pp. 368–69.

72. See Social Democratic Party, *Socialist Campaign Book 1900*, pp. 50, 57.
73. "The World of Labor," *International Socialist Review*, 1 (August, 1900), 117.
74. William Butscher to Harry Crandall, August 16, 1900, SPP Duke.
75. Butscher often urged locals to unite as diplomatically as possible. "I desire to inform you that we have a local in your town now and it might be well to see our comrades there before you take any definite action," he wrote one member. "Perhaps you can all get together in one local and then be better able to make a fight against capitalism." Butscher to Peter [?], August 6, 1900, SPP Duke.
76. Butscher to Max Hageman, August 13, 1900; to Albery G. Clifford, August 6, 1900, *ibid. Appeal to Reason,* December 15, 1900; *Workers' Call,* September 1, 1900.
77. Harriman to Hillquit, August 18, 1900, Hillquit papers.
78. Butscher to R. A. Morris, August 16, 1900, SPP Duke.
79. *Workers' Call,* October 27, 1900.
80. Kipnis, *American Socialist Movement,* pp. 97–98.
81. Washington *Post,* September 24, 1900; *Workers' Call,* October 13, 1900.
82. Boston *Globe,* October 29, 1900; clipping from the Eugene V. Debs Scrapbooks, Tamiment Institute, New York.
83. New York *Times,* October 31, 1900.
84. *Workers' Call,* November 3, 1900.
85. *Ibid.*
86. "Growth of the Socialist Vote," *Public Opinion,* 28 (May 10, 1900), 584.
87. *Social Democratic Herald,* December 1, 1900.
88. "What Debs Sees," *The Miners' Magazine,* 2 (December, 1900), 20–21.
89. See Kipnis, *American Socialist Movement,* p. 373; Bell, in *Socialism and American Life,* I, 266; Social Democratic Party, *Socialist Campaign Book 1900,* p. 118.

90. Nathan Fine, *Labor and Farmer Parties in the United States 1828–1928* (New York, The Rand School of Social Science, 1928), p. 218. Cited hereafter as Fine, *Labor and Farmer Parties*.

91. [San Francisco] *Organized Labor*, November 10, 1900.

92. *Workers' Call*, November 10, 1900.

93. Fine, *Labor and Farmer Parties*, p. 217.

94. Ginger, *The Bending Cross*, p. 212.

Chapter III

1. See Kipnis, *American Socialist Movement*, pp. 100ff; Quint, *The Forging of American Socialism*, pp. 374–88; David A. Shannon, *The Socialist Party of America* (New York: Mac-Millan Company, 1955), chaps. 1 and 2.

2. The name "Socialist Party of America" was chosen because several states had outlawed the use by a minor party of any part of the name of a major party, thus "Social Democratic Party" might have been illegal.

3. Socialist Party, *Proceedings of the National Convention, 1912* (Chicago, 1912), p. 4. In point of fact, some 6546 socialists, most claiming adherence to the "united party" with headquarters in Springfield were represented at the unity convention. See Kipnis, *American Socialist Movement*, pp. 105ff, 153–54.

4. Bell, "Marxian Socialism," 257; Kipnis, *American Socialist Movement*, pp. 105ff.

5. *Social Democratic Herald*, November 29, 1902.

6. *Ibid.*, December 5, 1903.

7. American Federation of Labor, *Report of the Proceedings of the 23rd National Convention of the American Federation of Labor* (Washington, 1903), p. 198.

8. Eugene V. Debs, "The Western Labor Movement," *International Socialist Review*, 3 (November, 1902), 258.

9. Hillquit, *History of Socialism*, p. 310.

10. Kipnis, *American Socialist Movement*, pp. 145–46; So-

cialist Party, *Proceedings of the National Convention . . . 1904* (Chicago, 1904), p. 327; "Socialism in the New York Campaign," *The Outlook*, 84 (November, 1906), 541–42.

11. New York *Times*, March 12, 1916; Socialist Party, *Proceedings of the National Convention . . . 1904*, p. 260.

12. See Louis Filler, *Crusaders For American Liberalism* (New York: Harcourt, Brace and Company, 1939).

13. Hillquit, *History of Socialism*, p. 313; Socialist Party, *Proceedings of the National Convention . . . 1904*, pp. 329–30.

14. Quint, *The Forging of American Socialism*, pp. 175–209.

15. Kipnis, *American Socialist Movement*, p. 148.

16. Socialist Party, *Proceedings of the National Convention . . . 1904*, p. 56.

17. Debs, *Writings and Speeches*, p. 94.

18. See Coleman, *Eugene V. Debs*, p. 221.

19. Ella Reeve Bloor, *We Are Many* (New York, International Publishers, 1940), p. 52.

20. Haywood, *Bill Haywood's Book*, p. 95.

21. Young, *On My Way*, pp. 161–62.

22. See Ginger, *The Bending Cross*, p. 230; *International Socialist Review*, 4 (May, 1904); Fine, *Labor and Farmer Parties*, p. 264; Socialist Party, *Proceedings of the National Convention . . . 1904*, pp. 301–05; *Social Democratic Herald*, May 7, 1904; *Chicago Socialist*, May 20, 1904.

23. Socialist Party, *Proceedings of the National Convention . . . 1904*, p. 13.

24. *Ibid.*, pp. 214–15.

25. Harriman to Hillquit, May 3, 1904, Hillquit papers.

26. Socialist Party, *Proceedings of the National Convention . . . 1904*, pp. 220–21; David Karsner, *Debs: His Authorized Life and Letters* (New York: Boni and Liveright, 1919), p. 180. Cited hereafter as Karsner, *Debs*.

27. Debs, *Writings and Speeches*, pp. 73–76.

28. Socialist Party, *Proceedings of the National Convention . . . 1904*, pp. 9–10.

29. *Ibid.*, pp. 258–61.

30. *Ibid.*, p. 300.

31. "The First Political Convention of the Year," *The Arena,* 32 (July, 1904), 90; "Debs' Speech of Acceptance," *The Miners' Magazine,* 5 (June, 1904), 8.

32. Eltweed Pomeroy, "A Political Forecast," *ibid.,* 32 (September, 1904), 581–82; "The Socialist Party," *ibid.,* 32 (September, 1904), 315–17.

33. *Chicago Socialist,* June 4, 1904.

34. *Appeal to Reason,* October 8, November 19, 1904.

35. Eugene V. Debs, "The Social Democratic Party's Appeal," *The Independent,* 57 (October 13, 1904), 836; Floy Ruth Painter, *That Man Debs and His Life Work* (Bloomington, Indiana: Indiana University Press, 1929), 88, cited hereafter as Painter, *That Man Debs;* Socialist Party, *Proceedings of the National Convention . . . 1904,* p. 279.

36. Upton Sinclair, "The Socialist Party," *World's Work,* 11 (April, 1906), 7431.

37. *Chicago Socialist,* March 12, July 23, 1904.

38. *Appeal to Reason,* October 15, 1904.

39. *Ibid.,* October 29, 1904.

40. *Ibid.,* October 8, 1904.

41. Coleman, *Eugene V. Debs,* pp. 224–25; Upton Sinclair, "The Socialist Party," *World's Work,* 11 (April, 1906), 7432.

42. Socialist Party, *Proceedings of the National Convention . . . 1904,* p. 55.

43. Upton Sinclair, "The Socialist Party," *World's Work,* 11 (April, 1906), 7431.

44. *Ibid.*

45. *Chicago Socialist,* May 14, 1904.

46. *Appeal to Reason,* October 8, 1904.

47. *Ibid.*

48. New York *World,* September 7, 1904.

49. *Chicago Socialist,* September 24, 1904.

50. *Appeal to Reason,* October 8, 15, 1904.

51. *Chicago Socialist,* October 8, 1904.

52. "Debs Urges 'Colorado Day,' " *The Miners' Magazine,* 6 (July 7, 1904), 5–6.

53. "Debs' Great Speech at Indianapolis," *ibid.,* 6 (September 15, 1904), 5–8; "Debs on the Socialist Vote," *ibid.,* 6 (October 20, 1904), 7–8.

54. *Appeal to Reason,* October 8, 1904.

55. Algie Martin Simons, "The Socialist Outlook," *International Socialist Review,* 5 (October, 1904), 217.

56. *Appeal to Reason,* October 8, 15, 1904.

57. Debs, *Writings and Speeches,* p. 126.

58. Eugene V. Debs, "The Social Democratic Party's Appeal," *The Independent,* 57 (October 13, 1904), 836.

59. Coleman, *Eugene V. Debs,* pp. 200–21.

60. Painter, *That Man Debs,* p. 90; Debs, *Writings and Speeches,* p. 126.

61. Ginger, *The Bending Cross,* p. 231; Debs, *Writings and Speeches,* pp. 130–37.

62. See Theodore Roosevelt, *Theodore Roosevelt: An Autobiography* (New York: Charles Scribner's Sons, 1920), p. 489.

63. Debs, *Writings and Speeches,* p. 136; *Chicago Socialist,* September 3, 1904. Oyster Bay was Roosevelt's home, and Buzzard's Bay was Cleveland's retreat.

64. Debs, *Writings and Speeches,* p. 136.

65. *The Miners' Magazine,* 6 (August 25, 1904), 5.

66. See *The Commoner Condensed* (Lincoln, Nebraska: The Commoner, 1905), IV, 163–69.

67. *Chicago Socialist,* August 13, 1904.

68. Debs, *Writings and Speeches,* p. 129.

69. "Senator Hanna on Labor Unions and Socialism," *Literary Digest,* 28 (January 30, 1904), 136–37.

70. Debs, *Writings and Speeches,* p. 64.

71. *Ibid.*, p. 66.

72. See H. Wayne Morgan, "The Utopia of Eugene V. Debs," *American Quarterly*, 11 (Summer, 1959), 120–35.

73. *Debs: His Life, Writings and Speeches* (Girard, Kansas: *Appeal to Reason*, 1908), p. 59.

74. Upton Sinclair, "The Socialist Party," *World's Work*, 11 (April, 1906), 7431.

75. Ginger, *The Bending Cross*, p. 232.

76. Karsner, *Talks With Debs*, pp. 113–14.

77. *Chicago Socialist*, October 22, 1905; *Appeal to Reason*, November 5, 1904.

78. *Ibid.*, October 29, 1904.

79. Karsner, *Debs*, p. 182.

80. *Debs: His Life, Writings and Speeches*, pp. 69–70.

81. *Ibid.*, p. 69.

82. *Chicago Socialist*, November 5, 1904.

83. *Ibid.*, November 26, 1904.

84. Socialist Party, *Socialist Congressional Campaign Book* (Chicago, 1904), p. 19.

85. "The Socialists," *The Independent*, 57 (November 17, 1904), 1165–1166.

86. "What the Socialist Vote Means," *Public Opinion*, 37 (November 17, 1904), 617.

87. Chicago *Times*, November 11, 1904.

88. *Appeal to Reason*, November 20, 1904.

89. "The Growth of Socialism," *The Nation*, 80 (April 27, 1905), 324–25.

90. "The Socialist Party," *The Arena*, 32 (September, 1904), 315–16.

91. *Appeal to Reason*, November 19, 1904.

92. "Comment," *Harper's Weekly*, 48 (November 19, 1904), 1757.

93. "The Growth of Socialism," *The Nation*, 80 (April 27, 1905), 324–25.

94. Fine, *Labor and Farmer Parties*, pp. 217–18.

Chapter IV

1. See N. W. Ayer and Sons, *American Newspaper Annual* for 1908 for circulation figures for the socialist press.

2. Ginger, *The Bending Cross*, pp. 269–70; Grady McWhiney, "Louisiana Socialists in the Early Twentieth Century: A Study of Rustic Radicalism," *Journal of Southern History,* 20 (August, 1954), 315–16; Oscar Ameringer, *If You Don't Weaken* (New York: Henry Holt Company, 1940), pp. 255–56.

3. Ernest Poole, "Harnessing Socialism," *American Magazine,* 66 (September, 1908), 427–32; Upton B. Sinclair, "The Socialist Party," *World's Work,* 11 (April, 1906), 7431–7432; "Why I Left the Ministry for Socialist Propaganda," *The Independent,* 58 (June 8, 1905), 1284–1288; "The Socialist Leaven in the Church," *Current Literature,* 45 (July, 1908), 71–73; J. O. Bentall, "Why I Am a Christian Socialist," *The Arena,* 38 (June, 1907), 600–604.

4. David A. Shannon, "The Socialist Party Before the First World War: An Analysis," *Mississippi Valley Historical Review,* 38 (September, 1951), 279–88.

5. Fine, *Labor and Farmer Parties,* 242; *American Labor Yearbook 1916* (New York, 1916), pp. 156–57; Kipnis, *American Socialist Movement,* pp. 257ff, 259ff.

6. Robert Hunter, "The Socialist Party in the Present Campaign," *American Review of Reviews,* 38 (September, 1908), 295–96.

7. By 1908, there were six socialists in the Wisconsin legislature and twelve socialists on the Milwaukee city council. A total of forty-eight socialists held elective office in the state as a whole. Roland Phillips, "Unfurling the Red Flag," *Harper's Weekly,* 52 (September 26, 1908), 14.

8. *Ibid.;* see also "Socialism in the New York Campaign," *The Outlook,* 84 (November 3, 1906), 541–42.

9. Socialist Party, *Proceedings of the First National Congress*

. . . *Chicago, May 15–21, 1910* (Chicago, 1910), 27; Morris Hillquit, *Loose Leaves From a Busy Life,* p. 55.

10. Elting Morison (ed.), *The Letters of Theodore Roosevelt,* 8 vols. (Cambridge, Massachusetts: Harvard University Press, 1951–1954), IV, 1113.

11. *Appeal to Reason,* July 8, 1905.

12. Ginger, *The Bending Cross,* p. 223.

13. Debs to Benjamin Fay Mills, February 28, 1905, Theodore F. Gerson papers, Department of Special Collections, University of California, Los Angeles.

14. *Chicago Socialist,* December 23, 1905.

15. Fine, *Labor and Farmer Parties,* pp. 275–76; Haywood, *Bill Haywood's Book.*

16. Haywood, *Bill Haywood's Book,* pp. 176–78, 189.

17. Debs, *Writings and Speeches,* pp. 175–81.

18. Haywood, *Bill Haywood's Book,* p. 182.

19. IWW, *Proceedings of the First Convention of the Industrial Workers of the World* (New York, IWW, 1905), pp. 142ff.

20. Karson, *American Labor Unions and Politics,* p. 210.

21. Samuel Gompers, *Seventy Years of Life and Labor,* 2 vols. (New York: E. P. Dutton Company, 1925), I, 424–27.

22. Letter from Debs dated April 13, 1906 in possession of Mr. Elbert Hubbard II, East Aurora, New York. Debs appealed to Elbert Hubbard, "The Sage of East Aurora," to plead the cause of these men in his magazine, *The Philistine.*

23. Haywood, *Bill Haywood's Book,* p. 207; Young, *Life and Times,* pp. 257–58; Debs, *Writings and Speeches,* pp. 256–59.

24. Young, *Life and Times,* p. 289.

25. Robert Hunter, "The Socialist Party in the Present Campaign," *American Review of Reviews,* 38 (September, 1908), 293–99.

26. N. W. Ayers and Sons, *American Newspaper Annual* (Philadelphia: Ayers Company, 1908), pp. 293, 615. The *Appeal*

was published in Girard, Kansas, and *Wilshire's* was edited in New York. Many labor and independent papers carried material favorable to socialism.

27. David A. Shannon, "The Socialist Party Before the First World War: An Analysis," *Mississippi Valley Historical Review,* 38 (September, 1951), 279–88.

28. Kipnis, *The American Socialist Movement,* pp. 86–106.

29. Robert Hoxie, "The Convention of the Socialist Party," *Journal of Political Economy,* 16 (July, 1908), 442–50; Charlotte Teller, "The National Socialist Convention," *The Arena,* 40 (July, 1908), 26–39. One reason for the lack of worker delegates may have been the party's failure to pay the delegates' living expenses while at the convention. See also Charles H. Kerr, "Socialist National Convention," *International Socialist Review,* 8 (June, 1908), 721–38. Of the delegates, seventy-one per cent were American born, with the rest scattered among the Germans, Scandinavians, English, Finnish and others. Sixty-two per cent belonged to labor unions; seventeen per cent were farmers; nine per cent were businessmen; and five per cent were professionals. But the large labor union contingent was composed of editors, typographers, writers, and others who belonged to craft unions. Thirty-five per cent of the delegates were former Republicans; forty per cent former Democrats; fifteen per cent former Populists; six per cent Independents; and four per cent former Prohibitionists. Socialist Party, *A Political Guide For the Workers* (New York, 1920), p. 45; Hillquit, *Loose Leaves From a Busy Life,* p. 290.

30. The origins, importance and alignments of socialist party factions between 1900 and 1914 is an extremely complex subject best dealt with in Kipnis, *The American Socialist Movement,* pp. 164–213.

31. Socialist Party, *Proceedings of the National Convention of 1908* (Chicago, 1908), pp. 93–102.

32. *Ibid.,* pp. 147–48.

33. Haywood, *Bill Haywood's Book*, p. 230. Haywood made it clear that he would not stand against Debs.

34. Socialist Party, *Proceedings of the National Convention of 1908*, pp. 148–50.

35. *Ibid.*, pp. 151–52.

36. Harriman to Hillquit, June 10, 1908, Hillquit papers.

37. Debs, *Writings and Speeches*, p. 298.

38. *Ibid.*, p. 299.

39. *Ibid.*, p. 304.

40. Ginger, *The Bending Cross*, p. 265; Young, *Life and Times*, p. 216.

41. A discussion of the candidates and issues of the campaign of 1908 can be found conveniently in Eugene Roseboom, *A History of Presidential Elections* (New York: Macmillan Company, 1957), pp. 347–55. The Taft campaign can be traced in Henry F. Pringle, *The Life and Times of William Howard Taft*, 2 vols. (New York: Farrar and Rinehart, Inc., 1939), I, 358–78; William Howard Taft, *Political Issues and Outlooks* (New York: Doubleday, Page and Company, 1909); and Edgar Hornig, "Campaign Issues in the Presidential Election of 1908," *Indiana Magazine of History*, 54 (September, 1958), 237–65.

42. Bryan's stand on the issues of the day in 1908 can be found in *The Commoner Condensed*, VII.

43. "Debs—the 'Living Link,'" *Current Literature*, 45 (July, 1908), 35–39.

44. "The Surprising Campaign of Mr. Debs," *ibid.*, 45 (November, 1908), 483.

45. Lincoln Steffens, "Eugene V. Debs On What the Matter is in America and What to do about it," *Everybody's Magazine*, 19 (October, 1908), 455–69.

46. *Ibid.*, p. 462.

47. With characteristic fervor, Debs read the proofs of the article and said that Steffens was a socialist, a label that the muckraker spurned. See Ella Winters and Granville Hicks

(eds.), *The Letters of Lincoln Steffens,* 2 vols. (New York: Harcourt, Brace and Company, 1938), I, 150, 202–204.

48. Socialist Party, *Proceedings of the National Convention of 1908,* p. 227.
49. *Ibid.*
50. Ginger, *The Bending Cross,* pp. 254–55.
51. *The Letters of Lincoln Steffens,* I, 209–11.
52. Kipnis, *The American Socialist Movement,* p. 212; Ginger, *The Bending Cross,* p. 269; Allan J. Benson, "A Socialist on Aspects of the Presidential Campaign," *The Arena,* 40 (October, 1908), 321–24; Hillquit, *History of Socialism,* p. 351; Socialist Party, *Proceedings of the First Congress . . . . 1910,* p. 28.
53. Coleman, *Eugene V. Debs,* p. 245.
54. New York *World,* October 4, 1908.
55. Coleman, *Eugene V. Debs,* pp. 245–48; Ginger, *The Bending Cross,* p. 274; Karsner, *Debs,* p. 191.
56. Karsner, *Debs,* p. 196.
57. *Ibid.,* pp. 191–92.
58. Hillquit, *History of Socialism,* p. 351.
59. *New York Socialist,* September 19, 1908.
60. Los Angeles *Times,* September 11, 1908.
61. *Ibid.,* September 13, 1908.
62. Painter, *That Man Debs,* p. 96; Karsner, *Debs,* p. 197.
63. *Berkeley Gazette,* September 9, 1908.
64. [Berkeley] *Daily Californian,* September 14, 1908.
65. Los Angeles *Times,* September 14, 1908.
66. *Ibid.,* September 16, 1908; Ginger, *The Bending Cross,* pp. 276–77.
67. Charles Lapworth, "The Tour of the Red Special," *International Socialist Review,* 9 (December, 1908), 401–15.
68. Karsner, *Debs,* p. 197; Coleman, *Eugene V. Debs,* p. 245.
69. Coleman, *Eugene V. Debs,* p. 246.
70. "The Socialist Party's Campaign," *The Public,* 11 (October 2, 1908), 635.

71. *Appeal to Reason,* October 10, 1908.

72. Allan Nevins (ed.), *The Letters of Brand Whitlock* (New York: D. Appleton-Century Company, 1936), p. 96; Karsner, *Debs,* p. 197.

73. See the photograph of Debs on page 295 in Debs, *Writings and Speeches.*

74. Ameringer, *If You Don't Weaken,* pp. 255, 266–67; Ginger, *The Bending Cross,* pp. 269–70.

75. "The Surprising Campaign of Mr. Debs," *Current Literature,* 45 (November, 1908), 481.

76. New York *World,* October 17, 1908.

77. "The Surprising Campaign of Mr. Debs," *Current Literature,* 45 (November, 1908), 481–82.

78. *Ibid.,* 482.

79. "Mr. Debs' Appeal," *The Outlook,* 90 (October 17, 1908), 323–24.

80. "The Surprising Campaign of Mr. Debs," *Current Literature,* 45 (November, 1908), 481–85; Karsner, *Debs,* 200–204.

81. Debs to Hillquit, October 15, 1908, Hillquit papers.

82. Karsner, *Debs,* p. 198.

83. Los Angeles *Times,* October 23, 1908; Karsner, *Debs,* p. 204.

84. Debs, *Writings and Speeches,* pp. 317–18.

85. Pringle, *Life and Times of William Howard Taft,* I, 367.

86. Henry Pringle, *Theodore Roosevelt* (New York: Harcourt-Brace Company, 1931), pp. 367–68.

87. Roosevelt's attitude toward the socialists was typical. Though he was never a socialist or even radical, he distrusted what he called the lunatic fringe of the socialist movement more than socialism itself at this time. Privately he sometimes showed considerable sympathy with much of the socialist program. Publicly he insisted that his own reform administration had saved the country from socialism. When the election of 1908 showed that socialism seemed to be on

the decline, it was safe for him to write that not all the socialists' works were bad and that they often had much to offer reformers. See Theodore Roosevelt, "Where We Can Work With Socialists," *The Outlook,* 91 (March 27, 1909), 662–64; Pringle, *Theodore Roosevelt,* p. 543.

88. *The Letters of Theodore Roosevelt,* VI, 1080.

89. *Ibid.,* pp. 1080–1081.

90. Socialist Party, *Socialist (Perpetual) Campaign Book* (Chicago, 1908), p. 7.

91. *Appeal to Reason,* September 5, 1908.

92. Painter, *That Man Debs,* p. 98.

93. *The Commoner Condensed,* VII, 48–49. This hardly squared with the standard socialist statement in 1908 that "Individual competition inevitably leads to combinations and trusts. No amount of government regulation, or of publicity, or of restrictive legislation will arrest the growth of modern industrial development." Socialist Party, *Socialist (Perpetual) Campaign Book,* p. 134.

94. *Appeal to Reason,* October 31, 1908.

95. *Ibid.,* January 18, 1908.

96. Gompers, *Seventy Years of Life and Labor,* I, 424–27.

97. Socialist Party, *Socialist (Perpetual) Campaign Book,* p. 9.

98. Samuel Gompers, "Debs—The Apostle of Failure," *American Federationist,* 15 (September, 1908), 736–40.

99. Painter, *That Man Debs,* p. 98. In after years, Gompers delivered a harsh judgment of Debs. He attributed much of Debs' radicalism to sentimentality and emotion, all of which, in Gompers' view, detracted from his success in the labor movement. See Gompers, *Seventy Years of Life and Labor,* I, 406. The AFL leader was fond of calling Debs a "leader of lost causes," and felt that Debs' whole mentality may have been warped by his stay in prison in 1895, *ibid.,* I, 415–16. For his part, Debs was never silent on Gompers either in public or private, especially after their clash in 1905 over the IWW. "Let me intreat you not to get excited about so

trifling a matter," he wrote a friend in Texas who was out-raged at Gompers' attacks. "Of course, I appreciate your loyalty, but we have got to learn to keep cool even under the smart of a flea bite." Debs to F. X. Holl, April 14, 1905, Debs collection, Barker History Center, University of Texas.

100. Samuel Gompers, "Editorial Notes," *American Federationist,* 15 (November, 1908), 972.

101. Karson, *American Labor Unions and Politics,* p. 60; Hillquit, *History of Socialism,* p. 331; Karsner, *Talks With Debs,* pp. 58–59.

102. Karsner, *Debs,* p. 190.

103. *Current Literature,* 45 (November, 1948), 471.

104. Fine, *Labor and Farmer Parties,* p. 324.

105. Cf. "Minor Parties," *The Nation,* 87 (August 20, 1908), 152–53.

106. "The Red Campaign," *Current Literature,* 45 (October, 1908), 365.

107. George England, *The Story of the Appeal* (Girard, Kansas: Appeal to Reason, 1912), p. 282.

108. Ginger, *The Bending Cross,* pp. 278–79.

109. Victor Berger, *Broadsides* (Milwaukee: The Social-Democratic Publishing Company, 1912), pp. 157–58.

110. Hillquit, *History of Socialism,* p. 350.

111. Ginger, *The Bending Cross,* p. 282.

112. *Appeal to Reason,* November 7, 1908.

113. Ginger, *The Bending Cross,* pp. 282–83.

114. Coleman, *Eugene V. Debs,* p. 248; Karsner, *Debs,* p. 205.

115. Chicago *Tribune,* October 15, 1908.

116. "The Presidential Election," *The Public,* 11 (November 13, 1908), 779.

117. Robert Hunter, "The Socialist Party in the Present Campaign," *American Review of Reviews,* 38 (September, 1908), 293–99; Socialist Party, *Socialist (Perpetual) Campaign Book,* pp. 5–10.

118. Cf. the figures in Socialist Party, *Socialist Congressional Campaign Book 1914*, p. 19.
119. "Interesting Election Results," *Current Literature*, 45 (December, 1908), 588.
120. *Ibid.*, "The Socialist Showing," *The Nation*, 87 (December 3, 1908), 540–41.
121. "Progress of the World," *American Review of Reviews*, 38 (December, 1908), 643–56.
122. "The Election Interpreted," *The Outlook*, 90 (November 7, 1908), 519–20.
123. Robert Hoxie, "President Gompers and the Labor Vote," *Journal of Political Economy*, 16 (December, 1908), 693–700.
124. Hillquit, *History of Socialism*, pp. 348–49; Socialist Party, *Proceedings of the First National Congress . . . 1910*, p. 30.
125. Karsner, *Debs*, p. 206.

CHAPTER V

1. Wachman, *History of the Social Democratic Party of Milwaukee*, pp. 67–76; Kipnis, *The American Socialist Movement*, pp. 345ff; Bloor, *We Are Many*, p. 95.
2. Fine, *Labor and Farmer Parties*, p. 231.
3. *Ibid.*, p. 220.
4. *The Letters of Lincoln Steffens*, I, 244.
5. In 1910, the socialists elected twelve representatives and two senators to the Wisconsin legislature, and one representative in the legislatures of Massachusetts, Pennsylvania, Minnesota, and California each. Kipnis, *The American Socialist Movement*, p. 345.
6. Fine, *Labor and Farmer Parties*, p. 223.
7. See the large number of letters in the box marked "1911–1913," SPP Duke.

8. Charles Edward Russell, "Socialism: Where It Stands Today," *Hampton's Magazine,* 27 (January, 1912), 754; Robert F. Hoxie, "The Rising Tide of Socialism: A Study," *Journal of Political Economy,* 19 (October, 1911), 610.

9. "Advance of Socialism in the United States," *The Chautauquan,* 64 (September, 1911), 18–19; "The Tide of Socialism," *World's Work,* 23 (January, 1912), 252–53; "The Warning of Socialism" *Century Magazine,* 83 (January, 1912), 472–73.

10. The party grouped them as follows: 10 city auditors; 4 city attorneys; 145 aldermen; 61 assessors; 2 collectors; 18 city commissioners; 1 Congressman; 25 clerks; 1 court clerk; 7 coroners; 160 councilmen; 3 comptrollers; 57 constables; 1 director; 45 election officials; 2 city judges; 55 justices of the peace; 2 listers; 1 magistrate; 18 marshals; 56 mayors; 4 pound keepers; 22 police officials; 6 presidents of council; 6 road overseers; 4 recorders; 2 deed registrars; 18 state legislators; 155 school officials; 2 surveyors; 2 state senators; 1 sheriff; 40 city, county and township supervisors; 1 assessment supervisor; 29 treasurers; 2 library trustees; 39 city and township trustees; 28 town officials; 1 vice-mayor. Socialist Party, *Socialist Campaign Book* (Chicago, 1912), p. 36.

11. Robert Hoxie, "The Rising Tide of Socialism," *Journal of Political Economy,* 19 (October, 1911), 610.

12. Debs, *Writings and Speeches,* pp. 333–34.

13. "Eugene V. Debs, "Danger Ahead," *International Socialist Review,* 11 (January, 1911), 413; Bloor, *We Are Many,* p. 112.

14. Robert Hoxie "The Rising Tide of Socialism," *Journal of Political Economy,* 19 (October, 1911), 610–11; J. H. Andrew to Carl Thompson, July 11, 1912; SPP Duke.

15. Elizabeth Gurley Flynn, "One Boss Less," *International Socialist Review,* 12 (July, 1911), 11.

16. Karson, *American Labor Unions and Politics,* p. 130.

17. Fine, *Labor and Farmer Parties*, p. 243.

18. Socialist Party, *Proceedings of the First National Congress . . . 1910*, pp. 32–33.

19. "The Growth of Socialism in Alaska," *International Socialist Review*, 12 (January, 1912), 405–406.

20. Socialist Party, *Proceedings of the First National Congress . . . 1910*, pp. 76ff; Kipnis, *The American Socialist Movement*, chap. 13.

21. Young, *Life and Times*, pp. 285–88.

22. "The National Socialist Convention of 1912," *International Socialist Review*, 12 (June, 1912), 807–28; "Convention Notes," *ibid.*, 828–31.

23. Bloor, *We Are Many*, pp. 94–95. Every state except Tennessee was represented at the convention. Of the 293 delegates, 32 were newspapermen, 21 were lecturers, 20 were lawyers, 12 were mayors, and 11 were party officials. Sixty were doctors, dentists, ministers and small businessmen. The remainder were workers, though only 30 were unskilled. More than a third were over 45 years old and only 31 were less than 30. This was in contrast to the group that had founded the party in 1901, most of whom were less than 35. Nothing better illustrates the party's capture of middle-class support than the members of this convention. New York *Call*, May 5, 1912.

24. "The Compromises of the Socialist Convention," *The Independent*, 67 (May 30, 1912), 1181–1182.

25. Debs, *Writings and Speeches*, p. 353.

26. *Ibid.*, p. 352. Debs did feel that expulsion was not the proper answer for syndicalism in the party. Eugene V. Debs, "This is Our Year," *International Socialist Review*, 13 (July, 1912), 16–17.

27. "The National Socialist Convention of 1912," *ibid.*, 12 (June, 1912), 826.

28. Brissenden, *The I.W.W.*, p. 254.

29. John S. Gambs, *The Decline of the I.W.W.* (New York:

Columbia University Press, 1932), p. 11; Haywood, *Bill Haywood's Book*, pp. 222, 257, 279; Bloor, *We Are Many*, pp. 94–95.

30. See New York *Call*, August 2, 1910.

31. Socialist Party, *Proceedings of the National Convention of 1912*, pp. 137–318.

32. *Ibid.*, pp. 138–41. Debs had supported Fred Warren of the *Appeal* staff for the nomination, but his support came too late, was merely a token, and did not take him out of the race himself. See Ginger, *The Bending Cross*, pp 309–310.

33. "The Socialist Platform and Candidates," *The Outlook*, 101 (June 1, 1912), 235.

34. Of the $66,000, the party spent $24,000 on literature, $17,000 on speakers, $21,000 on advertising, and $4,000 in grants to state organizations. The party emerged from the campaign with a small deficit. See Kipnis, *The American Socialist Movement*, p. 365.

35. "The Socialist Party Must Be Officially Clean," *The Miners' Magazine*, 12 (June 20, 1912), 8.

36. Eugene V. Debs, "Statement of a Presidential Candidate," *International Socialist Review*, 13 (August, 1912), 167–169. Theodore Debs protested formally that the whole affair was but an attempt to smear his brother indirectly and to hamper his campaign, and warned privately that Eugene would protest the choice. W. J. Ghent to Morris Hillquit, June 27, 1912, Hillquit papers. The party headquarters was flooded with letters protesting Barnes' selection, but conservative leaders felt that the whole affair was a tempest in a teapot and were especially gratified by Debs' weak protest and ultimate willingness to go along with the Barnes appointment. John Spargo to Morris Hillquit, July 17, 1912, *ibid.*

37. "This Thing Must Be Settled," *International Socialist Review*, 13 (September, 1912), 276–77; "Berger's Love for Debs," *Common Cause*, 2 (September, 1912), 330; *Social Democratic Herald*, August 10, 1912.

38. Barnes to Carl Thompson, January 7, 1913, SPP Duke.

39. [Phoenix] *Arizona Republican,* September 8, 1912.

40. *Bisbee Daily Review,* September 9, 1912.

41. San Francisco *Call,* September 6, 1912.

42. *Appeal to Reason,* September 14, 1912.

43. *Ibid.,* September 26, 1912.

44. New York *Times,* September 22, 1912; "The Presidential Campaign," *The Public,* 15 (October 4, 1912), 947.

45. New York *Times,* September 30, 1912.

46. *Ibid.*

47. Marcus O'Brien, "Our 'Gene,' " *Common Cause,* 1 (June, 1912), 9–12.

48. Socialist Party, *Socialist Campaign Book 1912,* p. 38.

49. Kipnis, *The American Socialist Movement,* p. 247; A. W. Ricker, "The Socialist Press," *The Miners' Magazine,* 12 (May 16, 1912), 7–8.

50. England, *The Story of the Appeal,* p. 282.

51. Socialist Party, *Proceedings of the National Convention of 1912,* p. 218; J. Mahlon Barnes to Carl Thompson, July 1, 1912, SPP Duke.

52. Ginger, *The Bending Cross,* p. 311.

53. *Appeal to Reason,* October 12, 1912.

54. *Ibid.*

55. *Ibid.,* November 9, 1912.

56. Chicago *Tribune,* October 22, 1912.

57. New York *Times,* November 3, 1912.

58. Bloor, *We Are Many,* p. 100.

59. New York *Times,* August 14, 1912. On September 5, 1912, the New York *Times* released a story to the effect that Robert Bruere, prominent socialist writer, former muckraker and authority on settlement work, had helped draft Roosevelt's platform. According to the story, Bruere had conferred with Roosevelt personally and suggested changes in the preliminary text of the platform and also in the draft of Roosevelt's "Confession of Faith." Bruere denied the whole

story, which supposedly had been fabricated by a fellow socialist who did not feel that Bruere was sufficiently radical. The affair was of minor significance but well illustrates the willingness of some party members to support Roosevelt and the care with which they were watched by their fellows for signs of "deviation."

60. Eugene V. Debs, "Roosevelt's Heartless Tyranny," *The Miners' Magazine,* 12 (September 12, 1912), 7–8.

61. New York *Call,* August 8, 1912.

62. *Bisbee Daily Review,* September 9, 1912.

63. *The Letters of Theodore Roosevelt,* VII, 663.

64. Eugene V. Debs, "The Socialist Party's Appeal," *The Independent,* 73 (October 24, 1912), 950.

65. Victor Berger, "Socialism, the Logical Outcome of Progressivism," *American Magazine,* 75 (November, 1912), 19–21.

66. Herbert Morais and William Cahn, *Gene Debs: The Story of a Fighting American* (New York: International Publishers, 1948), p. 87.

67. Ginger, *The Bending Cross,* p. 312.

68. New York *Times,* October 15, 1912.

69. *The Letters of Theodore Roosevelt,* VII, 676.

70. New York *Times,* September 26, 1912.

71. *Ibid.,* October 17, 1912; Los Angeles *Times,* October 18, 1912.

72. "Flying Red Flags," *The Public,* 15 (September 20, 1912), 892.

73. Los Angeles *Times,* October 1, 1912.

74. *Ibid.,* October 23, 1912.

75. New York *Times,* September 30, 1912.

76. Chicago *Tribune,* November 6, 1912.

77. Los Angeles *Times,* November 5, 1912.

78. New York *Call,* October 10, 1912; "Election Results," *The Public,* 15 (November 15, 1912), 1089.

79. "The Socialist Vote," *Literary Digest,* 45 (November 23, 1912), 943–44.

80. Socialist Party, *Socialist Congressional Campaign Book 1914,* pp. 19–20.

81. *Ibid.*

82. *Ibid.,* pp. 19–20, cf. the figures; *American Labor Yearbook 1916,* pp. 98–100.

83. "The Election," *International Socialist Review,* 13 (December, 1912), 461–63.

84. Roosevelt estimated that ten per cent of his followers were drawn for the socialists and was keenly alive to the loss of most of California's electoral vote due to the socialists. *The Letters of Theodore Roosevelt,* VII, 648, 650, 651n, 703.

85. "Labor Union Contribution to the Campaign in 1912," typescript in SPP Duke, shows that smaller labor groups donated $1968.68 to the socialist campaign fund. Many local socialists insisted that much of their vote had been thrown out. See R. E. Dooley to John M. Work, November 21, 1912, *ibid.*

86. "The Socialist Vote in the United States," *The Chautauquan,* 69 (January, 1913), 135–36.

CHAPTER VI

1. *Social Democratic Herald,* May 25, 1912; Haywood, *Bill Haywood's Book,* p. 258; New York *Call,* October 6, 1912.

2. At the Socialist national convention of 1912, Haywood had said: "I have likewise urged that every worker that has a ballot should use that ballot to advance his economic interest. In Lawrence, Massachusetts, while only fifteen per cent of the workers had a vote before the strike, since the strike we have taken into the Socialist Party as many as one hundred members at a meeting." Socialist Party, *Proceedings of the National Convention of 1912,* p. 100.

3. Twenty-five per cent of the membership voted on the proposal, with 22,000 voting against Haywood and 11,000 for him. Kipnis, *The American Socialist Movement,* p. 417.

4. New York *Call,* May 8, 1912; "The Motion to Recall Haywood," *International Socialist Review,* 13 (February, 1913), 625; Haywood, *Bill Haywood's Book,* pp. 259–60; Bloor, *We Are Many,* 113; Theodore Draper, *The Roots of American Communism* (New York: The Viking Press, 1957), p. 308; *American Labor Yearbook 1916,* p. 95. Kipnis attributes great significance to Haywood's recall, but is challenged by Shannon, *The Socialist Party of America,* pp. 70–79.

5. *Letters of Theodore Roosevelt,* VII, 719n.

6. Socialist Party, *Socialist Campaign Book 1914,* p. 321.

7. *Ibid.,* pp. 13–14; Fine, *Labor and Farmer Parties,* p. 228.

8. *Ibid.,* p. 225.

9. See N. W. Ayers and Sons, *American Newspaper Annual, 1915.*

10. Ginger, *The Bending Cross,* p. 313.

11. *The Letters of Theodore Roosevelt,* VII, 959.

12. Fine, *Labor and Farmer Parties,* pp. 325–33; *American Labor Yearbook 1916,* pp. 129–144; Shannon, *The Socialist Party of America,* pp. 44–47, 135–37.

13. Debs, *Writings and Speeches,* p. 373.

14. Haywood, *Bill Haywood's Book,* p. 280.

15. Rogoff, *An East Side Epic,* p. 66.

16. *American Labor Yearbook 1916,* p. 126.

17. *American Socialist,* January 9, 1915; New York *Call,* December 5, 1915; Rogoff, *An East Side Epic,* pp. 74, 96.

18. New York *Times,* March 12, 1906; Shannon, *The Socialist Party of America,* pp. 91–92; *American Labor Yearbook 1916,* p. 92.

19. Fine, *Labor and Farmer Parties,* p. 306.

20. *Ibid.,* p. 303.

21. *American Labor Yearbook 1916,* p. 127.

22. New York *Times,* March 14, 1916.

23. Shannon, *The Socialist Party of America,* pp. 91–92.

24. *American Labor Yearbook 1916,* p. 335.

25. New York *Times,* September 25, 1916.

26. *Ibid.*, March 20, 1916.

27. *Ibid.*

28. *Ibid.*, May 2, 1916.

29. Socialist Party, *Socialist Handbook* (Chicago, 1916), p. 3.

30. New York *Times,* November 5, 1916.

31. Debs, *Writings and Speeches,* p. 397.

32. *Ibid.*, p. 392.

33. Ginger, *The Bending Cross,* pp. 334ff. The Debs Scrapbooks in the Tamiment Institute have many clippings dealing with his 1916 campaign.

34. "Benson and Hanley, Minor League Pitchers in the Great Presidential Game This Year," *Current Opinion,* 61 (September, 1916), 162–63; F. M. Davenport, "Presidential Choice for the Socialists," *The Outlook,* 112 (April 12, 1916), 865–69; *American Labor Yearbook 1917–1918,* 335; Socialist Party, *A Political Guide for the Workers,* p. 47.

35. *American Labor Yearbook 1917–1918,* p. 335.

36. *Ibid.*

37. *Ibid.*

38. *Ibid.*, pp. 360–63. The League operated in twenty-one states and had some 5,000 members.

39. *American Labor Yearbook 1916,* p. 156.

40. New York *Times,* April 5, 1916.

41. *Ibid.*, November 5, 1916.

42. *Ibid.*, October 20, 1916.

43. *American Labor Yearbook 1917–1918,* p. 335.

44. *Ibid.*, pp. 336–37.

45. Ginger, *The Bending Cross,* pp. 334ff.

46. Socialist Party, *A Political Guide for the Workers,* p. 47.

47. Socialist Party, *Proceedings, Emergency Convention of the Socialist Party of America at St. Louis, 1917* (Chicago, 1917); Shannon, *The Socialist Party of America,* p. 97.

48. Socialist Party, *Proceedings, Emergency Convention,* April 12, Evening Session.

49. Fine, *Labor and Farmer Parties,* p. 316.

50. Socialist Party, *Proceedings, Emergency Convention,* April 12, Evening Session.

51. *Ibid.,* April 11, Afternoon Session; Ginger, *The Bending Cross,* p. 342.

52. Roger Butterfield, *The American Past* (New York: Simon and Schuster, 1957), p. 375.

53. Hillquit, *Loose Leaves From a Busy Life,* p. 171.

54. *Ibid.,* p. 169.

55. Bloor, *We Are Many,* pp. 144–50.

56. Young, *Life and Times,* p. 340.

57. Fine, *Labor and Farmer Parties,* pp. 317–18.

58. James Oneal, *American Communism* (New York: The Rand Book Store, 1927), p. 41.

59. See Victor L. Berger, *The Voice and Pen of Victor L. Berger* (Milwaukee: The Milwaukee Leader, 1929), *passim;* New York *Times,* December 20, 1919.

60. Los Angeles *Times,* December 9, 1917.

61. Gambs, *The Decline of the I.W.W.,* pp. 21–74.

62. San Francisco *Examiner,* August 11, 1917; Haywood, *Bill Haywood's Book,* pp. 291–326.

63. Robert Murray, *Red Scare* (Minneapolis: University of Minnesota Press, 1955), pp. 30–31.

64. See Debs, *Writings and Speeches,* p. 406.

65. Hillquit, *Loose Leaves From a Busy Life,* p. 206.

66. Fine, *Labor and Farmer Parties,* p. 226.

67. *Ibid.,* pp. 225–26.

68. *The Letters of Theodore Roosevelt,* VIII, 1249.

69. *American Labor Yearbook 1923–1924,* p. 125.

70. Ginger, *The Bending Cross,* p. 350.

71. Shannon, *The Socialist Party of America,* pp. 114–16.

72. See *Debs vs U.S.,* 249 US 211 (1919).

73. New York *Times,* July 1, 1918; Eugene V. Debs, *Walls and Bars* (Chicago: Socialist Party, 1927), pp. 29–30; Ginger, *The Bending Cross,* p. 359.

74. Bloor, *We Are Many,* p. 145; Theodore Debs to Mary E.

Gallagher, September 12, 1929, Tom Mooney papers, Bancroft Library, Berkeley, California; Young, *Life and Times*, pp. 347–48; John Reed, "With Gene Debs on the Fourth," *The Liberator*, 1 (September, 1918), 7–9.

75. Debs, *Writings and Speeches*, pp. 433–39; Max Eastman, *The Trial of Eugene V. Debs* (New York: n.p., n.d.); New York *Times*, September 11, 1918; H. C. Peterson and Gilbert C. Fite, *Opponents of War* (Madison, Wisconsin: University of Wisconsin Press, 1957), p. 252; David Karsner, *Debs Goes to Prison* (New York: I. K. Davis and Company, 1919).

76. "The Trial of Eugene V. Debs," *The Survey*, 40 (September 21, 1918), 695–96.

77. Murray, *Red Scare*, p. 26.

78. Karsner, *Debs Goes to Prison*, p. 48.

79. Darrow, *The Story of My Life*, p. 72; Ginger, *The Bending Cross*, pp. 386–89; Bloor, *We Are Many*, p. 148; Debs, *Walls and Bars*, p. 15.

80. Joseph P. Tumulty, *Woodrow Wilson as I Knew Him* (New York: Doubleday, Page and Company, 1921), p. 505; Josephus Daniels, *The Wilson Era: Years of War and After* (Chapel Hill, North Carolina: The University of North Carolina Press, 1946), pp. 365ff; Norman Thomas, "Political Prisoners in the United States," *The Intercollegiate Socialist*, 7 (February–March, 1919), 11–12; Darrow, *The Story of My Life*, p. 70; Debs, *Walls and Bars*, pp. 95–96; New York *Times*, March 12, 1919.

81. Hillquit, *Loose Leaves From a Busy Life*, p. 277.

82. Shannon, *The Socialist Party of America*, p. 128.

83. Berger, *The Voice and Pen of Victor L. Berger*, p. 595.

84. Two excellent studies of the American communist movement have recently appeared, Theodore Draper, *The Roots of American Communism* (New York: The Viking Press, 1957), and Irving Howe and Lewis Coser, *The American Communist Party* (Boston: The Beacon Press, 1957).

85. Bloor, *We Are Many,* p. 142; Young, *Life and Times,* pp. 362–63; Shannon, *The Socialist Party of America,* pp. 126–50.

86. Ginger, *The Bending Cross,* p. 397.

87. Debs, *Writings and Speeches,* p. 442.

88. Karsner, *Talks With Debs,* pp. 164–65.

89. Draper, *The Roots of American Communism,* p. 326.

90. David Karsner, "The Passing of the Socialist Party," *Current History,* 20 (June, 1924), p. 404.

CHAPTER VII

1. Karsner, *Debs Goes to Prison,* p. 23. See also Virginia Ottini, "The Socialist Party in the Election of 1920," unpublished M.A. Thesis (Stanford University, 1948), for a full discussion of the socialist position in 1920.

2. Karsner, *Talks With Debs,* p. 18.

3. David Karsner, "Debs in 1920," *Socialist Review,* 9 (June, 1920), 19–23.

4. *American Labor Yearbook 1921–1922,* p. 393.

5. David Karsner, "Debs in 1920," *Socialist Review,* 9 (June, 1920), 19–23; *Appeal to Reason,* May 24, 1919; New York *Call,* February 2, 1920.

6. Theodore Debs to David Karsner, March 19, 1920, Karsner papers.

7. New York *Times,* March 21, 1920.

8. *Ibid.,* May 3, 1920.

9. *Ibid.,* May 10, 1920.

10. David Karsner, "Debs in 1920," *Socialist Review,* 9 (June, 1920), 19–23.

11. *American Labor Yearbook 1921–1922,* pp. 393–94; New York *Times,* May 9, 1920; New York *Call,* April 15, 1920; Coleman, *Eugene V. Debs,* pp. 316–17.

12. The New York *Times,* May 13, 1920, lists delegates by origin and occupation.

13. *American Labor Yearbook, 1921–1922*, p. 393; New York *Call*, May 9, 1920.

14. New York *Times*, May 11–14, 1920.

15. *Ibid.*, May 14, 1920.

16. W. Harris Cook, "The National Convention," *Socialist Review*, 9 (June, 1920), 24–26; New York *Times*, May 14, 1920; New York *Call*, May 14, 1920.

17. "The Socialist Convention," *Weekly Review*, 2 (May 22, 1922), 534.

18. New York *Times*, May 15, 1920.

19. Hillquit, *Loose Leaves From a Busy Life*, p. 293.

20. *American Labor Yearbook 1921–1922*, p. 403; Henry W. Laidler, "The Socialist Convention," *Socialist Review*, 9 (June, 1920), 26–36.

21. New York *Times*, May 11, 1920.

22. *Ibid.*, May 14, 1920.

23. *Ibid.*, May 11, 1920.

24. *Ibid.*; *American Labor Yearbook 1921–1922*, pp. 397–400; Socialist Party, *A Political Guide for the Workers*, pp. 27–32.

25. New York *Times*, May 16, 1920.

26. *American Labor Yearbook 1921–1922*, pp. 403–404.

27. *Ibid.*, p. 404; New York *Call*, May 16, 1920.

28. New York *Times*, May 15, 1920.

29. New York *Times*, May 30, 1920; Debs, *Walls and Bars*, pp. 101–103; "The Candidate in Denims," *Socialist Review*, 9 (July, 1920), 73–74; Jessie Wallace Hughan, "Debs, the Candidate," *ibid.*, 9 (October, 1920), 157–59.

30. "Candidate Debs is a Beneficent Influence in Prison but Still a Revolutionary," *Literary Digest*, 67 (October 23, 1920), 57–58.

31. Coleman, *Eugene V. Debs*, p. 317.

32. New York *Times*, June 12, 25, July 22, 1920; Shannon, *The Socialist Party of America*, p. 157.

33. Debs, *Walls and Bars*, pp. 106–107.

34. Theodore Debs to Rena Mooney, November 23, 1920.

Mooney papers; *Appeal to Reason,* July 31, 1920; New York *Times,* May 16, August 28, 1920.

35. Michael Rudolph to T. Perceval Gerson, August 6, 1920, Gerson papers.

36. Lewis Gannett, "The Socialist Campaign," *The Nation,* 111 (October 13, 1920), 401–402.

37. *Ibid.,* p. 401.

38. *Ibid.*

39. New York *Times,* October 4, 1920.

40. Theodore Debs to Winnie Branstetter, July 28, 1920; and Eugene Debs to Otto Branstetter, October 23, 1920, SPP Duke.

41. New York *Times,* August 2, 1920.

42. Seymour Stedman, "Nine Steps to a New Age," *The Independent,* 104 (October 9, 1920), 39–40.

43. Seymour Stedman, "Letter of Acceptance," *Socialist World,* 1 (August, 1920), 9–10.

44. New York *Times,* June 25, 1920.

45. Unknown Addressee to Seymour Stedman, November 1, 1920, Seymour Stedman papers, State Historical Society of Wisconsin, Madison.

46. Lewis Gannett, "The Socialist Campaign," *The Nation,* 111 (October 13, 1920), 401–402.

47. New York *Call,* June 1, 17, 18, 24, 27, July 1, September 13, 1920.

48. New York *Times,* October 10, 1920.

49. "Eugene V. Debs: A Presidential Impossibility," *Literary Digest,* 65 (May 22, 1920), 53–58.

50. New York *Times,* May 15, 1920.

51. *Ibid.,* August 24, 1920.

52. *Ibid.,* October 10, 1920. The International Ladies Garment Workers Union and the Amalgamated Clothing Workers of America endorsed Debs in 1920. New York *Call,* May 13, 14, 1920.

53. Rogoff, *An East Side Epic,* p. 180.

54. New York *Times,* August 24, 1920; Socialist Party, *A Political Guide for the Workers,* pp. 25–32.

55. New York *Times,* July 19, 1920.

56. Theodore Debs to David Karsner, October 15, 1920, Karsner papers.

57. New York *Times,* February 20, 1920.

58. *Ibid.,* November 1, 1920.

59. "National Executive Committee Plans for the Campaign," *Socialist World,* 1 (July, 1920), 16; "Party Plans Aggressive Campaign," *ibid.,* 1 (September, 1920), 13–14; New York *Call,* August 23, October 2, 1920.

60. Shannon, *The Socialist Party of America,* p. 157.

61. New York *Times,* June 12, 1920.

62. New York *Call,* August 9, 1920; "Summary of Revenue and Expenses, 1920 Campaign," Typescript, SPP Duke; New York *Times,* October 4, 1920; *American Labor Yearbook 1921–1922,* p. 406; "Campaign Contributions Received by the National Executive Committee of the Socialist Party," Typescript, SPP Duke, shows that receipts for the campaign barely exceeded expenditures.

63. Debs, *Walls and Bars,* p. 101. "Eugene V. Debs personifies and represents the American Working Classes," wrote an official. "Nominated on the ticket of the Socialist Party, the real Third Party, Debs stands a living challenge to the statement of the Washington Peacock [Wilson] that under the Democratic administration no one has been imprisoned for his opinion." Michael Rudolph to T. Perceval Gerson, August 6, 1920, Gerson papers.

64. John Spargo, "Democracy Must Not Be Vindictive," *The Independent,* 103 (September 11, 1920), 303.

65. "Wilson has vision," Debs told a friend. "There is light on his social horizon, however much it may be obscured by the clouds that hover over and around him. He sees that the liberties of the people cannot be crushed by repressive measures. But there are tremendous forces behind the

President, or before him, I don't know which, that won't let him be free." Karsner, *Debs Goes to Prison*, p. 9.

66. Debs, *Walls and Bars*, p. 105.

67. New York *Times*, October 14, 1920. See correspondence in boxes marked "1918–1920) in SPP Duke for letters dealing with such persecution.

68. Michael Rudolph to T. Perceval Gerson, August 6, 1920, Gerson papers.

69. Karsner, *Talks With Debs*, pp. 155–61; Eugene V. Debs, "Socialist Unity," *Socialist Review*, 9 (June, 1920), 15–16.

70. Theodore Debs to David Karsner, March 20, 1920; Eugene Debs to David Karsner, April 30, 1920, Karsner papers.

71. Socialist Party, *A Political Guide for the Workers*, p. 49.

72. New York *Times*, October 5, 1920.

73. "Candidate Debs is a Beneficent Influence in Prison but Still a Revolutionary," *Literary Digest*, 67 (October 23, 1920), 58.

74. "Eugene V. Debs: A Presidential Impossibility," *ibid.*, 65 (May 22, 1920), 53–58.

75. Karsner, *Talks With Debs*, pp. 64–65.

76. Ginger, *The Bending Cross*, p. 406.

77. " 'Gene wishes me to say to you that personally he owes nothing to the Communists," Theodore Debs wrote Louis Engdahl in 1922. "When he was in that hell-hole at Atlanta the Communists with but few exceptions ignored him and the rest of the political prisoners, and their papers, including the one you now edit, were cold-bloodedly silent, not raising a voice nor lifting a finger to secure their release, and so far as they were concerned, 'Gene would still be rotting in his dungeon in Atlanta." Karsner, *Talks With Debs*, pp. 199–202.

78. New York *Times*, February 9, 1920.

79. *Ibid.*, May 16, 1920.

80. *Ibid.*, October 31, 1920; "Socialist Hopes," *Literary Digest,* 65 (May 29, 1920), 18–19.
81. Debs, *Walls and Bars,* p. 108; New York *Times,* November 3, 1920; Debs, *Writings and Speeches,* p. 468.
82. Ginger, *The Bending Cross,* p. 403; New York *Call,* November 4, 1920.
83. New York *Times,* December 18, 1920.
84. *Ibid.*, November 4, 1920.
85. *Weekly Review,* 3 (November 10, 1920), 432.
86. Hillquit, *Loose Leaves From a Busy Life,* p. 300.

CHAPTER VIII

1. "Debs," *The Independent,* 108 (January 14, 1922), 31; William Allen White, *Autobiography* (New York: Macmillan Company, 1946), 622–23; *The Letters of Lincoln Steffens,* II, 556–57, 575–77.
2. New York *Times,* April 5, 1921.
3. Theodore Debs to Bertha Hale White, November 25, 1921, SPP Duke.
4. Robert A. Hoffman to Anna Mooney, October 11, 1931, Mooney papers; *Annual Report of the Attorney General* (Washington, D.C.: Government Printing Office, 1922), p. 415.
5. Debs, *Walls and Bars,* p. 108; Debs to Karsner, December 6, 1924, Karsner papers.
6. Debs to Mooney, February 1, 1922, Mooney papers.
7. Karsner, *Talks With Debs,* p. 31.
8. *The Letters of Lincoln Steffens,* II, 579–80.
9. Karsner, *Talks With Debs,* pp. 66.
10. Louis Waldman, *Labor Lawyer* (New York: E. P. Dutton and Company, 1944), p. 153.
11. Karsner, *Talks With Debs,* pp. 171–72; Theodore Debs to Karsner, July 24, 1922, Karsner papers.
12. Karsner, *Talks With Debs,* pp. 27–28.

13. Bloor, *We Are Many,* p. 180.
14. Fine, *Labor and Farmer Parties,* p. 275.
15. Membership in 1921 was 13,484; in 1922, 11,019; in 1923, 12,000 estimated. *American Labor Yearbook 1925,* p. 141.
16. "American Socialism in the Wilderness," *Weekly Review,* 5 (July 16, 1921), 49–50.
17. Draper, *The Roots of American Communism,* p. 394.
18. David Karsner, "The Passing of the Socialist Party," *Current History,* 20 (June, 1924), 402–407.
19. New York *Call,* June 19, 1921.
20. Theodore Debs to David Karsner, February 14, 1922, Karsner papers.
21. Eugene V. Debs to Comrade Tuvim, March 22, 1922; Debs Collection, Tamiment Institute, New York.
22. New York *Call,* October 8, 1922.
23. David Karsner, "The Passing of the Socialist Party," *Current History,* 29 (June, 1924), 403.
24. Eugene V. Debs to Tom Mooney, February 1, 1922, Mooney papers.
25. Theodore Debs to David Karsner, May 4, 1923, Karsner papers.
26. Mary D. Brite, "Anyhow Debs Spoke in Cincinnati," *The Nation,* 117 (July 29, 1923), 87; Waldman, *Labor Lawyer,* pp. 147–55.
27. Eugene V. Debs to David Karsner, June 7, 1923, Karsner papers.
28. Shannon, *The Socialist Party of America,* p. 164.
29. Waldman, *Labor Lawyer,* p. 154; William Hard, "Third-Party Vibrations," *The Nation,* 118 (June 11, 1924), 679–80; "Third Party Ideas in the North West," *Literary Digest,* 81 (April 19, 1924), 14–16.
30. The standard study is Kenneth Campbell McKay, *The Progressive Movement of 1924* (New York: Columbia University Press, 1947).
31. *American Labor Yearbook 1925,* pp. 134, 137; "LaFollette

Nominates LaFollette," *The Outlook,* 137 (July 16, 1924), 414–416.

32. *American Labor Yearbook 1925,* pp. 138–43; "LaFollette's Labor Support," *Literary Digest,* 82 (August 16, 1924), 12–13; Shannon, *The Socialist Party of America,* pp. 177–79.

33. *Ibid.*

34. Fred E. Haynes, "LaFollette and LaFollettism," *Atlantic,* 134 (October, 1924), 539.

35. *American Labor Yearbook 1925,* p. 140.

36. See correspondence in the file marked "January–November, 1924," SPP Duke.

37. New York *Times,* January 2, 1925.

38. James H. Shideler, "The Disintegration of the Progressive Party Movement of 1924," *The Historian,* 13 (Spring, 1951), 189–201.

39. *American Labor Yearbook 1925,* p. 137; Eugene V. Debs to T. Perceval Gerson, September 22, 1925, Gerson papers.

40. Eugene V. Debs to David Karsner, January 17, 1923; November 11, 1925, Karsner papers.

41. Murray B. Seidler, *Norman Thomas, Respectable Rebel* (Syracuse: Syracuse University Press, 1961), p. 74.

42. See Bell, "Marxian Socialism," p. 254.

43. See Karson, *American Labor Unions and Politics,* p. 286; Kipnis, *The American Socialist Movement,* pp. 421–29; Shannon, *The Socialist Party of America,* pp. 62–80, 249–68.

44. Ginger, *The Bending Cross,* p. 261.

Index

253

H. Wayne Morgan specializes in American history from the
Civil War to World War I, and has written a variety of articles
for historical journals. He received his B.A. from Arizona State
University, his M.A. from Claremont Graduate School, and his
Ph.D. from the University of California at Los Angeles. He has
taught at both UCLA and San Jose State College, California, and
is presently on the faculty of the University of Texas.

SYRACUSE UNIVERSITY PRESS
SYRACUSE 10, NEW YORK